W9-BXO-424

God and the Knowledge
of Reality

GOD
AND THE
KNOWLEDGE
OF
REALITY

BY

Thomas Molnar

Basic Books, Inc., PUBLISHERS

NEW YORK

© 1973 by Basic Books, Inc.
Library of Congress Catalog Card Number: 72–97406
SBN 465–02684–2
Manufactured in the United States of America
DESIGNED BY VINCENT TORRE
73 74 75 76 10 9 8 7 6 5 4 3 2 1

To the memory of
my Mother

CONTENTS

INTRODUCTION

Even a rudimentary reading in philosophy shows that the impulse prompting a philosopher to formulate a system is very often a personal experience which crystalizes previously accumulated speculation. Plato was decisively influenced by the encounter with Socrates; Augustine was as if thunderstruck by the *tolle, lege* he heard one day in his garden; there is Pascal's testimony of his conversion on a piece of paper sown in his doublet; Descartes's system came to a sudden maturation in the *cheminée* in the winter of 1619; and Hegel saw in Napoleon on horseback "history marching through the streets of Iena."

The last instance—Hegel's vision of Napoleon as the force incarnating and terminating history—has had an incalculable impact on the subsequent age, which is still ours. It is a different impact from the continuing influence of Plato, Augustine, Pascal, and Descartes; it has its origin in Hegel's conception of history and philosophy, a conception which was not altogether new in his own time, but which remains nevertheless striking in its bold formulation and far-reaching implications. The Iena episode merely crowned the system which had been prefigured in the impact the French Revolution had made on the youthful Hegel, as he recalls in the *Philosophy of History*: "As long as the sun stands in heaven and the planets revolve around it, has it not happened that man stood on his head, that is on his thought, and built reality in conformity to it. Anaxagoras had been the first to say that *nous* governs the world; but only now

[ix]

has man gained the insight that thought should govern spiritual reality. This was a splendid sunrise; all thinking beings shared in celebrating the epoch. The age was ruled by a sublime emotion, the world trembled as the enthusiasm of the spirit pervaded it, as if only now had the divine been truly reconciled to the world."

The impression could not become any more intense, and it remained the governing principle of Hegel's thought: to every accomplishment of *reason*, the universal mind, there corresponds a higher degree of *historical* maturation just as to his own great intellectual performance, the *Phenomenology of the Spirit*, there corresponds the Napoleonic empire, the nucleus of the imminent World-State. Thus Hegel came to regard philosophy not as a systematized albeit never completed apperception of reality, a high articulation of human experience, but as a means of promoting the gestation of history—until mankind reaches its destination and philosophy liquidates itself.

This grandiose view has found easy accreditation with philosophers and intellectuals. They accept as the irrefutable character of the age and of all future times what Hegel wrote at the end of the Preface to the *Phenomenology*: We live in an epoch in which universality has been consolidated by all the accumulated richness provided by science while the singular, the individual, has correspondingly faded; henceforth "individual participation in the total achievement of the spirit can only be minimal." The philosopher's honor and duty must then be to help the universal (the collective) in its final accomplishments; philosophy must give its total support to history. Up until Hegel, history's pressure was bearable because it was ascribed to man's weakness and sinfulness, his willful separation from God's design. This was the Augustinian view which excluded perfection from the *civitas terrena* and saw it achieved in the *civitas Dei*, beyond history. After Hegel, the pressure of history has redoubled because the tragedies that continued befalling mankind

[x]

Introduction

could now be justified by reference to the processes of reason in its historical unfolding. The chasm that Augustine and other historians saw between the two *cities* was closed in the Hegelian system. Thus a new and unheard of legitimacy came to be formulated for the man—philosopher or leader—who speaks in the name of historical reason, the absolute mind.

The nearly universal acceptance of this conception indicates that we live inside the Hegelian world-view. The trouble with this world-view is that it is based on a philosophically unauthorized *transposition* of the speculative order onto the historical sequence: what the philosopher discovers as the processes of reason, he applies to the structure of the world. One can say of this Hegelian procedure what Hans Leisegang wrote of gnostic logic: that it is grounded in the conviction that man is able to discover the secret unity of the world on condition that he penetrate behind the cosmic scenario and, mobilizing all his spiritual powers, tear away the veil of false knowledge.

Hegel, too, believed in the analogical law permitting him to conclude from one set of processes to the other. He was consequently tireless in his search for the hidden harmonies between the absolute mind and the actions of men. Formulating the system by which the first proceeded, he thought he detected the same system in the movements of the second. The philosopher thus pierced the veil of Maya; he could give orders to History.

We have, therefore, two reasons to disengage ourselves from the *fascinatio* Hegel exercises on our contemporaries: to save history from the grip of doctrine and to save philosophy from the destructive *hybris*. The first task is not ours in this book, and we shall outline it here only briefly.

In 1806 Hegel saw history coagulating around the figure of Napoleon and his empire as the Spirit found rest in the World-State. As we noted already, in Hegel's view the stage was filled with the universal, so that henceforth individual participation would be reduced to inessentials. History would go on even after its culmination in the Napoleon-Hegel pair, the *Phenomenology* suggests, but it would be a history without a motive force, without anything essentially new. As Hegel puts it in *Reason in History*, there is still work to be done, but this belongs to the "empirical side." Since the early nineteenth century Hegel's many followers have agreed with this view, differing only on one detail: they saw the great turning point not in 1806 and the empire, but in dates, events, regimes contemporary to their own lifetimes. The "turning point" always seems to be the immanentist thinker's own *now*.

If historical experience taught Hegel the contents of what became the *Phenomenology*, the intervening one hundred seventy years have taught *us* a lesson which contradicts that most influential book. This lesson too is derived from historical experience, and it is this: history "uses" only temporary catalysts, and uses them only in a limited fashion; history is not the conflict of the universal and the individual, and the first is not the victor, nor the second the vanquished; there are always new motive forces, for history does not coagulate and serve as a form of expression to a philosophical doctrine.

The task of this book is the restoration of the philosophical enterprise. Its author cannot claim to have elaborated his thought from the nucleus of a compressed personal experience of the kind mentioned in the first paragraph. In fact, I have come only gradually to conceive the subject of this book as being the restoration of philosophy through a return to reason, and hence to the possibility of knowledge. In the past dozen years or so I was engaged in digging to deeper and deeper strata while searching for the causes of philosophy's derailment. Several other works completed during this time testify that this "archaeological" ac-

Introduction

tivity, in its attempt to discern the essentials, turned up intriguing finds but did not yet hit rock bottom.

At first, in *The Decline of the Intellectual* (1961), I had sketched out the typology of the modern intellectual, but only to conclude, erroneously as I see it now, that there may be valid reasons for distinguishing between *intellectuals* and *social engineers*. In the first type I saw men who, though they had forsaken their search for the constitution of being in order to search for the Ideal Society, nonetheless were the philosophers' legitimate heirs. To the second type I attributed the objective of *building* the Ideal Society. I thought the intellectuals had reached an impasse because they could not have intended the search for wisdom to end in the compulsory happiness of a Utopia. In short, by their "decline" I meant their abdication to, and replacement by, the social engineers.

By degrees, however, I came to the conviction that it was not the activity of intellectuals or of social engineers which caused philosophy's derailment, but the philosophers themselves. They —or at least some of the most prestigious among them—were the ones whose ambition, independent of time, space, and circumstance, has been to remake not merely society, but the constitution of being in search of *total knowledge*. Yet such a knowledge implies a fusion of self and world and can be attained only by what I call the "ontological promotion," in a world differently constituted from ours. Thus I found that Utopia, the ideal society, is not the real and ultimate objective: it serves merely as a framework for the philosophers' "noetic promotion." The problem is fundamentally epistemological and must be formulated primarily in epistemological rather than political terms. We discover then that the speech (*logos*) of many philosophers (in reality, ideologues) is not human speech, but either silence, indicative of a world devoid of meaning, or ideology, the false speech of a superindividual: History. Both silence and ideology suppress the validity of the *logos* because they deny reality as a

God and the Knowledge of Reality

point of reference. But, as Professor Stanley Rosen argues, if reasons have no external, objective reference and are altogether self-certifying, then they are arbitrary utterances, lacking in rational justification or human value.[1] In other words, they do not amount to a philosophy; on the contrary, they invite the invasion of antiphilosophy and with it the nihilism of the barbarians.

When we examine how this happened, we again meet at the crucial point Hegel and his epigones (as well as the ancestors of his thought). In elaborating his world-historical theory, Hegel obviously was motivated by philosophical premises which determined his reflections on mankind's destiny and destination. By examining these premises as well as Hegel's ontology and epistemology, and by finding them defective, we may not only reach conclusions different from his theory of man and history, but also discover the causes of contemporary philosophy's derailment. In other words, instead of undertaking the thankless task of showing our contemporaries the dimensions of the Hegelian "cave" where they sit in speculative chains, we may, more helpfully, show them its epistemological substructure with its esoteric, gnostic, mystical, and archaic-religious components.

Hegel's theory of knowledge (of which, naturally, more will be said later on) follows a well-known line from these types of thinking. Schematized, it is this: the *ens perfectissimum* is the Spirit remaining in its primordial compactness.[2] This perfect condition, however, is not found in reality, for the Spirit set out on movement and thus the second best thing happened: desiring to know itself, the Spirit produced history in which it unfolds and reflects itself—until it returns to an enriched compactness, the final synthesis of movement and being. Thus Intelligence (reason) and History (the world of events and of change) mature together toward the moment of fusion or compactness, generator of the Absolute Spirit. The last universal fusion is prefigured and promoted by others: the fusion of male and female

[xiv]

Introduction

(androgyne), of subject and object, of thesis and antithesis, and of other polarities resolved as *coincidentia oppositorum*. Thus the underlying theme and secret favorite of Hegelian epistemology—and of other theories of knowledge preceding it or taking it as a model—is *coalescence*: the soul's absorption in God, the absorption of change in the One, of history in the timeless absolute, of the mind in the world-spirit, the convergence of all human endeavors in the World-State. In these *termini* everything, from individual thought to the citizen's initiative, comes to a final rest.

Disengagement from the Hegelian *fascinatio* must, therefore, begin with the proposal of a different epistemology, one whose ideal is not fusion but *distinction*. It is through distinction that the mind operates, concepts are articulated, and being is understood. It is through distinction that we recognize the objective reality of the extramental world (as distinguished from the self), of the moral elements in human situations, and of the inherent limits of human beings in thought and action.

The precondition of elaborating an epistemology on this basis —and of a philosophy grounded in this epistemology—is the humble acceptance of the extramental world, as also of the self, as *real*, not as inventions or projections of the mind. Only in such a way can we constructively criticize the Hegelian concept of fusion and point justifiably at the individuality of things as they appear in our experience. We may assume, then, that they were created; what we may not assume is that they—the world and history—are stages in the dialectical unfolding of Absolute Reason. Because if they *are* such stages, then we must conclude, with Hindu mysticism and other esoteric doctrines, that they are phantoms, traps for the self, while the self is a trap for the World Soul; and conclude also, with a sophisticated fatalism, that the history of philosophy is the biography of the Absolute Mind, written in advance. The philosopher would then be a scribe, hesitantly tracing words under dictation.

[xv]

It is only fair to warn the reader about two things that this book is *not* intended to be.

The first is that he should not conclude from the above that this book is either about Hegel's philosophy or about its refutation. Hegel's system is, after all, only the culminating moment in the vast history of a certain mode of thinking, illustrated by great speculative minds; but *our* discussion aims at gaining insight into the nature of *two* modes of speculation, only one of which, the non-Hegelian, may, in our view, validly be called philosophical. It would be, however, unphilosophical and also contrary to the canons of scholarship to dismiss the other mode; in fact, its exploration is indispensable if we want to anchor the philosophical enterprise in the ground of reality.

The second warning is that this work was not meant to "cover" the entire history of philosophy nor to devote at least one section to every philosophical issue. The reader will note—perhaps with surprise, perhaps with relief—that many of the great names (Schopenhauer, Jaspers, Whitehead, Russell, James, Hartmann) are not even mentioned: while others are given only a cursory attention. The main reason for these omissions lies in the nature of the book: it is a *thesis*, elaborated with the intention of rescuing the enterprise of philosophizing from two antiphilosophical positions. True, the two positions are manifest in a very large number of old and new speculative systems, among which the contemporary ones occupy a place out of proportion; yet it seemed to me sufficient to discuss the *nature* of the antiphilosophical positions and to provide only a limited number of illustrations, although spread along much of the history of philosophy. It seemed, further, that the reader may be trusted to scrutinize the systems not mentioned here and decide for himself which among them display the characteristics of a genuine philosophy and which do not.

[xvi]

Introduction

A disagreement on some points between the reader and the author perhaps cannot be avoided. The author will find satisfaction, however, in the hope that, once raised in this particular way, the question of genuine philosophy versus pseudo-philosophy will not be solved by the exclusive criteria of the so-called "critical" philosophy, but by those of "realistic" philosophy. The very rareness of such an approach may at least make the reader stop; it may even, who knows, wake him up from his neo-dogmatic slumber.

NOTES

1. Stanley Rosen, *Nihilism* (New Haven: Yale University Press, 1969), p. 47.

2. Alexandre Koyré argues, it seems to me correctly, that the *ens*, being, in the Hegelian system is disquiet: it does not rest in itself, it is not itself, it is other than itself, dissatisfied with itself. Being escapes from itself, tries to become other, to realize itself through self-negation. ("Hegel à Iéna," *Revue d'Histoire et de Philosophie religieuses*, 1934.)

Part One

Part One

THE INACCESSIBLE

GOD

GENERAL conclusions that one may draw from the reading of philosophical works have always been of several kinds. Some readers are struck by the variety of themes and by their contradictoriness; others regard the history of philosophy as a process with a climax that has been reached or will be reached at a predictable future date. It is, however, also possible, and to my mind more constructive, to view the philosophical enterprise as centered around one vast theme with which philosophers try to come to terms.

The central theme appears to me what I shall call the *God-problem*. This problem should be stated in its phenomenological starkness, without prejudging it from any point of view: religious, anthropological, mystic, archaeological, or atheistic. The God-problem, at least in its first rough formulation, is the manner in which one conceives the existence of a supreme being, his role in the creation of the world, and his relationship to man. It is intriguing to note that despite the reputed emancipation of philosophy in the West from mythology and theology, the God-problem is as vigorously debated today as at any time in the past, although the debate is couched in varying and changing terminologies. The problematics of philosophy was several times emancipated from theological speculation: in Greece by Xenophanes and again by the Sophists; in India by Yajnavalkya and the Hindu metaphysicians; in the medieval West by thinkers who delimited the spheres of reason and faith and pronounced discursive knowledge disqualified to approach matters of religious belief: the existence of God, miracles, prophecy, grace, and the like. Another attempt to emancipate philosophy from religious discourse and the God-problem occurred in the eighteenth century and has continued without interruption ever since. Such thinkers as Vico, Condorcet, Comte, Hegel, and others divided history, including the history of philosophy, into "ages," and they concluded that the beginnings are characterized by religious, mystical, or metaphysical speculations but that the end (*now*) is the mature stage of positive or scientific thinking.

For all these efforts at outlawing the God-problem, it has remained—this is an elementary observation—a central theme in the history of Western and non-Western philosophy up to the present. Its demise is frequently announced, as is its replacement: the explanations of science, a mankind purged of atavistic fears, a society without conflicts—or indeed the combination of these. Nevertheless, a simple and attentive reading of philosophical works disproves these contentions: the God-problem remains anchored in speculation even when, paradoxically, death-of-God systems are proposed. This documented fact must have some importance for adherents of religions, theologians, and religious mystics; the question that interests us here is not, however, formulated from their point of view, but from that of the philosopher. We find the God-problem in the forefront of the philosopher's speculation no matter to what school he belongs. It may then be correct to assume that joined to religious affirmations are philosophical affirmations that may not be detachable from them. As if the philosophers felt they must try to solve the God-problem, the premise, before elaborating the speculative edifice with no debt to religion, but they find that the problem

[4]

obtains even after the premise seems to have settled its fate. It obtains not merely in ethical and political discourse but also in the theory of knowledge, the foundation stone of the edifice.

The philosophies that constitute the material of this discourse —Hindu, Middle Eastern, Greek, Western—have their roots in religious and theological speculations. These speculations at first split the God-problem into two fundamental positions, affecting thereby the philosophical systems that emerged from them. Later, a third religious-theological position was articulated and added to the original two. The three positions represent such basic speculative attitudes that they have remained embedded in philosophical discourse throughout the ages. Our interest in them warrants a detailed exposition of all three positions regarding the God-problem, not, by any means, in order to decide which has chronological precedence over the others, but because they affect, each in its specific manner, the problem of knowledge and the problem of the good society, both eminently philosophical topics.

The three positions may be identified in the following manner. *A* holds that God (or the gods) has a certain role to play in the universe and in the life of men, but that essentially he (or they) is remote from both; I shall call it the position of the *inaccessible God*. *B* holds that God is not only not remote from man, but that he is not even distinct from him. This position has been variously described, among others, as pantheism, and R. C. Zaehner, the Oxford historian of religion, has termed it *pan-en-henic* (all-in-one), or immanentist. I shall refer to it as the position of the *immanent God*. Finally, *C* holds that God is neither remote nor one-with-man, but that he is *transcendent and personal*; crudely phrased, he is an "anthropomorphic" God.[1]

My objective is to examine the philosophers' reaction to these ways of envisaging the God-problem and to show, as I said before, that they react to them in a manner decisive for their entire speculation. This will be shown in Part Two, regarding the

God and the Knowledge of Reality

epistemological problem, and in Part Three regarding the political problem. Part Four, *in fine*, is an attempt to draw conclusions from the three fundamental positions for a possible reformulation of the philosophical enterprise in our time.

The first approach to the God-problem, designated *A*, conceives of a being whose existence is not in question, but who remains remote from human affairs, and who may even be nameless and unknowable. This is a theologically sophisticated position, and, in fact, the theme is first embroidered on the fabric of the great cosmogonic myths that describe creation as the emergence of an intelligible world from primeval chaos. The world is intelligible because a god or a hero sponsored and aided by the gods destroyed the monster—usually a sea monster—whose *disjecta membra* (scattered parts) constitute the solid ground on which mankind builds its physical and moral abode. In a Mesopotamian myth, Marduk kills Tiamat; in the Rig Veda, Purusha is dismembered; and so on. But the creator god does not necessarily remain in the visible world, sustaining it. Indeed, the creation of the world, "the most immense of realities," as Mircea Eliade comments,[2] is a tremendous act by which a community explains its own origins and by which it has become a structured reality, a cosmos. Thus through the cosmogonic myth more than the community's own existence receives an explanation: the world, regarded as coeval and coextensive with it, also becomes intelligible. Things can only decline after this primordial event because the emergence from timelessness into time erodes the primordial model represented in the origination myth. Together with the erosion of man's world, that of the gods also loses gradually the vividness of its representation until the gods fade into less and less distinct memory. The vicious circle continues as worship of the god also fades, while his place is taken by a son, a deputy, or a demiurgos; or, indeed, the place of

[6]

The Inaccessible God

these *dei otiosi* who had been the creator gods, and as such favorable to men, is taken by malignant spirits whom the community has great difficulty to propitiate.

The cosmogonic myth is extremely rich in meanings that various branches of learning may utilize. One is that for archaic man the world became comprehensible, therefore organizable and manageable, with the help of myth. Thus, myth is not a gratuitous fabulation—the fantasies of primitive mentality—as it used to be assumed, but a means of philosophic apprehension. This point was brought to light by the researches of Mircea Eliade, Walter Otto, Rudolf Otto, Erwin Rohde, Henri Frankfort, Eric Voegelin, Gerardus van der Leeuw, and others. Another lesson is that the presence, or at least the vivid memory, of the creator gods seems to be a crucial factor of this comprehension. In order to arrest degeneracy and abolish time in which it takes place, the archaic community periodically reenacted the primordial events (of creation), so that the ceremony, regarded as sacred, might help the community's return to Being. During these ceremonies, from which the community was to gain new vitality and strength, the performers and the community in whose name they performed the primordial acts became "the contemporaries of god."[3] This is a clear indication that for archaic man, Being, the gods, and reality were quasi-interchangeable and perhaps not yet articulated notions.

The third lesson to be drawn is that there seems to be a temptation—or is it rather the weight and pull of passing time?—to forget the gods, to allow them to wither away, and to look elsewhere for elements of a new comprehension. The transcendent deity that guaranteed the reality of the model becomes increasingly distant and deficient in Being, making room for the irruption of doubt concerning the reality and the meaningfulness of what man is and does. It seems as if archaic man, at least, needed the assurance that whatever he did had a parallel or a replica more anchored in Being than his own existence and his

[7]

own acts, and without which these acts and this existence would lose their validity. Modern man, in contrast, has all but discarded the roots in Being and has relegated the *sacred* to one small corner of his existence. Modern philosophy reflects—or generates?—this distance from *being* when it casts discredit on the reality of the world and regards it, together with human life, as meaningless, absurd. Consider, in contrast, the myth of the Dayak in Borneo: the world is good and meaningful because it is sacred, and it is sacred because it was born from the Tree of Life, that is, from the divinity. This primordial divine totality is alone perfect. If the cosmos (that is, the Dayak's intelligible universe) must be periodically abolished and then re-created, this is not because the first creation was a failure, but because the pre-creation state represents a fullness and happiness not accessible in the created world.

There are other reasons and other examples also. It was entirely possible for archaic man to believe in his and his society's renewal through participation in Being, which was always (that is, periodically) present in the form of the gods. The strongest impulse was thus received from an eternal model, unchanging and immobile, explaining and sustaining the ever-recurrence of experiences. Even today the Indonesian author S. Takdir Alisjabana can write of his tradition-bound society that "harmony with tribal life and with the surrounding natural order was viewed as coinciding with the harmony of the holy cosmic order. Life was static and conservative, since the decisive moment lay in the past, when the holy cosmic order had made itself manifest at a holy moment and at a holy place through holy persons."[4] This description explains archaic man's extreme reluctance to break out of the rhythm of "eternal return" and to lose his mooring in the experience of the *noumenon*. At the same time it makes clear that even a slow modification of profane experience may erode the credibility of the primordial model, the re-creation of which becomes then increasingly difficult. The solution, if it is one, may lie in a retreat of the gods and their re placement by other spirits and forces. What is lacking in this conception is not the transcendence of god or of gods, but his or their active participation in the affairs of men. As a result, the community is left to its own devices and to its bad conscience between two instances of the renewal ceremony; it is unable to "repair" (reform) what went wrong during degenerating time without the laborious restoration of original purity. Thus the Egyptians, as Frankfort remarks, were obliged to look for the normative in the past: no pharaoh could hope to achieve more than the establishment of the conditions "as they were in the time of Ra," that is, at the beginning.[5]

This difficulty does not exist for Jews and Christians, consequently one would think that within the sphere of culture permeated by monotheistic concepts the phenomenon of the "inaccessible god" does not present itself. True, the Lord of the Hebrews seems to stand so high above them that Hegel was led, incorrectly, to the conclusion that he is a master and that the Jews are his slaves. True also, the Jews are not to pronounce his holy name (since about the fourth century B.C.), not to carve his likeness in wood or stone; not even to his best servant, Job, were God and his decisions quite comprehensible. The Hebrew *noumenon* is so tremendous (*tremenda majestas*) that Abraham is nothing but "dust and ashes" in its presence. Yet, even though this God appears in the Old Testament as the "wholly other," he is also wholly accessible and is a participant in human experience on the numinous and on the daily level. Contrary to the ancient traditions of India, for example, which dealt essentially with worship and were independent of considerations of time, those of Israel are fixed in the framework of history. This is because for Jews and particularly for Christians the *model* is no longer in the past, nor is it situated in the cosmic order;[6] the norm is now in the eternal order that unfolds in time and includes the future. God himself participates in time, that is, in history, pulling men and nations toward his design, which, for Christians at least, presents no preordained or "ideal" model whatever.

Nevertheless, in this conception too, the God-problem is often formulated as if it were about an unknowable god, which is, naturally, not at all the same as a numinous, awe-inspiring god. The reason is not the erosion of the primordial model or its juxtaposition, like that of a norm, with changing experience, since in this conception both god and man are creators of history, while time is not subjected to the weight of degeneracy. Time renews itself under the combined impulse of human freedom and divine providence.

Yet, there are several ways within the Judeo-Christian tradition to assert God's remoteness. Some of these ways are identical with, or similar to, those of other religions. The Ismaelian branch of the Chiite sect considered God as unknowable, ineffable, unable to create; creation was the work of two eternal principles God had produced, the Universal Reason and the Universal Soul. The Aranda of central Australia recognize the "Great Father" as the supreme deity but judge him to be so far and unconcerned (*deus otiosus*) that they fear their totemic ancestors more than they fear this inhabitant of heaven. Similar notions prevail among African tribes in Central Africa, namely in Eastern Angola. Several mystical systems in India and Tibet also posit a God (Isvara), but they attribute to him no role and do not aspire to reach him. In fact, he is only a hypostasis of the world-spirit, the *Brahman*.

Thus the problem of the "inaccessible God" appears as a phenomenon spread over the entire earth in the form of a paradigmatic experience whose basic meaning is that transcendence no longer is in a normative relationship with the world. It should be mentioned at this point, however, that the same psychological force that "expels" God from the sphere of human action may also be responsible for the seemingly opposite move, the absorption of God in the human *pneuma*, which we shall examine in the next section. It will be necessary in the course of describing positions *A* and *B* to call attention to their similarities and similar motives. This is so true that the French historian of religion Festugière, studying Hermetism and pagan gnosis, distinguishes between a "pessimistic" and an "optimistic" branch by which he approximately designates the distinction made on these pages between *A*, the remote God and *B*, god absorbed in man's soul. This close relationship of two seemingly opposed positions may be stated also of other than gnostic ways of envisaging the problem.

I

Methodologically, it may be right to investigate first the gnostic way of expressing the loss of transcendence and the relegation of God to a remote corner of the totality. As it is known, the Gnostics, partly influenced by Jewish apocalyptic writers after the fall of Jerusalem, partly under Christian inspiration (the so-called Christianizing Gnostics), partly assimilating various Iranian and oriental traditions, proclaimed the created world to be incurably evil, the necessity to withdraw from it with contempt, and the knowledge (*gnosis*) that the elect, consubstantial through their spirit (*pneuma*) with God, must purge themselves of their material bodies (*sarx*) in order to rejoin him. Several consequences followed from this position that, incidentally, show some variations from one Gnostic school to another. The most important consequence is the assumption that there are two gods: One the original, "distant god" who is not responsible for creating this evil world, who in fact was compelled to yield up some of his substance so that the world might be fashioned; and the other god (described variously as prince of darkness or demiurgos) who had overcome the "good" god and who, mixing evil matter with god's spiritual substance, is responsible for the creation of the world, of nature, and of man.

The similarity with archaic man's cosmogonic myth is striking: the original, good god retires (or is compelled to retire), and an inferior, malevolent but more active god or spirit takes his place—in proportion as reality is no longer viewed as tied to transcendence, that is, as being exemplary. To be noted here is Harnack's remark that the Gnostic system is an attempt of Greek philosophy to hellenize Christianity: indeed, Xenophanes, Plato, and Aristotle did not find it incompatible to speak of the One God and of other gods at the same time. Yet, it seems to me that there was here much more than a Greek intellectual influence; the Gnostic position welled up from greater depths, and it is indubitably more universal than Greek philosophy itself.

All leading Gnostics agree that the world, separated from God and renewing itself by the continued dispersal of the divine sparks through the sexual intercourse of material, that is, evil, bodies is not worthy of being lived in and of knowing. One of the more influential sects, the Valentinians, asserted that what the world calls knowledge is grasping the illusory, and that true knowledge (*gnosis*) was man's original condition, now lost through sinking into the world of matter. The objective was, of course, to regain the original condition available to the elect. But even so, the knowledge to be attained differed from the intellectual knowledge to which the Greek philosophers, and after them other philosophers, aspire. It is, writes Rudolf Bultmann about Gnosticism, "a form of occultism, learned in a mystical way rather than a philosophical. Its teaching demands faith rather than hard thinking. . . . [It] guarantees the soul of the Gnostic access to heaven after death; at a later stage the initiate is born again through the operation of the mystical or magical formula of the regenerating world."[7]

This is what Plotinus in the first book of his *Ennead* (8, 1) asserts also. The Spirit does not gain its content from logical propositions, by processes of thought and reflection on cause and effect; the Spirit is all and has all, and possesses all things in the sense that it *is* all things. The ninth-century Indian mystic San-kara denounces the multiplicity of things as false and to be re-solved in the unity of the *Brahman*. The Gita (9,2) proclaims too that the royal knowledge, the kingly secret, is the knowledge of *Brahman*: an immediate self-knowledge, self-perception. Ti-betan mystics concentrate in their meditation on the idea that all substances are unreal, false, without fixity, and that phenom-ena are mere illusions.

Not only are intellectual knowledge and mastery of subject not required of the Gnostic (and of various adepts of mysticism and esoterism), he can also ignore, on his way to coalescence with God, the moral teachings, the distinction between good and evil, and what religions generally call love and good works. Since the world as it is is evil, the Gnostic must abstain as completely as possible from worldly actions, and consider all moral teaching regarding existence in this world as *ipso facto* evil. Thus the Christianizing Gnostics rejected the Old Testa-ment together with the Ten Commandments as being the rev-elation of the inferior God (Yahweh, or the demiurgos who created the world); likewise, a thousand years later, the Albigen-sian sect was to reject the church as the invention of Satan (the inferior God), who, with his tricks, subdued the true church of Jesus Christ—the Albigensian church.

The theme of the "two gods" runs through the entire Gnostic tradition, one of the gods being good but remote, the other evil but the immediate creator of the world. The Gnostic Sat-urninus maintained that the one unknown Father made the angels, but that seven angels, in their turn, made the world and men. The Carpocratians argued that they were at least as pow-erful as Jesus Christ because they despise the creator of the world even more than he is supposed to have done. In the *Book of Baruch*, Elohim and his wife Eden are named as creators of the world; in the course of time Elohim perceived a greater light (perfection) than his own and ascended to its source, the Good.

He begged permission to remain and offered to destroy his own creation, which he now perceived as evil: "My spirit is imprisoned among men and I wish to take it back," he pleaded. He finally stayed near the Good, leaving the created world to Eden who, out of revenge, caused the angel Naas (serpent) to torment the spark of Elohim, that is the spirit, in men, her subjects.

One may legitimately suggest another variant of the "two gods" theme, present among Gnostics, as we just saw, but also in late medieval Christian mysticism and in Indian mysticism as well. The personal God, surrounded by worship and by an organized church, comes to be regarded, in the words of the thirteenth-century mystic Meister Eckhart, as an "idol," too near and anthropomorphic for the mystic's fine spiritual palate, too compromised also in mundane affairs. In such cases some mystics search for a God above God, indescribable and unknowable, more spiritual than the first. This "Super-God" is in the tradition of the so-called *negative theology* to which the names of Denys the Areopagite and John Scotus Erigena are associated. According to them God remains above all categories, he is supergoodness, superessence, and so forth, terms placing him beyond all words. The fifteenth-century cardinal and philosopher Nicholas of Cusa approached this Super-God through *docta ignorantia*, or "not-knowing"; for Eckhart and for Sankara he is infinitely above the personal Lord: "Grasp the unheard-of," exclaims Eckhart, "God and Godhead are as distinct as heaven and earth!" For obvious reasons, the Godhead (or Super-God) is the one with whom the Eckhartian kind of mystic wants to fuse his soul: not just in a temporary *unio mystica*, but as the same substance —hence as superior to the personal God.

II

Another attempt to remove God from the sphere of natural and human events may be described as the oriental, or Indian, way. *Brahman*, the world spirit or absolute spirit, is indeed very far removed from men and their worldly cares, consequently Hindu metaphysicians, like the Gnostics, were not interested in mundane problems or in problems of epistemology. The objective of the *atman* (self or ego) is to detach itself from the *maya* (the illusion of this world) that *avidya* (not-knowing; the source of error and appearance) built around the *Brahman*, thus screening it from direct knowledge, and to create a void that isolates it for the purpose of a more concentrated meditation. The ultimate goal is reached when the *atman* is absorbed in the *Brahman* (having pierced the *maya* and overcome *avidya*), which can be understood as meaning that "the individual soul is substantially and essentially identical with the unqualifiable Absolute. From the point of view of the Absolute the phenomenal world has no true existence in itself."[8] All that exists is the *atman* and the *Brahman*—the two are the same, according to Sankara's celebrated formula—the rest is, or rather *was*, from the point of view of the *atman*, reabsorbed in the *Brahman*, a fictitious net of multiplicity.[9] Needless to say, this is also the Gnostics' cosmogony.

In Gnostic systems it was the demiurgos, a self-interposing force between God and man, that separated the first from the second and expelled God—with important consequences for mundane existence—into a place of exile accessible only to those contemptuous of this world. In Hindu metaphysics there are no first and second gods (although some vague god-figures like Isvara, the eternal and absolutely transcendent God, do appear in several, more-or-less theistic currents of speculation), and the self itself, with its consciousness, is the obstacle separating it from the one all-embracing spirit. But with these notions we are already near the position we shall examine later, position *B*, according to which God and man, or at least man's soul, are of the same substance and only artificially separated in this evil world. As I said before, at times it is difficult to perceive a clear separation between the two positions and not to conclude that in both instances the outcome is the same—namely, that

God is remote, inaccessible. Even when no god is posited by speculation, as in the Brahmanic and Buddhist systems, the suspicion must arise in Western man that there may be in these systems an adumbration of a divine being, only that he is not accessible either through love or through intellect, hence that he has no effect on our mundane existence, intellectual search, and moral action. The existence, although veiled, of a god or gods ought to be nevertheless assumed because—for example, in Yoga—the objective is unity with the (nonpersonal) substance of the One. To be sure, this does not seem to be the ultimate objective but a mere *point d'appui* (a leverage) for further self-concentration, and therefore the "God" so reached is neither transcendent nor personal; it belongs to the category of the "distant God." Louis Bouyer's statement that if God cannot communicate with man, man remains locked in inner solitude[10] seems to be borne out by Buddhist doctrine and practice. A French observer, Friar Frois in the seventeenth century noted that many times a year the bonzes deliver themselves up to a certain kind of meditation lasting an hour and a half, and that they meditate the axiom "There is nothing."[11]

III

The third way of excluding God from man's nearness is to conceive of him as apprehensible only to one faculty of man—for example, to faith—but not to the other, reason; or to the speculative faculty but not to faith. In both instances God remains an abstraction, and man who tries to reach him appears more like an athlete or a champion than a real human being. In turn, God too seems to be a geometrical point to which no tangible qualities are attributed. As a term, writes Evelyn Underhill, it is as attractive and impersonal as a mountain peak; and the mystic attaining it has something of the aristocratic self-satisfaction of the successful mountaineer.[12] Without a doubt, this is a Platonic heritage strengthened and popularized by Plotinus, who did not realize that on several points his teaching would converge with the Gnostic thesis he warned against and combatted. It was Plato who insisted on the separation of the real god from creation, even from Being, so that it is little surprise that, deprived of the vitality of classical Greek philosophizing, this god degenerated, in the hands of Neoplatonists and Plotinus himself, into an aloof abstraction, the One. True, Plotinus, a mystic, was able to establish a *synousia* (union) with the transcendent, but this mystical contact exploded when exposed to discursive knowledge and to description in words: the mystic fell back on the duality, and the union was decomposed into subject and his mystical object. Again, like in the complementary case of man's identity with the divine, in Plotinus's teaching the soul enters in contact with the One only by losing the contours of all noetic vision, in other words by sacrificing its intellectual part. Indeed, Plotinus transcribed the few mystical experiences he had in erotic terms, trying to convey the sensation of an unmixed joy.

The One, however, is so distant that it is the source of Being, not Being itself. Consequently, it is never conceived as Augustine's God: lover, helper, and savior. It needs nothing and desires nothing, least of all worship by man. It is therefore somewhat difficult to conclude that Plotinism is a typical variety of the position called an "inaccessible God"; as we have seen, a distant God discourages mundane existence, intellectual effort, and desire for moral or even meaningful action. Plotinus, on the contrary, was harsh with the Gnostics, who believed that, "taking flight toward God on the wings of dream," one may escape the human condition. In his eyes, the wise man never mistakes the illusion of instant purity for the state one obtains at the end of a long effort. He strikes a Pascalian note when he says that those who believe themselves to be above intelligence fall below it; nature must not be despised.

There is in the third book of Plotinus's *Ennead* a beautiful passage that agreeably contrasts with the teaching that man is either isolated from a distant god or is consubstantial with a god indistinguishable from the human spirit. "Without being the best of living beings," writes Plotinus, "man occupies the middle order he has chosen and where Providence does not allow him to lose himself but brings him always back to the divine through virtue. Thus Providence safeguards the reasonable character of the human race, making it participate, with some degree of wisdom, art, and justice, in social relations. Man is a beautiful accomplishment, and his destiny is better than that of any other earthly being."[13]

Yet, as one of Plotinus's distinguished French commentators, Maurice de Gandillac, remarks, this last of the great Greek philosophers is the inspirer of various currents of thought that he would have probably rejected with the same firmness with which he criticised Gnostic dualism. There is a monist mystical tradition in the Middle Ages that claims Plotinus as one of its ancestors, the tradition of Meister Eckhart, Nicholas of Cusa, and others, counting adepts up to the Renaissance and beyond.[14] Meister Eckhart's statements (mostly in his justly famous *Sermons*) are as ambiguous—belonging, measured by our categories, to both *A* and *B*—as Plotinus's, if not more. He speaks according to the position of the unknowable God, as for example in Sermon 15: "Nothing we say of God is true. . . . If you would catch the spirit of truth, pursue it not with the human senses. It is so swift, it comes rushing." And in Sermon 56: "The inner and the outer man are as different as heaven from earth. God is a thousand times more different. God becomes and unbecomes." Then in Sermon 87 he speaks as a Plotinian, indeed as an adept of Indian metaphysics: "To keep a place of one's own is to keep up a difference. Wherefore I pray to God to quit me of God (so that I may return to sheer being which is above God and above difference). . . . I am my own cause, both of my being which is eternal and of my being which is in time. . . . I can never die. . . . In my birth all things were born. . . . Had I willed it, I had never been, nor all things with me. Had I not been, God had not been."¹⁵

Thus it is difficult to situate Meister Eckhart exactly, although it is clear that his position from the church's point of view was unorthodox. In contrast to a par excellence orthodox mystic, Ruysbroeck (a theistic mystic, according to Zaehner's classification; a "constructive" mystic, in the terminology of Delacroix), Eckhart, like the Gnostics or the Indian mystics, taught that the pure must go beyond the ethical commandments because "God commands no external act, such acts being neither good, nor divine." Eckhart's disciples and successors, Henry Suso and John Tauler, also taught that "internal man" is purged of the vices of "external man." Tauler, who acknowledged his debt to the fifth-century Neoplatonist, Proclus, expressed the view that when we enter in contact with our inner self, we recognize God there at once, more clearly than the eye can see the sun.

Partly from the influence of the Muslim philosophers Averroës and Avicenna, as the Middle Ages were drawing to an end the Christian God became the target of indirect attacks, which, for being indirect, were no less sharp. The two positions I distinguish as *A*, the inaccessible God, and *B*, the immanent God, gained ever clearer outlines and were proposed with increasing boldness as the church became divided by schisms and relaxed its vigilance. (The third position, *C*, the transcendent and personal God, continued meanwhile to be presented by orthodox theologians.) The theme of the "unknown God" became the favorite of philosophers, and the theme of the mutual absorption of the divine and the human remained the chosen way of mystics, as Eckhart's examples show. Philosophers (chiefly, William Ockham and the Ockhamists) were impatient to investigate the secrets of nature, made doubly difficult to them, first, by the injunction that the findings of reason and experience may not contradict the tenets of faith and, second, by the church's

God and the Knowledge of Reality

vigilance lest natural science undermine or bypass the contents of the scriptures and the belief in miracles. Yet, the desire to explore, and thereby to enlarge, the natural world, was growing, and in proportion of its growth the domain of faith was respectfully, but already impatiently, pushed further back. As Gandillac remarks, *volens-nolens* the Plotinian mystical themes converged with the Ockhamist revolution: man's termless effort to reach the One (which, let us keep in mind, was *not* God, but the "source of Being") came to be interpreted as a justified effort to expand the known universe as indeed a "Promethean effort of the divinized human being."[16] The objective was no longer the mystic's contemplation of the One, it became now the natural philosopher's method to understand nature, to transform and dominate it. This resulted, as Ernst Cassirer notes, in the monism of the Renaissance, in the reduction of the intellectual and of the historical world to the natural world and its laws.[17]

Nicholas of Cusa played an essential role in this process. It is difficult to decide whether his God is that of the church or the Plotinian One, "above every limit and finite thing." A sharp gap is thus created between the conditioned world and the Unconditioned, so that every statement concerning the latter could only be a negation of the empirical predicates that the believer, the mystic, or the Christian philosopher might apply to the Godhead. "How shall he attain unto You?" asks Nicholas. "Does he not enter, by ascending above the limit, into the undefined and confused, and thus, *in regard to the intellect, into ignorance and obscurity*? [My italics.] So that the intellect ought to become ignorant and abide in darkness if it wants to see you. . . . Is this not a wise, a knowing ignorance? You, God, who are infinity, can only be approached by him whose intellect is in ignorance, to wit, by him who knows himself to be ignorant of you."[18]

This is a striking passage because Nicholas of Cusa, in the

most admirative and worshipful words, addressing himself to what appears to be a personal God, definitively shuts the door of knowledge on him. The *docta ignorantia* records a radical opposition between God and every form of rational, conceptual knowledge: the "vision of God" is definitely not a noetic vision, it stands perhaps closest to Kant's notion of God and knowledge. Indeed, the Kantian Cassirer remarks apropos of Nicholas that in his vision knowledge gained from experience and empirical data is sufficient to organize these data without, however, reaching the essence of things.

With regard to God, it is very clear that for Nicholas of Cusa he was distant and inaccessible. The content of faith, made up of human representations, is conjectural, expressing mainly the "otherness" of the Absolute, always differently from the previous expression. He gives us a most original description of God who must be imagined, he says, as one of those skillfully done paintings of a human face that seems always to look at us no matter from what angle we view it. All these "images," however, do not add up to a knowledge of God, even through a glass, darkly: truth, ungraspable and inconceivable in itself, can only be known in its otherness. This radical otherness is not mitigated by the catchword: learned or wise ignorance. If this is counted as knowledge, it only grasps a nonknowledge, that is, it grasps itself as completely *other* than the Absolute.[19]

A near-total separation between God and the world was thus effected in the mysticism of Eckhart and the quasi-mysticism of Nicholas of Cusa, a separation not very different in description or intention from what the Gnostics proposed. Scandalized, Iranaeus in the second century had written that Gnostics "imagine that they discovered another God beyond God . . . whom nobody can recognize as holding communication with the human race or as directing mundane matters."[20] Nicholas of Cusa and Ockam do not find it necessary to discover another God. They wish to remain within a loosely interpreted Christian discourse; therefore they put God out of bounds for reason, yet communicating with man through faith. The immediately accessible God for them will, in a sense, be man himself, to whose reason now everything must be reduced (except the Christian God, of course), whose reason finds no insurmountable obstacles. Ockham's thought, writes Louis Bouyer, is a radical empiricism that reduces all being to what is perceived. Hence God, his grace and the dogmas, not being part of empirical experience, are emptied out, unless they are perceived as changes effected in us; but in that case the changes really come from us, and the transcendental, in order to intervene, must become part of ourselves.[21]

IV

Spinoza's system is a brilliant variation on the "distant God" theme. Unlike Nicholas of Cusa, he teaches that God is accessible to reason but not to faith. Let us make this observation more precise. Spinoza abolishes religion and leaves no room for faith. His *Tractatus theologico-politicus* demonstrates that such beliefs as prophecy, miracles, and the election of the Jews by God are only manifestations of universal necessity that man ought to adore, not through faith but through clear comprehension. Since ordinary people have only superstitions and only the philosopher possesses knowledge, it follows that the adoration of God is equivalent with the philosopher's act of comprehension that God is necessity and that his own knowledge of God is itself part of this necessity. Hence the philosopher's serene state of mind, which, however, has nothing to do with faith. Spinoza writes in his third chapter: "To say that everything happens according to natural laws, and to say that everything is ordained by the decree of God, is the same thing."[22]

One may, naturally, debate whether a God conceived as pure necessity is a "distant God" or an "immanent God," one who

leaves us anguished or one who reassures us through the mathe-
maticity of his decrees that are equivalent to laws of nature.
One is reminded of the quarrel around Plato's view of the celestial bodies: were they divine on account of their immutability
and unchanging course, or were they, as Augustine said, inferior
to men because unfree? At any rate, Nietzsche mocked Spinoza's
love for this God of necessity ("amor intellectualis Dei") as
bloodless. Nothing remains, indeed, of God's attributes by which
the non-Spinozist philosopher might grasp him other than
through an abstract awe: "Nothing in the universe is contingent,
but all things are conditioned to exist and operate in a particular
manner by the necessity of the divine nature." (*Ethics*, Part I,
prop. XXIX.) "Will no more appertains to God than anything
else in nature, motion, rest and the like . . . which follow from
the necessity of divine nature." (Part I, prop. XXXII/cor. II.)
"A thing can in no respect be called contingent, save in relation
to the imperfection of our knowledge." (Part I, prop. XXXII./
note I.)

The intimation that this is a distant God comes not only from
direct philosophical proof but also from reactions to Spinozism
from those whom it repelled and from those whom it attracted.
Spinoza's English correspondent, Oldenburg, kept reminding
him, unsuccessfully, of what presumably educated and philosophically knowledgeable people, himself included, thought of
Spinoza's system (of the *Tractatus* and other minor writings;
the *Ethics* was published posthumously). "You confuse God and
Nature," Oldenburg writes (Letter XX.), "you take away the authority and value of miracles whereby alone the certainty of
divine revelation can be established." "You appear to set up a
fatalistic necessity for all things and actions. If so, the sinews of
laws, virtue and religion are severed, all rewards and punish-
ments are in vain." (Letter XXII.) "The tenor of Holy Scripture
seems to imply that man can abstain from sin and avoid pun-
ishment. If this were denied, it would have to be said that the

human mind acts no less mechanically than the human body."
(Letter XXV.) And so on, more letters and more anti-Spinozist
arguments.

The tone of Spinoza's correspondence with the burgher Blyenbergh is not different, except that Spinoza shows himself more
impatient with him than with Oldenburg. "You remove all the
sanctions of virtue and reduce us to automata," writes Blyenbergh. "Your doctrine, that strictly speaking we cannot sin
against God, is a hard saying"; and so on.

From Spinoza's attitude as it affects his correspondents the
same features transpire as from the Gnostic attitude with its denial of God's presence in life and history. And it affected Oldenburg and Blyenbergh much the same way as the Gnostics' system or systems affected the early fathers of the church, Iranaeus,
Clement of Alexandria, Hypolitus, and Augustine. At first sight,
there seems to be a considerable difference: in diverse ways, all
Gnostics agreed that God is distant, unknowable, unnamable, in
short, a nonparticipant in the manner of Epicurus's *deus otiosus*; at times two gods were conceived, one inferior, the other
real; the Christian Gnostics—for example, Basilides—held that
Yahweh was the inferior God (*archon*) and Christ the genuine
God, bringing salvation from on high; the Bogomils of the
twelfth and thirteenth centuries (who spread from northern
Italy into the Balkans) believed that the Father, the good God,
simply abandoned the present cycle of seven thousand years to
Satan.

The upshot of all this was that man, wretched in his state of
abandonment and a stranger (*allogenes*, alien) in this world, has
two options if he is an elect, a *pneumatikos*, a *gnostikos*: either
reach God through strenuous asceticism or abandon himself to
immoral license since evil (matter, body; *hyle*, *sarx*) cannot affect him anyway. Thus the concept of a distant God seems to
have an immediate impact on man's behavior. And, after all,
this is what his critics brought up against Spinoza, in whose equation, God is Necessity, they saw a God so distant as to author-

ize the worst. The philosopher answered that in his own view this God authorized only the best, the kind of near-ascetic conduct, indeed, that some Gnostics also adopted. He wrote, "Men who are governed by reason and seek what is useful to them in accord to reason, desire for themselves nothing they do not desire for all mankind, and thus are just and honorable in their conduct."[23] As we have seen, this did not convince his critics. Even the less philosophical Blyenbergh writes to him that if our essence is equivalent to our state at a given time, we are as perfect when sinning as when virtuous: God would wish for vice as much as for virtue. Both the good and the evil man execute God's will.

The reasons that led Oldenburgh and Blyenbergh to oppose Spinozism were the very same ones that endeared the philosopher from the Hague to a number of later thinkers. No trace of transcendentalism remains, indeed, in Enlightenment philosophy, whether German or French. In seventeenth-century English thought, as in Continental thought too, the Bible still ranked as the book, next to nature's "book," in which God's design may be read. By the eighteenth century nature was honored, to the exclusion of scripture, "with a religious reverence."[24] This is what the Baron d'Holbach wrote in 1780: "Let us be content to say that matter has always existed, that it moves in virtue of its own essence, and that all the phenomena of Nature are due to the different movements of the various kinds of matter of which Nature consists."[25] Could this not have been a comment from an enthusiastic Spinozist schoolboy's copy on the master's most important thought: "Men think themselves free in as much as they are conscious of their volitions and desires, and never even dream, in their ignorance, of the causes which have disposed them so to wish and desire."[26]

Together with nature, reason too was the royal road to understanding. Understanding no longer God's will, but, indeed, causes why some people still believed in him. The German divine Samuel Reimarus, whose posthumous manuscripts Lessing was to edit, declared that Jesus taught a rational religion—a statement rather out of harmony with his other remark that Jesus was a fanatic Jewish peasant. We are, of course, here at the end of the degeneracy of the idea of the distant God, and partly, in a different tradition, that of Lucretius. But Lessing and Hegel (and of course Goethe), the best minds of the age, are Spinozist, not Lucretian. Well known is Jacobi's letter to Mendelssohn, bringing the scandalous news of Lessing's conversion to Spinozism. "The orthodox ideas of Deity are no longer possible for me," Lessing reportedly said. The transcendent God made no special revelations and was only known through the book of nature. In one word, he was no longer necessary. He may have been the first cause, but he had not intervened since. "There is no other philosophy except the philosophy of Spinoza." And Lessing added: "I have no desire for free will."[27]

What was the end of the road for Lessing became Hegel's starting inspiration. These are some of the statements he made in his lectures on the history of philosophy, statements pertaining to our topic: "Spinozism is accused of atheism because no distinction is made in it between God and the world. . . . God disappears and only nature remains. . . . Spinoza maintains that there is no such thing as the world, it is merely a form of God. . . . This is the Eastern view of things, which first found expression in the West with Spinoza. To be a follower of Spinoza is the essential beginning of all philosophy. For when man begins to philosophize, the soul must bathe in this ether of the One substance, in which everything we hold true has disappeared. This negation of all particulars, to which every philosopher must have come, is the liberation of the mind and its absolute freedom."[28]

We must examine, finally, one more method of conceiving God as distant, a method to which allusions were made earlier and repeatedly; let us now review it in a more systematic manner.

The Inaccessible God

V

If it can be proved that the created world is illusory, or if at least it can be downgraded, shown as relegated by God to a position inferior to all other created beings (angels, powers, and so forth), then the result will be identical with the previously outlined attempts: the isolation of man from God. In most of these attempts the Greek influence played a dominant role: to a greater or lesser extent, from Parmenides to Plato and to Plotinus the abyss between the One and the Multiple was left wide; this accounted considerably for the Gnostic exaggeration of regarding God as perfect but impotent, and nature as the *locus* of all evil.[29] Attempts were, of course, made by the Gnostics to narrow the gap: they invented an entire hierarchy of more-or-less divine beings who become degraded in proportion with their distance from the Father. But even with Plotinus man stands on a low echelon. Note how different this pessimistic conclusion is from the Christian teaching where between God and man there exist various creatures who are superior to men in knowledge, spirituality, and in the ability to see God face to face, yet man is God's genuine object of interest, even when he delivers man—Job, for example—to one of the superior creatures, Satan. In this sense Meister Eckhart was right, together with the entire orthodox tradition: God needs man.

There is a negligible difference between a god compelled to create (or, what is the same, a god robbed of his substance that is then used for creation) and a god separated from his creation. The distinction is clear, on the contrary, between these two conceptions and the biblical one where creation is understood as the overflow of divine love. In Gnostic systems the passage from the One to the Multiple is far from being regarded as a free divine decision to create; creation is a cosmic catastrophe, literally a fall (of the One or of God). Again, we face here more than a Gnostic and Neoplatonic concept: it is a certain way, irrespective of the epoch and the place, of conceiving the God-problem. It is one of the fundamental themes of Neoplatonic metaphysics from Plotinus to Bergson.[30] It was taken up in the third century by Origen, in the ninth by John Scotus Erigena, and its most recent exponents were the German Idealists. The notion that creation is a fall condemns the diversity of beings and things, their materiality, their time-bound and sexual nature. It is obvious that such evil things can proceed only from an evil source, or, as in the case we are considering, from a good source fallen and compelled to bring forth evil things.

The fall is, first, a fall into temporality.[31] The eternally immobile and self-contained suddenly glides, as it were, into time.[32] This catastrophe is simultaneous with the fall of souls into matter by which physical multiplicity (dispersal) arises, while the existence of time measures now the chronological differentiation. Much of Greek philosophy, and the whole of Gnosticism, consisted in having the soul reintegrate the One from which the fall had torn it; with reintegration the cosmic drama is wrapped up again like a carpet after the juggler's performance: time is abolished, and with it multiplicity, that is, creation. To be sure, the latter did have an existence; but regardless of how long it lasted, even if for millions of years like a Brahmanic "great cycle," this existence was either an illusion or a degradation, or both.

Indian metaphysics is, as usual, more radical, and some scholars speculated that it was the transfer of Indian thought to the Mediterranean world, mainly through Alexandria, that "radicalized" also the Gnostic tenets. In the Upanishads, the fall signals individuation: once imprisoned in the body, the spirit recognizes itself as a *self*, as an *ego*, and begins to attribute to himself—falsely—qualities that distinguish him from other selves. The reign of evil, of worries, and of wretchedness begins, man now says "*I* am such and such," or "this or that belongs to *me*."

The Inaccessible God

The soul has now established contact with the non-I (nonself; object-world) and has become wretched. The created world and (individualized) man stand thoroughly condemned in these systems. "Whereas Jewish and Christian tradition," writes Claude Tresmontant, "establishes personal and ethical relationships between the transcendental Absolute and the human persons, the Upanishads persuade the sage to surmount the illusion of personal existence as well as the ethical demands which it entails."[33] The Brahmans alone may rise to the knowledge of the Light that is God, after having rejected the vanity of physical existence. It is questionable whether this spiritual knowledge is a sufficient guideline: in some Gnostic systems salvation, the possession of gnosis, was interpreted as a liberation, in others as license, the first leading to ascetic life, the second to extreme libertinism. Members of the Valentinian sect, writes Iranaeus, claim that they are saved not by means of conduct, but because they are spiritual by nature. As seen before, this theme runs through the entire Western tradition as a way of solving the God-problem.

N O T E S

1. "Many of our contemporaries who acknowledge the existence of a God, have substituted for the transcendent and permanent God an immanent and impersonal one. Never before were there so many different forms of monism." Maurice de Wulf, *Introduction to Scholastic Philosophy: Medieval and Modern*, trans. P. Coffey (New York: Dover Publications, 1956), p. 223.
2. Mircea Eliade, *The Sacred and the Profane: The Nature of Religion*, trans. Willard Trask (New York: Harcourt Brace Jovanovich, Inc., 1968), p. 81.
3. Ibid., p. 87.
4. S. Takdir Alisjabana, "Sukarno's Melanesia: A Few Years in a Long History," *Quadrant* (March 1969): p. 66.
5. Henri Frankfort et al., *Before Philosophy* (New York: Pelican Book, Inc., 1949), p. 35.

God and the Knowledge of Reality

6. "This conception of God," writes Henri Frankfort, "represents so high a degree of abstraction that, in reaching it, the Hebrews seem to have left the realm of mythopoeic thought." Ibid., p. 243.

7. Rudolf Bultmann, *Gnosis* (New York: Fernhill House, Ltd., 1963), pp. 10–11.

8. R. C. Zaehner, *Mysticism: Sacred and Profane* (New York: Oxford University Press, Inc., 1961), p. 28.

9. Rudolf Otto, *Mysticism East and West* (New York: Macmillan Co., 1970), p. 103.

10. Louis Bouyer, *The Spirit and Forms of Protestantism*, transl. A. V. Littledale. (Cleveland-New York: Meridian Books, 1964), p. 152.

11. Henri de Lubac, *La Rencontre du Bouddhisme et de l'Occident* (Paris: Aubier-Montaigne, 1952), p. 85.

12. Evelyn Underhill, *The Essentials of Mysticism and Other Essays* (New York: E. P. Dutton & Co., Inc., 1960), p. 130.

13. Plotinus, *Ennead*, III, 2, 9.

14. In our time Bergson referred to Plotinus as one of the chief influences on his philosophy.

15. Meister Eckhart, *Sermons*, trans. Raymond B. Blakney (New York: Harper Torchbooks, 1941).

16. Maurice de Gandillac, *La Sagesse de Plotin* (Paris: Librairie Philosophique J. Vrin, 1966), p. 267. My translation.

17. Ernst Cassirer, *The Individual and the Cosmos in Renaissance Philosophy*, trans. Mario Domand (Philadelphia: University of Pennsylvania Press, 1972), p 109.

18. Nicholas of Cusa, *The Vision of God* in *Opera*, 3 vols. (1514; reprint ed., New York: Johnson Reprint Corp., 1962). My translation.

19. Even incarnation cannot be said, then, to have taken place as a concrete event because nothing may be stated of Christ if not negatively. According to Nicholas of Cusa, incarnation occurs in man's soul; it is renewed in every ego, every time, in our depth that is the true "child-bed" of divinity. The same idea occurs in Hegel's thought and today in Bultmann's "demythologized" theology.

20. Iranaeus, *Adversus Haeresos* 3. 24. 2. My translation.

21. Bouyer, *Spirit and Forms of Protestantism*, p. 153.

22. Benedict de Spinoza, *Theological-Political Treatise* in *Chief Works*, 2 vols., trans. R. H. Elwes (New York: Dover Publications, 1955), 1: 45.

23. Spinoza, *Ethics* in *Chief Works*, 2: Part VI, Prop. XVIII/Note.

24. Basil Willey, *The Eighteenth Century Background: Studies on the Idea of Nature in the Thought of the Period* (Boston: Beacon Press, 1966), p. 157.

25. Quoted in B. Willey, *ibid.*, p. 158. My translation.

26. Spinoza, *Ethics* in *Chief Works*, 2: 94–99.

27. The conversation between Lessing and Jacobi took place in July 1780, the year before Lessing's death.

The Inaccessible God

28. Georg W. Hegel, *Lectures on the History of Philosophy*, 3 vols., trans. E. S. Haldane and F. H. Simson (New York: Humanities Press, Inc.; London: Routledge and Kegan Paul, 1955), III: 256, 280, 286–87.

29. Quispel points out that the Gnostics of the first centuries, even the more important among them, such as Valentinus, Basilides, and Marcion, learned their philosophy from rather poorly vulgarized Platonic textbooks circulating in the Hellenic-Roman world. Gilles Quispel, "Gnostic Man: The Doctrine of Basilides," *Eranos* 16 (1948): 210–246.

30. Claude Tresmontant, *La Métaphysique du Christianisme* (Paris: Ed. du Seuil, 1961), p. 420.

31. For the Gnostics, "time, the work of the Creator God, is at best a caricature of eternity, a defective imitation far removed from its model. In the last analysis, it is the consequence of a fall; it is a lie." H. C. Puech, "Gnosis and Time," *Eranos* 20 (1951): 38–85.

32. It is important to note that no philosophically satisfactory reason is ever given for the passage from the One, the changeless, to the Multiple and dispersed. It is explained as a momentary inattention or fatigue (by the Platonic schools), or as the result of a struggle between light and darkness (in Middle Eastern cosmogonies). In later speculation, including some of the modern political myths, the departure from primeval innocence (state of nature, archaic communism, and so forth) is the weakest, least clarified link in the chain of deduction.

33. Tresmontant, *La Métaphysique du Christianisme*, p. 265. My translation.

THE IMMANENT GOD

THE approach to the God-problem we shall examine next, position *B*, seems to be, at first, the opposite of position *A*, examined in the previous section. *A*, while assuming God's existence, insists that he is distant, removed from man's immediacy, so that he becomes irrelevant while man remains either agonizingly lonely or arrogantly independent. At any rate, he remains, from the religious point of view, an agnostic. The second approach, *B*, points, on the contrary, to the identity of God and man (his soul), that is, not merely to their analogous nature but to their identical nature.

Speculation about the "inaccessible God" divided itself into several possible approaches; speculation about God who is in the soul of man follows one method. This is not surprising. We may conceive God and man as *one* from the timeless beginning, or we may hold that man has fallen from this primordial and essential unity but that he will regain his exalted status through emancipation from his bodily prison. In both cases the spiritual substance is identical; also in both cases liberation from the body, and from all things that physical, fleshly existence entails, depends on the abolition of time. The "inner man" regains the divine status either by sudden illumination or by lengthy exercises the main aspect of which is liberation from time-bound existence. Three things prevent a man from knowing God, writes Meister Eckhart: "The first is time, the second corporeality, and the third is multiplicity."

[32]

The Immanent God

Am I describing the mystic experience? In a way, I am, for my point is that position *B* is derived from the conviction (experience) that God is in the soul or is identical with the soul. But this is not exclusively the mystic's experience; it may also be the philosopher's thesis, as the examples of Giordano Bruno, Hegel, and others suggest. In fact, if the terms in which the *unio mystica* is described are not the same as the philosopher's discursive description, the philosophical consequences of both—for example, regarding epistemology—are strikingly similar, even identical.

The mystic and the philosopher may then adopt a *pan-en-henic* position[1] through the experience that all is one, including the self. In Indian metaphysics the search for the One (*Ekam*) in fact precedes the search for the soul (*atman*) and for God (*Brahman*), although they later merge: the soul "becomes One" and assumes then the third experience, that of the divinity. Rudolf Otto admits, however, the frequency of the case when the mystic uses the term *God* merely "as a trimming upon the One" whose primacy in the experience he tacitly recognizes. The *atman* thus withdraws from selfhood and from discursive knowledge since it has grasped itself as pure consciousness, a superior kind of saving knowledge. As the sage Sankara said, the *atman* is the Real (or *Brahman*), it conceives reality in itself—a description useful for us to retain for the discussion of Hegel's theory of knowledge. The *atman* is then the "one, eternal, unchangeable and homogeneous *Brahman*," yet not God because the *Brahman* is the world-spirit, superior to God (*Isvara*). It is an *absolute* in a world where the personal God plays, at best, an ambiguous role and only in certain theistic trends. Indian metaphysics does not by necessity posit God's existence, certainly not a personal God's.

It is different with Jews, Christians, and Muslims. In their eyes God is a person so that man, tempted by the absolute, can better focus on certain precise attributes on which the Judeo-

God and the Knowledge of Reality

Christian and the Platonic traditions converge, like goodness, omniscience, and omnipotence, and then discover these elements in himself. Where the Indian sage regards absorption in the One as the chief objective of the mystic, a certain type of monotheistic mystic searches for union with God, finding him in his soul. What happens then is that he bends the dogmas, mysteries, and concepts of his (monotheistic) religion in such a way that he may acquire, so to speak, an inner light about them; instead of internalizing the tenets of his religion, following its commandments, and striving for a fuller comprehension and practice, he leaps *inside* his religious faith—and by the soul's naturally radical movement, to its center—so as to become its source and light. The tenth-century Muslim mystic, Abu Mansur el Helladj, prayed to God, saying: "Oh, God, you who are myself and of whom I am the He! Between my 'I am' and your 'he is' the only difference is that I am in time and you are perennial." Compare this with Meister Eckhart: "If I am to know God directly, I must become completely He and He I; so that this He and this I become and are one I." (Sermon 94.)

On the level of religious practice and of the church, this attitude is translated through the rejection of intermediaries between God and the faithful. The sacraments are denied validity, and the priesthood is regarded as an unnecessary interference between the soul and the in-dwelling God. We have seen that the Christianizing Gnostic's inner revelation authorized him to reject what he considered as the "externals," that is the Law, the entire Old Testament. The Valentinian prayers invoked the celestial origin of the initiate so that he stood in no need of any other knowledge than self-knowledge. "The Gnostic is a Gnostic because he knows, by revelation, who his true self is. Other religions are in varying measure God-centered. The Gnostic is self-centered."[2] This attitude is, of course, religious in nature, but it appears also in parareligious movements, for example, in those Western sects that were influenced by oriental systems,

[34]

the Rosicrucian fraternity, certain German Masonic sects of the eighteenth century, Helen Blavatsky's Theosophists, and other esoteric movements to be discussed in the first section of Part Two. The substance of their message is that the believer needs no mediator, no cult, nor any of the "grotesque divine ornaments." There is no other wisdom outside the one we discover in ourselves, no other divinity except the one we bear in our own depth.[3]

The philosophical expression of this position bypasses, naturally, the cultic language of religion, but their common origin would be hard to deny. We find the *pan-en-henic* position in men apparently as different as Empedocles, the Gnostics, Avicenna, Bruno, Spinoza, Meister Eckhart, Hegel, and countless others. In fact, Georg Misch noted that the Xenophantic formula *hen-kai-pan* (all-one) expresses the monistic principle that runs through European philosophy, and that in modern times it has even acquired a new luster as the symbol of the fight waged by the free spirit of philosophy against the otherworldliness of Christianity.[4]

A near-Gnostic position is expressed by Empedocles: the soul is of divine race, too noble for this world. It begins to live only after its escape from the body. But while confined therein, the soul has its separate existence: it has no concern with the everyday business of perception and sensation; it is active in the higher mode of knowledge, in ecstatic inspiration.[5] We recognize in this position one as old as mankind, in fact more than merely old, *natural* to our thinking the moment we are struck by the difference between the mind's life and the immediate "bodily" reactions to the outside world. Yet, the word *natural* does not mean "correct," and reference to the soul as superior to the body should not denote the former's divine nature. The demarcation line is hard to observe, perhaps because another basic experience of man is his misery. Romantic and existentialist moods usually exaggerate this feeling, and words are then

God and the Knowledge of Reality

found conveying its vagueness with a remarkable precision, if one may say. Such are expressions as *Weltschmerz, Sehnsucht, vague des passions, misery of consciousness*, anguish, *spleen*. The noteworthy thing is the translation of this feeling into the language of philosophy where it is explained by the soul's position and movements between a place that is its *home* and another place that is its *exile*. For example, the Gnostics held that in its unredeemed state the *pneuma* immersed in the soul (*psyche*) and in the flesh (*sarx*) is unconscious of itself, benumbed, asleep, or intoxicated by the poison of the world: it is ignorant. Its awakening and liberation are effected through knowledge. Knowledge, however, may not be instantaneous, it leads through "generations" that the spirit must endure before full knowledge (lost memory) is regained. "To the unredeemed soul this time perspective is a source of anguish. The terror of the vastness of cosmic spaces is matched by the terror of the times that have to be endured."[6]

Hence the great lament of Gnostics, as also of all those who share in approach *B* to the God-problem: the disrupted unity of God and man. Why did you create the world, they address God, when the price was to cast us out of your bosom? In Meister Eckhart's words, "When I came out of God into multiplicity, all things proclaimed: 'there is a God!' Now this cannot make me blessed, for I realize myself as creature." This thought also applies to Sankara's position, according to Rudolf Otto.[7] It is obvious that the exiled prince, son of the divine being, is unable to regard his place of exile, no matter how happy he may be in it, according to mediocre mundane standards, as comparable to his lost heavenly abode. His sole concern is to regain it, a process he calls salvation, redemption, return from the diaspora, going home, or, as Hegel calls it, *bei sich sein*. It is a regeneration in the sense of a gathering together (*syllexis*) of our luminous, divine substance,[8] a restoration of the original unity, a release from the world. The *Poimander* describes the process

[36]

as a gradual ridding of the naked self of the consequences of cosmic fall so that primal man may be free to become again one with God. In modern terminology this can be expressed as man's return from an alienated existence to his ontological condition, to the total and permanent reality of his ego. As Origenes said, this disincarnation, this abolition of bodies, means the loss of individuality too: the monads lose their names and their differences; they are reabsorbed in the divine substance.[9]

These themes continued far beyond the Gnostic era and were fed into an uninterrupted tradition. If they seem to be more sporadic in the first half of the Middle Ages, it is because this tradition too suffered from the West's general isolation, the disappearance from circulation of Greek philosophical writings, and, naturally, from the church's vigilance. This was not quite the case with Arab speculation although the official theologians of Islam were vigilant in their orthodox position. There the interpreters of Aristotle, particularly Avicenna, combined the Stagirite's teaching on form and matter with Neoplatonism and concluded that since matter is the principle of individuation our bodies disperse the soul-substance that would otherwise remain undivided. A few centuries later in Europe, too, the theme of the oneness of God and man was stressed by Muslim mystics—not by the orthodox ones, of course, but by later ones in the tenth and eleventh centuries. The later Muslim mystics reached conclusions similar to those of the Gnostics: the divine soul, whose passage in the world is a brief sojourn between two eternities in God, has no other duty and aspiration than purification from matter; it has no concern with worldly behavior and moral matters since it seeks liberation from life itself. Some mystics of Islam held the same ideas: the intimacy they had reached with God was supposed to absolve them of the duty of prayer, of abstention from wine, of obedience. Al Ghazali regarded them as more sinful than the infidels "for they open up a door to license which cannot be closed."[10] They, that is the adepts of Sufism, imagined themselves to be amalgamated with God, others to be identified with him, yet others to be associated with him.[11]

What was their sin in Ghazali's eyes? They took their state of enthusiasm, their elation, for a sign of union with God because it gave them the deceptive impression of emptiness that the divine presence would fill. The orthodox Muslim and Christian mystics contended, on their side, that not only God but the devil too may enter through the "door left open," because the expectation of purity, the soul's quietude, made the false mystics scorn the works of virtue. Ruysbroeck called them the forerunners of Antichrist who "wish to be free of the commandments of God, and to be empty and united with God without love and charity."[12]

Both the Muslim and the Christian world thus distinguished true and false mysticism, and the distinction can be made on practical grounds: the genuine mystic remained humble and obedient and turned with renewed fervor and certitude toward concrete forms of charity for his fellow men. In God he perceived the ultimate guarantee of the world's reality and the meaning of his own actions. The false mystic was rather similar to the Gnostic who took his state of elation for the divinity of his soul. He therefore concluded that the immobile (quiet) state of his soul is too exalted to be disturbed by action or by the need to test it through the works of virtue. Gordon Leff observes that the latter kind of mysticism, one of the main roots of unorthodoxy, surfaced in the West thanks to the thirteenth-century translations of Neoplatonist writings (Proclus, Plotinus, the pseudo-Dionysius). God was sought in the soul, emphasis was placed on inner experience: correspondingly, the sacraments were depreciated, the role of the priesthood denied validity. This was the first link with the Gnostic-Neoplatonist tradition; the second was to be established some two hundred years later when Plato and the Hermetic documents were introduced from the Greek world overrun by the Turks.

Meister Eckhart himself was the product of the first contact.

The Immanent God

A rather ambiguous mystic, who perhaps for this reason had an enormous influence, he walked the thin edge of two traditions. While an orthodox in many respects with whose teachings even the Thomists could find no fault, Eckhart the mystic followed a monist line, actually coming to identify the soul with the deity. This to such an extent that Rudolf Otto chose him as the chief representative of Christian mysticism, to show the similarity between it and an important mystic tradition in India. Defenders of Eckhart, among them Otto, argued that his more extreme utterances were emphatic ways of presenting the creature's fragility when confronted with God, the need for man to put all his valuation into a life celebrating God's all-importance. Yet, this is exactly the monist mystic's way once he yields to the temptation formulated here as position *B*: emphasis on what separates God from man results in despair over ever reaching God—so that a "more real" God (Super-God) is found, but this time in man's soul. The earlier adored God is dismissed then as inferior or as a false God. We saw that this was also the position of negative theology, that of the pseudo-Denys. According to Vacherot, Denys taught that to know God we must cease thinking of him. The devout is lost in ignorance because nothing can be said of the deity who is removed to an infinite distance from the human soul.*

---

* Since I wrote these lines (and made other references to Denys in this book), friends in Torino made me acquainted with the work of Fr. Ceslas Pera whom I had met shortly before his death, in 1963. According to Fr. Pera, Denys developed his "negative theology" to contradict Aetius and Eunomius who held that reason possesses the same power as revelation in knowing God. On the other hand, Denys, according to Fr. Pera, emphasizes a "positive theology" against the influence of such as Philo and Plotinus. If this interpretation is correct, Denys was an orthodox theologian (which would explain the high esteem in which Thomas Aquinas held him) and he would have to be situated not at the end of the fifth and beginning of the sixth centuries, but in the second half of the fourth, which would explain the controversy in which he was involved. See Ceslas Pera, "Denys le Mystique et la Theomachia," *Revue des sciences philosophiques*, XXV (1936), Paris, Lib. Phil. Vrin.

I quoted earlier a part of the Eckhartian statement: "Consider, I beseech you, by the eternal and imperishable truth, and by my soul: grasp the unheard-of. God and Godhead are as distinct as heaven and earth. Heaven stands a thousand miles above the earth, and so the Godhead is above God. God becomes and disbecomes." The last phrase has been many times commented by Eckhart scholars. I think the meaning is clear: it describes the German mystic's own experience of vacillation, of going to and fro, between the God whom his church adored and his own whom he saw as infinitely higher. "Had I a God whom I could understand," he exclaimed, "I would no longer hold him for God!" And: "Our Lord departed to Heaven, beyond all understanding, beyond all human ken. He who is thus translated beyond light of any kind dwells in the Unity."

This was, then, Eckhart's "Super-God." Compared to him, the creature is truly and only miserable dust, and as Eckhart says, he has no essence, no value; of himself he is nothing. But this is an untenable situation in which a man of the Western traditions—that is, one who requires not only faith and a state of being but also the use of reason—cannot remain for long. From dust and ashes he aspires to become—now that God is too far to intervene as a person—being and essence, beyond the *status creaturae* that was recognized as an essenceless void. Eckhart's extremist stance is clear: considering the *creatura* exclusively under one, negative, aspect—namely, that he is not-God —he concludes that he is also unreal, nonessential, vain. Under such circumstances, the creature cannot gain any reality unless he takes the leap from creatureliness into divinity. This is what Eckhart does. It is not enough, as he sees it, to be united with God (*Deo unitum esse*); one must be the same as God (*unum esse cum Deo*). Complete and absolute identity of soul and God. And Eckhart knew that he was preaching new and unheard-of things, a return to God through the birth of the Son in our soul, the renunciation of separateness and of the *status creaturae*.

[40]

The Immanent God

Although seemingly exalting God above all else, the act of creation was thus belittled—or, if one wishes to state it differently, man was recognized as a creator. This makes Gordon Leff conclude that for Eckhart every individual was just as much a part of God as Christ himself.[13] A variation on the theme is the view of Wyclif, who regards all creatures as merely temporal realizations of eternal archetypes. The result was a cumbersome system in which creatures and God are singularly tied together so that the distance between the divine and the created becomes blurred.[14]

We saw in "The Inaccessible God" the essential aspects of the position of Nicholas of Cusa. Like Eckhart—but more boldly after a whole century, most agitated for the church, had elapsed —he too set out to locate a God above God with whom the soul might identify itself. He approached the problem in what was to be the modern way, through epistemology, not directly through the soul's aspiration to reach the Godhead. But the epistemology of Nicholas was intended, first, to recognize as knowledge of God only the state when knower (man) and known (God) coalesce, which is also Eckhart's position, and second to emancipate scientific knowledge, which has no such exalted ambition, from the requirements of theology—themselves incorrectly presented as if the knowledge of God were the soul's monopoly, exclusive of the claims of rational thought.

For Nicholas, all things are spirit, though temporarily hidden from us by the sensory covering. With the removal of this covering, spiritual things can know spiritual things directly because now they know themselves in things with which they share the same substance. This is no longer a way of *knowing*, but a *not-knowing*, "beholding without grasping," a phrase in which *grasp* means intellectual apprehension, an inferior kind of knowledge. God is the object of "unknowing" (*docta ignorantia*) and he stands above being and not-being, the universe and its negation. Thus the God to whom we are accustomed to ascribe qualities, the God of scriptures, is not the true one; we arrive at the true God if we imagine a Super-God and reach him insofar as knowing flows into nonknowing.

All this takes place in the soul or self that is the organ through which the *universal essence* (Super-God) knows and expresses itself. The *self* (the *I*) is no longer a thing among things, a distinct entity, it is a form in which the universal essence (Super-God) has its life. This is what other leading German mystics and Paracelsians were also to say. There is nothing in heaven and on earth, Paracelsus maintained in the sixteenth century, that is not in man; God who is in heaven is really in man. Also in the sixteenth century Sebastian Franck and Caspar Schwenckfeld argued that it is not the Jesus whom the gospels preach who is of value, but the Christ who can be born in every man out of his deeper nature. A century later the radical mystic Angelus Silesius went beyond Eckhart's exalted statements: "I know that without me God cannot live for an instant; if I come to nothing, then He must give up the ghost." "When my will is dead then must God do what I will; I myself prescribe to Him the pattern and the goal." "Without me God cannot make a single worm; if I do not preserve it with Him, it must straightway fall to pieces."

It may be that such pronouncements indicate only that the mystic feels he is part of the chain of being that for him is God. He is, however, a privileged part, the point of concentration, and not merely as a God to whom magnified earthly attributes are allocated, but as a Super-God, beyond description and ineffable. It is easy to imagine that in later centuries, the same notion, albeit desacralized, was to serve the philosopher wishing to locate the absolutized self, the world-spirit whose sole interpreter he is. Rudolf Otto went to the core of this position when he asked whether Godhead and *Brahman* were not merely names for the soul that has found its own glory.

In spite of mounting persecution, the sects that popularized the immanentist position kept multiplying from the time of

Joachim de Fiore (twelfth century) to Wyclif in the fourteenth and beyond. One gains the impression that the officials of the Inquisition became less and less masters of the situation, although their task must have been rendered easier by the collection of testimonies that monotonously repeated the same kind of heretical theses, millenarist aspirations, and individual cases of exaltation. As if all sects had learned from one single manual, their members displayed the same behavior regardless of century and country, used the same words to describe their beliefs, blasphemed in the same way, asserted the same hopes. In every testimony we are struck by the same claim of being an elect and having God in one's soul.

The Brethren of the Free Spirit held that "God is all that is," and that "every created thing is divine." On the death of the body the soul was supposed to disappear in its Divine Origin like a drop of water in a jug. If not direct Gnostic influence, certainly an analogous system had led the Brethren to convictions that were articulated a millennium before: from eternity man was God in God, and, for more precision, they added that from eternity the *soul* of man was in God, and *was* in fact God. Man was not begotten but was from eternity wholly unbegettable; and therefore he is wholly immortal.[15] From this gnosis there followed a set of behavior for the Brethren, also familiar from earlier times: the Brethren and the female members of the sect went around hardly covering their nakedness, lived from begging, held all possessions in common, and engaged in sexual orgies. "They believed they were free from sin and could yield to desire with impunity."[16] John of Brünn, a leader of the sect, confessed that he acted not by external stimulation but by the spirit within. "The spirit is free, and I am a natural man," he declared. John Hartmann, another member cited before the Inquisition, asserted that God is everywhere and that one could find him in playing chess as much as in the eucharist, provided chess was more to the taste of the individual believer.[17] Leff

[43]

sums up this period when he writes that, under Eckhart's un-
guarded influence, the mystics lost the distinction between God
and creation so that they maintained that the "perfect man is
God."[18]

With the Renaissance (which was also the Renaissance of
Pythagorean, Hermetic, and other occult doctrines) and the Ref-
ormation, pantheism entered one of its most fertile periods.
Half of Europe's universities shut out scholastic philosophy and
began catering to a new type of wandering scholar, not fitting
into the old professional mold. These scholars did not teach
Aristotle, not even Plato, but the corrupted doctrines of the late
Empire, the syncretism of post-Hellenic Mediterranean world in
which not Athens was the cultural capital but Egypt, Syria, and
North Africa. Giordano Bruno, to whose role we shall return in
Part Two, was the prototype of these scholars, welcome at the
universities of the new Protestant England and Germany, where,
as I shall show later, philosophy began its career as a social and
political stimulant. Bruno's *De la causa, principio et uno* is a
pantheistic tract: "the being of the universe is one in the Infinite, and not less present in any one of the individual beings
which we see as parts of the same: so that the whole and every
part is one in substance. . . . The idea of the Infinite dissolves all
individualities and differences." One can say with Georg Misch
that Xenophanes' old formula, *hen-kai-pan* (all-one; all is one),
the first formula of monism in Western Philosophy, returned to
the scene with the Renaissance. With this comeback, Christian
transcendentalism received its first serious blow since the days
of Iranaeus and Augustine.[19] The fruits of Ockhamism began
to ripen. True, the mystics of Eckhart's tradition kept asserting
that God was all in all; yet, the individual gradually began to
usurp God's substance. To put it differently, it was easier to observe God *within* oneself than in the sphere of transcendence.
Ockham, approaching the problem from the opposite end, taught
that all we may know of God is his existence and that therefore
the study of nature is the only legitimate exercise of the intel-

lect. Thus God, while his goodness, wisdom, mercifulness, and sovereignly free creative power (*potentia absoluta*) were not denied, gradually yielded to nature as the primary means of conveying knowledge of the universe. Philosophers and paraphilosophers began to take nature as their basic datum and to turn only afterward to the Bible in order to seek confirmation. The "perfect knowledge" attributed to Paracelsus was supposed to consist in his ability to find the scripture texts in harmony with natural data.

From God manifesting himself in nature, interest shifted to God-in-nature, or God-nature. The Eckhartian mystics had prepared the way for man to identify himself with God; the Ockhamists were to have no difficulty to identify man with nature. The exuberant Giordano Bruno drew just these conclusions: God has nothing to do with man individually, he wrote in *Spaccio*, he communicates himself only through nature. He is the nature of nature, the soul of the soul of the world.

This is Spinozism *avant la lettre* because it denies the personal and merciful God who extends his providence over all living creatures, individually. God becomes the mechanism of nature, although in Bruno's case he is still accessible to magic manipulation. We remember that Oldenburg, Spinoza's correspondent, correctly understood the Hague philosopher's thesis that the human mind is part of an infinite understanding. From this point of view it makes hardly a difference whether God is conceived as personal or mechanical: the important thing is that, although the formulation of God changes, what does *not* change is the thinker's belief that man is part of God. Besides, consubstantiality even with a Spinozist God-nature may evoke from him occasional passages of serene expostulation. It is a kind of cold lyricism, hardly distinguishable from that elicited by the doctrine of Nicholas of Cusa, who disperses God in all men, making incarnation take place through a constantly self-generative process in the soul, the "child-bed of divinity."[20]

In the post-Renaissance centuries the gradual fading of religious belief and the affirmations of individualism did not prevent approach *B* to the God-problem from being fully represented in philosophy. Whatever new definitions of God became popular among thinkers, it was easy to conceive the consubstantiality of the divine and the human being according to the latest definition. Eckhart's daring formula, "God is because I am," authorized the displacement of emphasis onto man and onto whatever temporarily preoccupied him: nature, progress, history, or the *élan vital*. Besides, as stated before, the continuity with the Neoplatonic tradition was amply assured. We shall see in Part Two that a veritable flowering of eschatological conceptions, partly brought over from the Middle Ages, partly from Hellenistic times, took place and was preparing the way for the Enlightenment and the nineteenth-century philosophies of history. Hermetism, alchemy, magic, the Rosicrucean movement, and Freemasonry, among others, based their esoteric doctrines on the unity of man and God (or the God nurtured inside man), with important epistemological consequences.

True, the philosophy of the Enlightenment with its materialism overshadowed for a while the esoteric tradition, particularly in France. Remember, however, that this was precisely the reproach Hegel made against the eighteenth-century French *philosophes*: God and man are not antithetical, he told them, they are of a common substance, otherwise man would not be able to know God. "Faith in God is engendered by the believer's very divinity; only a modification of God [that is, man] may know God."[21] This was, of course, Hegel's main thesis from which everything else was later derived. Genuine being, in his view, is unified being, because each individual becomes himself only through another. Thus the ideal is a being that has no object (*Objektlosigkeit*)—since everything is absorbed in it as subject—hence also no consciousness to be reabsorbed when no object compels it to distinguish between the other and itself (*Bewusstlosigkeit*). This state is realized in God, and, according to Hegel, this is what Jesus meant by advising us to be like chil-

[46]

dren. Hegel regards it as the end of the misery of consciousness, the *conscience malheureuse*,[22] because it means a restoration of inner totality in opposition to the positivity (*Gesetzheit*) of the Jewish religion of the Law. Inner totality, inner unification, *conscience heureuse*, religion of love—that is, not of Law—are expressions describing what Hegel regarded as Christ's message through which man may recover his own divinity. The role of Jesus is that of a restorer, a rediscoverer: he is God, but so are we all. Hegel understood incarnation not as an isolated historical event, but as a manifestation of the Absolute Spirit, taking place in all human beings and at all time.[23] Hence, for Hegel consciousness is God, and this enables consciousness to be treated as Revelation.[24]

Before outlining, in "The Transcendent and Personal God," position *C*—God as transcendent and personal—I shall now attempt to show the basic similarity and, from a certain point of view, near identity of positions *A* and *B*. The two positions follow from similar and symmetrical assumptions, hence it is not surprising to find the practical consequences following from either to be the same.

Earlier, I quoted Festugière, who distinguished between a "pessimistic" and an "optimistic" gnosis. The first posits a heavy, material world from which the soul, rid of matter and thus lightened, attempts to escape to its *true home* in the immaterial divine world. The second posits a living and divine world in which everything is divine for all: the stars, the sun, nature, the earth itself are parts of God. We note that in both gnoses the soul is of divine nature—whether God is distant and hard to attain or is so near as to coincide with the world. The nucleus of positions *A* and *B* is the divinity of the soul, although in one case this is assumed of it at once, in the other case only after it has ascended to its "true home."

Both positions express the ontological obsession "to return to the presence of the gods, to recover the strong, fresh, pure world that existed *in illo tempore*"[25]—that is, at the beginning of creation. In short, they express a thirst for being. Two researchers of Gnostic ideology, Puech and Quispel, speak of the desperation to feel alienated, as indeed many moving texts show it. We concluded that this despair may lead in two directions: one posits God as absent or distant, so that man is authorized to set up his tent in a desert where only his own voice will be heard; the other is that God is one with man, so that man gains reassurance about his own status, he is, as Hegel says, *bei sich*, at home.

These forms of the "ontological obsession" may, however, be misdirected, inasmuch as through *A* and *B* man may reach not reality but a superreality in which he ceases being a distinct person and a perceiving intelligence. If *A* is identified with agnosticism and, *à la limite*, with atheism insofar as God remains distant for the (uninitiated) soul; and if *B* is identified with the denial of the world that is not absorbed in God, then we may argue that these positions are two extremes between which pantheism ceaselessly wavers. "Unable, without falling into a manifest contradiction, to identify God and creature, the finite and the Infinite, pantheism either absorbs God in the world, or the world in God."[26] If God is distant (atheism, agnosticism), only the world exists; if the world is in God, only God exists (acosmism). In both cases man is the glorified beneficiary: in the first, he remains the highest spiritual entity; in the second, he is the privileged spiritual part of the *pan-en-henic* reality. He is the intellect par excellence, he knows the world because he knows himself; he knows the world *in* himself.

It is for these advantages that philosophers so often choose *A* or *B*. Basically, it is not a religious choice: its object is not God but the absolute intelligibility of being that is found to be compatible with *A* or *B*, but not with *C*. It is, consequently, a philosophical choice: the whole philosophical enterprise would

The Immanent God

be worthless, as viewed by the majority of thinkers, if it did not deliver the perfect grasp, the supreme knowledge. God as a person, they think, is not only a self-limiting concept; it is also a limitation for man in his search for the absolute intelligibility of being.

We shall see in "The Transcendent and Personal God" that position *C*, taking the view that God is distinct from the world (and from the soul) and that man's intellect is turned first toward intelligible reality (the world), not toward the pure spirit of God, posits God as a principle of limitation as well as a guarantee of the limited knowledge thus acquired.

Because of this essential difference we are justified to hold the view that in regard to the God-problem the two main positions are *A* and *B*, on the one hand, and *C*, on the other.

NOTES

1. As indicated in "The Inaccessible God," R. C. Zaehner's term *"pan-en-henic* experience" seems to be preferable to "pantheistic experience." The phenomenological basis of the experience is not that everything is God but that "all is in one." For easier intelligibility, I shall, however, refer to the approach here discussed as pantheistic.

2. Robert M. Grant, *Gnosticism and Early Christianity*, 2nd ed. (New York: Harper Torchbooks, 1966), p. 8.

3. Maurice Magre, *Pourquoi je suis bouddhiste*, quoted in Henri de Lubac, *La Rencontre du Bouddhisme et de l'Occident* (Paris: Aubier-Montaigne, 1952), p. 219.

4. Georg Misch, *The Dawn of Philosophy* (Cambridge, Mass.: Harvard University Press, 1951), p. 236.

5. The soul is too noble even for the function of thinking, which is nothing else than the heart's blood.

6. Hans Jonas, *The Gnostic Religion* (Boston: Beacon Press, 1963), p. 53.

7. Rudolf Otto, *Mysticism East and West* (New York: Macmillan Co., 1970), p. 31.

8. See H. C. Puech, "Gnosis and Time," *Eranos* Jahrbuch 20 (1952): 38–85.

9. Christian Gnostics managed to insert Christ's redeeming role in this process by arguing that he came to awaken the true *pneumatikoi* to the fact that they belong to a superior sphere.

10. Quoted in R. C. Zaehner, *Mysticism: Sacred and Profane* (New York: Oxford University Press, Inc., 1961), p. 187.

11. Evelyn Underhill, *Mysticism* (New York: Dutton Paperback, 1961), p. 171.

12. These were to be charges later against the Quietists of Mme Guyon in the seventeenth and eighteenth centuries.

13. Gordon Leff, *Heresy in the Later Middle Ages: The Relation of Heterodoxy to Dissent, c. 1250–1450*, 2 vols. (New York: Barnes & Noble Books, 1967), 1: 262.

14. *Ibid.*, 2: 503.

15. Norman Cohn, *The Pursuit of the Millennium: Revolutionary Millenarians and Mystical Anarchists of the Middle Ages*, (New York: Harper Torchbooks, 1961), p. 180 ff.

16. Leff, *Heresy in the Later Middle Ages*, 1: 359.

17. One is reminded of the seventeenth-century English Ranters who held, among other things, that pigsties are as acceptable as churches as places of worship.

18. Leff, *Heresy in the Later Middle Ages*, 1: 379.

19. Renaissance rehabilitation of monism soon conquered some exclusive and scholarly circles among the intellectuals of the church, such as Erasmus and his companions. A historian of the Reformation, Joseph Lortz, notes Erasmus's role in interiorizing Christianity. "It cannot be overlooked," Lortz writes, "how fearfully easy it is to misinterpret the words of the New Testament: adoration in the spirit and in the truth. Here looms the very real danger in the Christian doctrine: to fall prey to an inner, man-made sublimation. Since the appearance of humanism, this human sublimation became more and more a threat to the Christian faith." *How the Reformation Came* (New York: Herder & Herder, 1964), p. 81.

20. In the sixteenth and seventeenth centuries, at the confines of faith and disbelief, such systems proliferated. For example, Robert Fludd who taught that since man's mind (*mens*) is made of life and light, when we arrive at full knowledge of ourselves we become like God. Fludd was an enthusiastic propagator of the Rosicrucean movement in England.

21. Georg W. Hegel, *L'Esprit du Christianisme et son destin*, trans. Jacques Martin, introd. by Jean Hyppolite (Paris: Librairie Philosophique J. Vrin, 1967), p. 89. My translation.

22. On this point, Jean Wahl writes, Hegel is near the Dionysian mysticism of Hölderlin and Novalis's Christian mysticism. *Le Malheur de la conscience dans la philosophie de Hegel* (Paris: Presses Universitaires de France, 1951), p. 167.

23. This is also the central thesis of Rudolf Bultmann's teaching, as well as of a number of contemporary existentialist theologians.

24. Eric Voegelin, "Immortality: Experience and Symbol," *Harvard Theological Review* 60, 3 (July 1967): 235–279.

25. Mircea Eliade, *The Sacred and the Profane: The Nature of Religion,* trans. Willard Trask (New York: Harcourt Brace Jovanovich, Inc., 1968), p. 94. We find that the Greek view of history is not essentially different from the archaic view: the cyclic movement of time (*anakyklosis*) is beautiful because it approximates the ideal, that is, immobility, but the eternal return of the same occurrences causes also weariness and increasing fragility.

26. Reginald Garrigou-Lagrange, *Le Sens commun: La Philosophie de l'être et les formules dogmatiques* (Paris: Nouvelle Librairie Nationale, 1922), p. 76. My translation.

THE TRANSCENDENT
AND PERSONAL GOD

O F the two main intellectual ways dealing with the God-problem, the one here designated as *A* and the other as *B* appear as forms of mankind's traditional methods of speculating about the supreme power manifesting itself in the universe. The transformations in man's thinking about God are governed by forces that will never be entirely fathomed. At any rate, it may seem in the light of my discussion so far that the advanced monotheistic religions form a synthesis between *A* and *B*, and that they also moderate what may appear as excessive in each position. Thus if monotheistic religions—Judaism, Christianity, and Islam—are characterized by their positing a God both *transcendent* and *personal*, these traits may be considered as the combination and respective moderation of the two earlier-mentioned positions. "God is transcendent" means then that he is radically different from man but is not an "inaccessible God"; "God is personal" means that he is knowable and accessible to man but is not identical with him. In Jacques Maritain's formulation: "[God's] sovereign personality is at once that which removes Him farthest from us—the inflexible infinite stands face to face with me, a wretched mortal—and at the same time brings Him nearest to us, since the incomprehensible purity has a countenance, a voice, and has set me before it so that I may gaze upon Him, so that I may speak to Him and He to me."[1]

Formulations of a third aspect of the God-problem, of a third way of conceiving God, are not the inventions of advanced monotheism; they were in evidence in much earlier times also, although under less clear labels than those that later mono-theisms were able to provide. While God was conceived by some civilizations or religions as distant or fading into distance, and by other civilizations and religions as being one with man, a third group developed beliefs in an "anthropomorphic" god (or gods) standing in a possibly more complex relationship with man than is the case in the two other systems of belief. It is of course also possible that *A* and *B* coexist in the same re-ligion, or that they represent subsequent phases of the same re-ligion in historical development. This is all the more probable as, in Mircea Eliade's words, "the transcendence of the Supreme Being has always served man as an excuse for indifference to-ward him."[2] Thus the *deus otiosus* may be a way of justifying man's disaffection from the deity after a period of faith, falsely described as God's disaffection (*Distanzierung*) from man.

A strong argument against the "anthropomorphic" god is that it has always caused a great embarrassment to philosophers, al-though not to the advocates of "common sense."[3] One may even make a case by arguing that philosophy was born, at least in India and Greece, from the indignation over a religion that had become—or had been from its origin—scandalously "human," that described the gods in all-too-human terms. Well known is Xenophanes' scornful statement that if cows or horses had re-ligious beliefs, they would picture their gods under bovine or equine features. And Plato was not alone in his time—philosophy was, of course, quite advanced by then—accusing Homer and Hesiod of transposing vulgar human characteristics into the na-ture and the lives of the gods. The philosophers' opposition did not, however, weaken the general belief in an anthropomorphic god. Walter Otto correctly appraises the function of the gods in the Homeric poems when he writes that the Greek perceived the outlines of the divinity in the delineations of his own nature. Well aware of the nature of reality as it is manifest also in human nature, the (Homeric) Greek believed in the special intervention of a god or goddess in his own life whenever it was obvious that something "superhuman," outside the ordinary concatenation of banal acts, was expected of him. "All objections to Greek religion," writes Otto, "on the ground of anthropomorphism are idle gossip. It [the Greek religion] did not make divinity human, but regarded the essence of humanity as divine."[4]

Naturally, such a conclusion is highly personal and debatable, and it is in fact contradicted by the many fascinating examples Otto brings to his thesis as illustrations. For he shows—in the episodes of Athene restraining Achilles, of Hermes appearing to Odysseus on Circe's island, and of Athene advising Telemachus —that Homer's gods intervene in human affairs when men are hesitant or filled with anxiety, so as to help, guide, and reassure them. This would hardly be necessary if men thought of themselves as endowed with divine powers. On the contrary, the gods appear at important junctures in human existence in order, so argues Otto, to underline the fact that outside support is needed in the generally precarious fabric of the human condition.

But Greek examples of the "anthropomorphic" god are by no means the only ones. We have seen that the very function of myth is to bridge the contingent and time-bound to an absolute and permanent, and that this was always done through the emergence of God in the human world and the emergence of men among the gods. Already at the most archaic stage of culture we find man's longing to behave like a spirit, to "transmute the corporeal modality into a spiritual modality."[5] But is it not equally true that men ardently desired to experience the *living God* in their midst, as either a vaguely or an entirely recognizable presence, or even as an incarnate God? This is because things and acts acquire value only by participation in a transcendent reality, or at least when they are witnessed by it. Take at random a passage from the Old Testament: Moses sends a messenger to King Sehon of Hesebon to request right of passage. The request is in reference to God's grant of land to the Hebrews. "But Sehon, King of Hesebon, would not let us pass; the Lord your God gave him a hard heart, a stubborn will, so as to put him at your mercy; and it has happened under your eyes. I am ready, the Lord told me, to deliver him into thy power. . . . And when Sehon offered battle at Jasa . . . the Lord our God gave us victory over him." (Deut. 2: 28–33.)

The similarity of the concept (and of the episode) is striking with the one Walter Otto mentions when Athene abandons Hector and joins Achilles. All that the bystanders see is that "luck flies from the one and supports the other. For the spacious mind of the Greeks these are gods who at the peak of an event can present themselves to their sole elect, even visibly, and whose activity is yet nothing else than the natural course of things and the mysterious consequences which must ensue under good omens and evil."[6]

As said before, philosophers, although by no means can they be placed collectively in any of three "camps" with regard to the God-problem, have generally been most reluctant to accept position *C*, the transcendent and personal God, even when it no longer appeared with the contours of an all-too-human, directly anthropomorphic, figure. The Greek philosophers objected to the Homeric gods' immorality, but later philosophers were just as dissatisfied with Yahweh's sternness or with the incarnate Christ. When Christianizing Gnostic sects in the first centuries placed Jesus Christ over the Jewish God, they not only insisted that the Jewish God was a fraud—because he was too unspiritual, too manlike—but also that Jesus was not really God either. They elaborated what Quispel calls a "mystique of Christ," not a mystique of God, since in their view God was "entirely different, to be described only in purely negative terms." The Gnostic Valentinus also affirmed that God is "abyss and silence," and another Gnostic, Basilides, taught that God, the real one above the false Jewish God, is unnamable. This God was obviously not identical with Jesus Christ either.

It is not surprising to find that the Christian concept of incarnation caused throughout two thousand years the greatest scandal of all in philosophers' eyes. The Christianizing Gnostics did not at first join the battle because for them the Jewish God was the real culprit, the evil creator who usurped the place of the true God. Marcion, in the second century, found the Old Testament full of anthropomorphism and its God the demiurgos whom Christ came to defeat. The Old Testament God was, according to Basilides, only an *archon*, the god of this world, hence not a god at all. But for most Gnostics Jesus Christ too was only a phantom since the real God, defeated "at the beginning" so that the world and men may come fraudulently in existence, could not be conceived as assuming flesh and blood and other human attributes. The distance between the real but unnamable God and man was stressed in every possible way by Basilides and his disciples so as to avoid any anthropomorphization of God—which would preclude the total spiritualization of man, the real objective. Of the three "filialities" created by God two at once rejoined him, and only the third remained in this world. When this too will rise to God, together with the *pneumatikoi*, then only psychic men will remain here, forever in ignorance of God because they cannot accept the *pneuma*, the spirit.[7]

There were many variations of Basilides and Marcion's doctrine. They emerged as so many ramifications of Judaism, but they soon abandoned the common origin under the double influence of the philosophers' propaganda and the preaching of the gospels, and became indistinguishable from one another. The sects of Ebionites, Nazarenes, Essenians, and generally the *improfessi* or nonsectarians were then further dispersed into yet smaller movements,[8] all unable to solve the many-angled problems posed by the nature of God, the destiny of man, the reasons for the creation, the contradiction between the One and the Many, God's perfection and a world where evil predominates. Such people were deeply disturbed by an incarnate Christ whose "incarnation" meant that God had seen fit to descend to the lowest level of creation (the last periphery of the emanations of the One), to men, in order to save them. But were they, the Gnostics, ordinary men—or elect already saved, and thus humiliated by the assumption of a God made flesh? All that Christ had to accomplish—and for this task incarnation was unnecessary—was to awaken the consciousness of the elect to their subjective resurrection. The Russian mystic philosopher, Vladimir Soloviev, is therefore correct in pointing out that in the Gnostic heresies the human character of Christ the mediator is changed into a phantom so that mediation is suppressed. The consequence, according to Soloviev, is that a gap is made and widened between God and creation, a gap that becomes an opposition.[9]

Soloviev may be right in arguing that the Gnostic opposition to incarnation was inspired by oriental religions: an infinitely distant God who does not participate in human affairs becomes an "inhuman God." Fact is, the church denounced the Gnostic opponents as "heretics" who, among other things, rejected the ecclesiastical structure—the institutional church—as mundane, that is, not justified by a God of whom we know nothing except that he is hidden innermost our bodily prison. The church argued against them that the incarnation is not only a symbolic center of all history, but that it was also a concrete, historical event attestable and duly recorded, so that the guarantee of Christian truth is the *theandros*, the God-man. It is the supreme proof of God's love for man, a renewed argument for the Old Testament thesis that God created the world from an overflow of love. He could give no greater proof of this love to a desolate mankind, the church fathers insisted against the Gnostics, than to become man, merging with history for a number of years and in concrete circumstances of time, place, and milieu. Even Origen, who later turned away from orthodoxy, understood the originality of the Christian religion as centered on the incarnation, which happened in historical time, not in cosmic time.

Thus from the beginning of the Christian era the entire problem of the "anthropomorphic" god has turned into the problem of the (Christian) incarnate God. This is an extremely important point for our discussion because, as we have seen, a comfortable majority of philosophers—and not only the modern ones—has found accommodation with the concept of the "distant God" and with that of the "God who is identical with man," but they balk at the concept of a transcendent and personal God who has appeared to them as the God of Judaism and Islam, and, with a particular emphasis, as the incarnate Jesus Christ.

The opposition to the Christian concept of God, and behind it to all divine figures anthropomorphically conceived, stems from many and complex causes. The response to this opposition was no less insistent and varied. In Part Two we shall be mainly concerned with the epistemological aspect of this high controversy, and in the subsequent Parts with the politico-philosophical aspects also. Here we must dwell on its religious foundations, not without considering, for the sake of the completeness of the picture, the religious aspects discussed so far.

Our examination of belief-systems presenting the God-problem from the archaic myth to the systems of Spinoza and Hegel reveals in retrospect—that is, in the light of the present chapter —that a god that ceases being "anthropomorphic" rapidly becomes an "inaccessible god" or an "immanent god." Since, however, the desire for a divine being does not cease, the newly conceived god-figure too needs interpreters who may shed light on him. This function has been filled by Gnostics, Hermetics, mystics of all kind, and esoteric speculators, and by philosophers. Rejecting *theandria*, these interpreters strove either to remove God from creation (Gnosticism) or to absorb God in creation (pantheism) or to absorb God in mankind (anthropotheism). These positions regard God, respectively, as distant, as being the totality of the universe, and as being man himself. According to any one of these positions man becomes, by default, by indirect or by direct appointment a divine being, insofar as he occupies the par excellence spiritual role in the universe. In contrast, an anthropomorphic God, an incarnate God, a *theandros*, presents to man an immediate form of the Absolute, outside him, that is distinct, yet near enough to him to be known and consulted.

Admittedly, the Gnostic, pantheistic, and anthropotheistic (immanent) God-concepts impose on man practically no limitation that would follow from the nature of their relationship. The *inaccessible god* opens the wide world to man's actions; it even authorizes him to combat and defeat the "false god" or *archon*, and thus liberate the true God whom he then joins by right of consubstantiality. The *pantheistic god* seems at first to impose on man a feeling of respect, even of veneration for all that exists, from the celestial bodies to the smallest insects; through observation of the world around him, however, man soon comes to the conclusion that of all existing things he is the highest because he alone possesses the power of reflecting on all the rest. He is also the most powerful, particularly when he is no longer surrounded by natural objects that teach him modesty; he then discovers means of creating a second, technological reality through which he acquires the power of transforming nature, once his equal, even his superior, into his servant. Finally, the *anthropotheistic god* lifts man's self-experience to exalted heights by instilling the conviction of the absolute uniqueness of his thoughts, emotions, aspirations, and enthusiasms. The idea of a supreme being finds then its embodiment in the individual —or the collectivity of individuals, mankind—and whatever this unique being thinks, does, or wills becomes *ipso facto* the highest form of thought, decision, or action—at least until he transcends himself toward still more exalted heights in the process of divine expansion.

In contrast again, the anthropomorphic and incarnate God-concepts impose on man decisive limitations. God's transcendence is then not interpreted as inaccessibility, but only as an ultimate reality never fully fathomed and known, yet permanent and steady like a background against which things and events are brought into relief. And God's personalness is the mediation of his transcendence so that man may find himself in a perpetual dialogue, free from God yet always *called back* to give an account of himself and his stewardship of creation. This is the concept we find, for example, in the Jewish thinker Martin Buber when he writes: "The further removed a concept [like God] seems from anthropomorphism, the more it must be organically completed by an expression of that immediacy and, as it were, bodily nearness which overwhelm man in his encounters with the divine."[10]

From the point of view of epistemology, the only one that interests us here, the incarnate God appears, then, as the best guarantee of the existence of reality. The philosophers' debate before and throughout the Christian era centered on this as its main issue, one school holding that the transcendent and personal God created reality, maintains it, and renders it knowable, the other school arguing that what man knows is a construct of his mind, will, or emotions—in short, of his subjective self.[11] Eric Voegelin formulates the first position categorically when he writes: "The constitution of being is what it is, and cannot be affected by human fancies. Hence, the metastatic denial of the order of mundane existence is neither a true proposition in philosophy, nor a program of action that could be executed. The will to transform reality into something which by essence it is not is the rebellion against the nature of things as ordained by God."[12] This is, naturally, what is denied by thinkers seemingly as diverse as Hegel, Spinoza, Joachim de Fiore, Ockham, at times Plotinus, and the idealistic and subjectivist (e.g., existentialist) schools, although their denial has gradations corresponding to the three positions distinguished above. Not only do these thinkers attack incarnation as a real event (in the religious discourse), they also insist on dissociating God and reality or on making reality a function of man's mind (in their theory of knowledge). As we shall see later in detail, the philosopher seeks perfect knowledge and expresses doubt in a religious position that speaks of an incarnate God: such a God imposes limitations on the human intellect, an intolerable barrier before the philosopher's search.[13]

Let us now look again at position *C*, which implies limitations of man's being and faculties. The figure of a transcendent and personal God appears then, in addition to being the object of faith, as an explanation why knowledge can never be total and exhaustive, a basic experience of the human condition. Such a God guarantees the validity of knowledge as far as knowledge goes, because he is the guarantor of the "constitution of being." Yet, he also explains, by the fact that he goes beyond man in every dimension, why man himself is limited in his faculties, first of all in his noetic powers. Corresponding to the two attributes: transcendence and personalness (most categorically and articulately stated in the phenomenon of incarnation), man finds his being and knowledge circumscribed by the nature of reality and by his own nature. In order to find this situation intellectually and existentially acceptable, he must invalidate those images and concepts of God that contradict incarnation, although they probably precede it in time as historical forms. We find the doctrine of transcendence forcefully asserted by Thomas Aquinas reacting to the teaching of Averroës. God, Aquinas teaches, is neither the *anima mundi*, the "world soul," nor the form of things, nor the center of a universe in which everything would be rigidly arranged according to a strict necessity. External to the world, God created it as a gigantic work of art, so that there is always a hiatus between the eternal order, Being in itself, and the universal order that is the *application* of the laws of being on the created world.

One can see that this thought was elaborated also as a refutation of the Neoplatonic tradition that explained the world-order via the theory of emanation. Subsequent emanations would be, according to this theory, a way for Pure Being to make itself explicit in the world and ultimately to reabsorb the world into itself. Thomas, however, after formulating what he meant by God's transcendence, turned to the problem of God as a person, the God of scripture. The Neoplatonic Pure Being is unable to participate in the human situation and in history, unable to conduct a dialogue with man. Man is privileged above all other creatures, argues Thomas; he is not one of the hypostases of Pure Being, condemned to remain at his appointed post, but belongs to several intersecting orders. The dialogue depends on him also, not on God alone. It is not difficult to conclude that incarnation is the most dramatic moment of this dialogue.

The dialogue—and the mutual trust it implies—is pursued in many ways and follows many methods because, again, God's transcendence and personalness offer a wide space, so to speak, within which man may comfortably move in his search for knowledge. The condition seems to be that this "wide space" should not be reduced by man's impatience to only one of its limit-points: transcendence—by which God would be "removed" to beyond man's reach—or personalness—by which man is tempted to "absorb" God. The dialogue has metaphysical and mystical preconditions. *Metaphysical*, insofar as the structure of reality contradicts any relationship between God and man not based on the essential difference of their nature and the subordination of the second to the first. "It is permissible for the believer," writes Buber, "to believe that God became a person for love of him, because in our human mode of existence the only reciprocal relation is a personal one."[14] The nonpersonal, so-called universal reason of Hegel never enters into a living relationship with man, although Hegel seems to make much of love when he holds that only "unified being," its union cemented with love, amounts to genuine being. But is this love genuine, bringing two independent persons into contact, or is it an absorption in which one of the protagonists is extinguished as a person?

If God is creator, then reality preexists us, or as Buber daringly asserts, "being is established, we are established, our meeting with it is established. This establishment of a universe, including ourselves and our works, is the fundamental reality of existence. Contrasted with this reality, the demand that man recover his creative freedom appears as a demagogic phrase."[15] The metaphysical relationship within the system we are discussing is then essentially the recognition of a preexistent reality. A reality—that is, neither a representation nor a phantom—that man did not make but that he can go a long way toward knowing—never, of course, absolutely. The mind, argues Plato in *Euthydemos*, can know things in themselves as they really are without distorting them into mental constructs. Knowing is not a creating but a finding, a discovery. This refutes the post-Cartesian popular view that argues that the reality we know is not a reality at all but a deceit, the veil of *maya* (a subjective representation, says Kant; an artificial fragmentation of the flux of becoming, says Bergson; and so on), and that "real" reality is still to emerge via the mechanism of immanent forces in history or is still to be constructed by the efforts of men. Knowledge, in this case, is "postponed" until it can submerge itself in the second reality—when however, it will no longer be reflective knowledge but union with God. For the Gnostics, and for Plotinus too, reflection is inattention because it *reflects* the myriad dispersed beings cut out, as it were, from God's substance. Reflection would cease if all being were reabsorbed in God.[16]

It is evident that this kind of knowledge does not take place if the intellect *enjoys* its distinctness from both God and reality, and if, in the second place, it is able to penetrate quite far into the nature of reality—without exhausting it but also without lamenting over this limitation. This is also the nature of *mystical knowledge* correctly understood, that is, as a way of holding a dialogue with God. We have seen in previous sections what separates true from false mysticism (Zaehner's distinction between "theistic" and "monist"). In the former, the mystic encounters God, effectuates the *unio mystica*, then returns from the voyage with his distinct, in fact strengthened, personality, power of judgment, and ethical orthodoxy intact. In the latter, he mistakes his *afflatus* for a permanent union with God and feels emancipated from the norms of ethical behavior as well as from ordinary human tasks, joys, and servitudes.

Plotinus's position is rather ambiguous concerning the two or three mystical experiences he reports. The mystic, he says, becomes suddenly included in Intelligence; the One appears then so near that the mystic feels *identical* with its light rather than having a *cognitive* grasp of reality. What he contemplates is light itself and not an external object. Yet we never know with Plotinus whether his mystic becomes one with the object he contemplates or remains unintegrated with Totality. His commentator Gandillac seems to solve the Plotinian ambiguity by stating that although for the Neoplatonic master reflection is man's characteristic dignity, it still must disappear in the *unio mystica*. The purity of the self consists in getting rid of time, place, and discursive knowledge—exactly the operation prescribed by the Gnostic program combatted by the third-century sage.

The Transcendent and Personal God

The question is, then, is mysticism a way of knowing reality through dialogue with God. Plotinus does not give a clear answer, precisely because his "reality" is limited to God (the One) and is not extended to creation. Creation, in Plotinus's view, is degradation, hence a low level of reality; it is the philosopher's task to suggest ways of denying the sign of degradation, the body, so that man's intellectual part may climb up the ladder of emanations and rejoin the real Being. Thus Plotinus belongs—although not completely, since he is an ambiguous mystic—to the category described by Zaehner as monist—that is, to the mystics who hold that soul and God are the same and all else is pure illusion. Zaehner sees an unbridgeable gulf between them and the theistic mystics who are aware that God is incomparably greater than they are, while he is also the root and ground of their being. Zaehner's most striking example of the first type is the following passage from *Wisdom, Madness and Folly: The Philosophy of a Lunatic* (1951) by John Custance: "In a sense I am God. I see the future, plan the Universe, save mankind; I am completely immortal; I am male and female. The whole Universe, past, present, and future, is within me; all nature and life are connected with me, all things are possible. I reconcile Good and Evil, and create light, darkness, worlds, universes. . . . The opposites are bridged—and my state of elation is itself a bridging of opposites—the watertight compartments of individuality tend to disappear."[17]

This, together with other examples Zaehner provides (Rimbaud's "universal mind," Aldous Huxley's "mind at large," the Cabala's pantheistic theory, certain types of Hindu mysticism) may be mystic experiences but are definitely not ways of knowledge. They end in false knowledge, illusion, self-aggrandizement, perception contrary to the nature of reality—and they do not end in positive action. They contribute to the impression that the inner reality, the self, becomes enlarged out of all proportion to the surrounding reality.[18] Knowledge, as said before, is based on the distinct existence of a subject and an object;

when the mystic's vision or the philosopher's system presents a complete union, one cannot speak of knowledge but of a mutual absorption. "Even when the philosophical act culminates in a vision of unity, philosophy is founded on the duality of subject and object. The duality of I and Thou finds its fulfillment in the religious relationship; the duality of subject and object sustains philosophy while it is carried on."[19] God, because he is a (transcendent) creator desires to be known, and because he is personal knows that he can be known. Thus the real mystic holds a dialogue with God and is aware that the condition of the dialogue as well as its reward is that he remains distinct from him. Not that this would require a particular effort or a consciously followed technique: its achievement can be verified in that it produces knowledge, a noetic act accompanied by the certainties of faith as it existed before the *unio mystica*. A new faith arising out of the union must be suspect. The mystic Ruysbroeck in the fourteenth century accused the Beghards of it, pointing at their state of quietism in which they claimed to have become "divine." This state usually does not last, and the aftermath, as in the case of John Custance, brings with it a terrible depression. But while it lasts, it is accompanied by the blissful feeling that the external world is not really distinct from the percipient subject, that "within and without are one."[20]

Position *C* implies, then, that true mysticism, like genuine metaphysics, leads to an "anthropomorphic" God whom one reaches both through faith and the noetic act. Ruysbroeck, the most transcendental of all mystics, writes Underhill, highly valued corporate and sacramental religion. He said that the supersensual illumination "is not God, but is the light whereby we perceive him."[21] How else could it be when, as St. Bernard also said (Cant. 41), the soul, transported out of herself, is granted a clearer vision of the Divine Majesty, yet only for a moment and with the swiftness of a lightning flash. Evidently, this kind of knowledge finds in God the ultimate reality, which guarantees that the mystic's vision and ordinary human perception converge and that they are not in error. The test we can apply to the ecstatic, Underhill suggests, is the question that Jacopone da Todi addresses to the mystic's soul: "What fruit do you bring back from your vision?" And the answer is: "An ordered life in every state. . . . Reality has become real to him."[22]

The positions examined in Part One yield three conclusions worth considering before we approach Part Two.

The first is that the philosophical enterprise can never definitively exclude from its scope the domain of the God-problem. This statement applies to premodern philosophy as much as to post-Cartesian and contemporary speculation. Many philosophers try, of course, to solve, and leave behind, the God-problem as not meaningful or not suitable for mature speculation; yet their apparent indifference—that of materialists, positivists, or skeptics—does not exempt them from the obligation of taking a position.

The second conclusion is that those philosophers who include the God-problem in their speculation favor, perhaps in the majority of cases, position *A* or *B*—and we have seen that the two are basically related—and attempt to escape from position *C*. Even Christian thinkers, in an effort to "save" their religion against accusations of obscurantism and consequently to modernize it, often adopt some variety of *A* or *B*—as indeed did many Christian philosophers of the Renaissance who found in esoteric doctrines another and better version of the truths propounded by their church.

The third conclusion is that so many philosophers' preference for *A* and *B*, and their opposition to *C* is motivated by their search for a perfect, that is *unmediated* form of knowledge. They reject *C* where the knowing self is understood to be limited while the object of knowledge is presented as guaranteed by a

God and the Knowledge of Reality

transcendental creator. The dissociation of subject and object exasperates many thinkers who see in it a limitation, a diminution of man, and a barrier set up against a reconstructed reality with its epistemological, moral, and political derivations.

NOTES

1. Jacques Maritain, *Les Degrés du savoir* (Paris: Desclée, De Brouwer & Cie, 1939), p. 466. My translation.
2. Mircea Eliade, *Myth and Reality* (New York: Harper Torchbook, 1968), p. 93.
3. See Reginald Garrigou-Lagrange, *Le Sens commun: La Philosophie de l'être et les formules dogmatiques* (Paris: Nouvelle Librairie Nationale, 1922).
4. Walter Otto, *The Homeric Gods* (New York: Pantheon, 1954), p. 236.
5. Mircea Eliade, *Myths, Dreams, and Mysteries: The Encounter between Contemporary Faiths and Archaic Realities* (New York: Harper & Row, 1967), p. 107.
6. Otto, *Homeric Gods*, p. 219. It must be pointed out that in such comparative passages I am not advocating any one system of beliefs and consequently do not argue for or against the truth-value of any religion. My concern is to show that most religions, specifically the advanced monotheistic ones, come to terms with some kind of "anthropomorphic" god.
7. Gilles Quispel, "Gnostic Man: The Doctrine of Basilides," *Eranos* 16 (1948), 210–246.
8. Jérôme Carcopino, *De Pythagore aux apôtres* (Paris: Flammarion, 1956), p. 352.
9. Vladimir Soloviev, *La Grande Controverse* (Paris: Aubier-Montaigne, 1953), p. 66.
10. Martin Buber, *The Eclipse of God: Studies in the Relation between Religion and Philosophy* (New York: Harper & Row, Publishers, 1957), p. 14.
11. These are two limit-formulations, not taking into account the various intermediate theories of knowledge.
12. Eric Voegelin, *Order and History*, vol. 1, *Israel and Revelation* (Baton Rouge: Louisiana State University Press, 1956), p. 453.
13. Recall the conflict between Spinoza and Oldenburg: for Spinoza it was absurd that God would have taken upon himself human nature "as a circle assuming the nature of a square"; for Oldenburg, a God who would

act merely by necessity implies "that the human mind acts no less mechanically than the human body." Benedict de Spinoza, *Selected Letters* in *Chief Works*, 2 vols., trans. R. H. Elwes (New York: Dover Publications, 1955), vol. 2.

14. Buber, *Eclipse of God*, p. 97. It is important to point out that this may be regarded as an existentialist argument with pragmatic undertones. The Thomist would not say that incarnation is the most *convenient* solution for man to feel the closeness of God (as Buber seems to imply here), but that it is a *fact*.

15. Ibid., pp. 68–69.

16. According to the Upanishads, the fall is individuation, the consequence of which is the fact of thinking of oneself as an individual, the fact of attributing to oneself features distinct from others.

17. Quoted in R. C. Zaehner, *Mysticism: Sacred and Profane* (New York: Oxford University Press, Inc., 1961), p. 91.

18. See in this respect Aldous Huxley's *The Doors of Perception* (New York: Harper & Row, Publishers, 1970), as well as the vast literature, both old and modern, of drugtakers.

19. Buber, *Eclipse of God*, pp. 31–32.

20. Zaehner, *Mysticism: Sacred and Profane*, p. 102.

21. Evelyn Underhill, *The Mystics of the Church* (New York: Schocken Books, Inc., 1964), p. 149.

22. Evelyn Underhill, *The Essentials of Mysticism and Other Essays* (New York: E. P. Dutton & Co., Inc., 1960), p. 23.

Part Two

THE MAGIC WAY TO
PERFECT KNOWLEDGE

IT is the rooted conviction of the West," writes C. G. Jung, "that God and the ego are worlds apart. In India, their identity was taken as self-evident (for India, man's mind is part of the world-creating mind). . . . The alchemists at least suspected man's hidden godlikeness."[1] The Swiss psychologist does not appear, in this passage, as "Jungian" as the facts in this case warrant: we have seen that the identification of God and man is a constant theme in the West too, indeed it is one of its main intellectual traditions. Jung's own reference to the alchemists' belief indicates this, and the alchemists were by no means alone in the Western world with their searches and conclusions. A universal symbolization is at work that has always and everywhere marked mankind's preoccupation with its origin and destiny.[2] The symbols (which, incidentally, Jung claims to have rediscovered in the "collective un-conscious") have been used by almost all civilizations, or rather, by movements and sects, and they were used with the same general intention: to penetrate to the ultimate meaning of being and to solve the fundamental questions of man's place in the universe. The reason is thus evident why there is basically only one esoteric tradition, manifest in literally uncountable movements, sects, heresies, legends, myths, and fantasies, and in speculative systems.

[73]

God and the Knowledge of Reality

All three foregoing sections argue that the safeguarding of the rights of a reflective mind and of discursive knowledge is linked to the recognition of a certain *distance* between God and man, a distance equal from the two limit-cases, *A* and *B*. We have noted, however, that the temptation is strong either to make this distance approach the infinite or to reduce it to nought. In proportion as either of these operations is carried out, the subject ceases to reflect and to know things in the ordinary sense and becomes instead a mystic, a divine being, a self-contemplating sage. It is then assumed that true wisdom is achieved only when reflection is abolished because reflection belongs to a lower order than wisdom, it is, in fact, the absence of wisdom since its objects are daily, vulgar phenomena, unworthy of the attention of the wise. Reflection is the dispersion, the inattention of the One, so that reabsorption in the One is to cease reflecting.

A similar doctrine appears in Plato's *Phaedrus*: the soul is older than the body to which it is chained after its fall from the spiritual state. This is an intellectual fall, taking place in the soul itself through the darkening of its cognitive part. The result is partial loss of essence, *amnesis*, and insertion in a lower sort of existence, characterized by earthly appetites. In Plotinus, the division is further sharpened: although the Nous (intelligence) is no longer the same as the One, it has come into existence by the One's "self-contemplation." It is understandable, then, that the Plotinian soul *reasons* only when locked inside the body. Reasoning or reflection is the result of a diminishing of intelligence that no longer suffices to itself. This is not merely a Plotinian way of thinking, it is present in much of Eastern and Western thought. The world is a product of reflection that creates the appearance of multiplicity. The world is thus an appearance, a nonreality, since only the undivided One is real. At the root of things (appearances, phenomena), the Cabala teaches, there is a schism (division, hence dispersion). The multiplicity of beings does not proceed from a real and positive creation; it is rather the consequence of fragmentation.

The sage is the one who delivers us from multiplicity and its root, reflection, and leads to real knowledge, gnosis. He removes the veil of appearances and shows us the Unity that is God; then he shows us that we are part of the Unity, one with God. We cease to be individuals and join the Whole. In the One, teaches Plotinus, there is no distance between project and act, between the possible and the real. In Hindu speculation too, the *atman* is (or becomes through purification) *Brahman* which means that the individual soul is substantially identical with the unqualifiable Absolute. For both Plotinus and the Hindu metaphysicians the phenomenal world is devoid of true existence. In the twelfth and thirteenth centuries the influential Averroist philosophy conveyed these various concepts—Hindu, Neoplatonist, Gnostic—to an intellectually isolated, medieval Christian world, arguing against the Aristotelian principle of individuality and against a self separated from the Absolute Unity. The genuine act of thought, for the Averroists, consisted in abandoning and overcoming this isolation so that the self may fuse with the One Absolute Intellect. True, Averroës parried the question why, if all men shared the same intellect, do they not think the same thoughts simultaneously, by showing that men differed according to their experiences and that therefore each possessed only one aspect of universal knowledge. He maintained, nevertheless, that the true subject of thought is not the self but the nonpersonal being common to all thinking beings. Only the fusion with the One can explain the process of thought and establish its validity.[3]

Before the fusion, or when deprived of the possibility of fusion because of "inattentive," "dispersed" life, we are not ourselves, we are "alienated"; whether the sage is Plotinus, Spinoza, or Fichte, he brings about the unification so that we may recover ourselves in the divine substance. What is more natural for most men than to desire this unification here on earth, without waiting for the distant and uncertain event that some religions promise? Reflection, which, as the word indicates, is a permanent and thus painful contact with this very imperfect world *reflected* by the senses and in the intellect, must be circumvented so as to eliminate the chief source of suffering and alienation. Discursive knowledge and the (imperfect state of the) world of which it is a knowledge become one in the eyes of the seeker-for-wisdom. Impatience inspired by pessimism impels him to look for formulas and shortcuts, magic means, through which the superior powers may be manipulated via the gnosis he expects to share with them. Jewish apocalyptic writers of the first centuries, for example, were more pessimistic about the world than the prophets of Israel had been, and they were also more confident about the imminence of God's action. They expected that God would shortly destroy the world and substitute a new one for the old. The contrast between the apocalyptic writers and the prophets transcends Judaism: the difference between ordinary Jewish and Christian view and that of the Gnostic is that neither Paul nor Rabbi Akiba was transformed by his mystic experience of ascent, whereas the Gnostic Valentinus came to be "in true and eternal life" while still on earth.[4] In conformity with what was previously said about mystical experience, Paul and Akiba are seen as retaining their this-worldly personalities, their individual separateness from the divine substance. While they have much to denounce in this corrupt world, neither are they, unlike Valentinus, looking for a substitute world nor are they impatient to be themselves transformed. They do not feel alienated in a "false life," hence they are not searching for shortcuts toward a true one.

Many centuries later we find that the enigmatic Rosicrucians practice contemplation "in order to attain here below already a sure and infallible felicity."[5] Contemplation for them includes the knowledge of nature, not in the physical sense, but as the knowledge of the occult universe, so that they may derive from it "a new language with which to explain the eclipse of Churches," that is, the laws transforming the world from imperfect to perfect. They try to grasp the harmony of the universe by studying the Great Adam (the Adam Kadmon of the Cabala), that is the correspondence between the microcosm and the macrocosm. One of their objectives was (I speak here of the seventeenth century) to "give orders to the spirits" that act according to universal laws.

The example of the Rosicrucians helps us to understand an important point in our argumentation. They (and the Gnostics, the Cabalists, the alchemists, and other esoteric adepts) were not ignorant men out of touch with their time, nor were they precursors of modern science—as it is still often alleged that the alchemists, for example, were the founders of modern chemistry. The esoteric search is a sui generis speculation, systematized at various times in perhaps all parts of the world; it is a way of thinking shared, at least partly, by many nonesoteric thinkers who, through some often crucial aspect of their system, reach very similar conclusions, since the object of their search and even their methods are similar to those of esoteric thinkers. The French authors Caron and Hutin make in this respect a remarkable observation in their compact little volume *The Alchemists*. They find parallel developments in alchemist doctrines between lands as distant as ancient Greece and China: "The simultaneous appearance of the Chinese hermetic art and of the Greco-Egyptian sacerdotal synthesis attributed to Hermes Trismegistus is due to the decadence of antique mysteries in both civilizations."[6] This would explain to some extent not why there is esoteric speculation, but that its flourishing periods coincide with the eclipse of orthodox theism in what Eliade identifies as periods of the "coarsening of the myth."

If the objective is to rid oneself of false knowledge and to attain true knowledge (and *this* is what esoterism is about), then the esoteric thinker wants to demonstrate his consubstantiality with God and the means of asserting it. This is how the mythical Hermes, the most important fictitious figure of the tradition, teaches his son, Tat, about the divinity of man's intellect: "The intellect, O Tat, is drawn from the very substance of God. In men, this intellect is God; and so some men are gods and their humanity is near to the divinity. . . . If man makes right use of [God's gifts], he differs in no way from the immortals."[7]

Plato and Aristotle freely spoke of *one God* and of *many gods*, and we do not quite know what they meant, at least by the latter. It would seem that this distinction was current in the Hellenistic world; yet a new emphasis enters with Hermetism, and perhaps as early as the theme found in the gospel of John where Jesus says: "Is it not written: You are all Gods?"— echoed by St. Basil who speaks of the command received by men to become Gods. At any rate, illustrations of this theme begin to abound with the early Hermetic literature. This quotation is from the *Asclepius*, a famous Gnostic text of indefinite origin: "Man is a *magnum miraculum* . . . as though himself God . . . familiar with the race of demons, of the same origin as he; he despises that part of his nature which is only human, for he has put his hope in the divinity of the other part." To be noted is that more than a thousand years later when Renaissance scholars discovered these texts, Pico della Mirandola was to base on the *Asclepius* his famous oration on the *Dignity of man*. More than that, he was to argue that hermetic science— that is, the *art* of reaching divine status and powers through magic manipulation—is the best proof of the divinity of Christ. In other words, by the time of the Renaissance the esoteric texts of the first centuries A.D. had acquired in scholarly and humanist circles an unparallelled prestige, confronting as equals the texts held sacred by the church. In Pico's estimation, "nulla est scientia que nos magis certificet de divinitate Christi quam magia et Cabala" (there is no science that would prove for us Christ's divinity better than magic and the Cabala). Robert Fludd, the English esoteric writer quoted earlier, was also thoroughly under the influence of the *corpus hermeticum.* He argued that the mind (*mens*) of man is made of life and light, so that when we ascend to the knowledge of ourselves (like the self-contemplation of the Plotinian One), we become like God.

Even Hermes Trismegistus was supposed to have had a teacher, Poimander. This is what he learned, among other things: "Unless you make yourself equal to God, you cannot understand God, for the like is not intelligible save to the like.[8] Make yourself grow to a greatness beyond measure, by freeing yourself from the body; raise yourself above all time, become Eternity. . . . Believe that nothing is impossible for you, think yourself immortal and capable of understanding all, arts, sciences, the nature of every living being. Mount higher than the highest heights, descend lower than the lowest depths. Draw into yourself all sensations of everything created, . . . imagining that you are everywhere, on earth, in the sea, in the sky, that you are not yet born, in the maternal womb, adolescent, old, dead, beyond death."[9] The reader has the impression of rereading the passage quoted in Part One, by John Custance who calls himself a "lunatic." In truth, the *Poimander* is the initiation of Hermes Trismegistus, as all other esoterics must also be initiated and must rise through successive levels of apprenticeship and adeptness to that of the magus and the master. This is generally achieved through initiation into the meaning of the pertinent symbols, the value of which cannot be explained by reference to "symbolism": the symbols are *instruments* for the manipulation of the higher world of true reality by someone (the magician) who is in the lower world.

Knowledge and manipulation are inseparably linked in esoteric doctrines, as it is evident from the word *art* by which both doctrine and its practice are designated. The Hermetic *artist* (or practitioner) strives first for separation of the soul from the body (purification) and, second, for the spiritualization of all matter, since, as we shall see, all substance is supposed to be basically one. Through self-purification he accedes to the highest rank in the hierarchy of divine power, after which the universe neither has secrets for him nor can it resist his art of transmuting the elements and objects of the lower order into those of the higher. The Brahman rejects the body and the vanities attached to it, and having become similar in nature to light (this transformation involves various elaborate techniques of letting the light circulate in his body), he knows God who is Light. Liberated, the Indian sage no longer is part of the cosmos and its laws, which are characterized by movement and conflict, tension between opposites; the immobile, contemplative attitude of the Sage expresses the reconciliation of opposites, their spiritualization. As Eliade remarks, spiritualization, the desire to "fly," universally present in all mankind, shows an invincible tendency to transmute what is "heavy" and earthbound in the human condition. The Sage is the man who has succeeded in making the body behave like a spirit, no longer bound by limitations.[10] In contrast to the spirit, which is *real*, the body is then the principle of unreality, so that esoteric knowledge must consist in the spiritualization of matter and the absorption of the spiritual substance (*pneuma, anima*) in the One. At once we understand the significance of the alchemical search predicated on the potentiality of all metals to grow and mature, that is, to become spiritual. This belief goes back to the earliest antiquity and was still very much alive in the seventeenth century.

The esoteric tradition is extremely rich in mythical and symbolic tales telling the story of the spirit's pilgrimage to reach its home. The Gnostics held that in its unredeemed state the *pneuma* is unconscious of itself, asleep or intoxicated by the poison of the world. Its ignorance is cured as it awakens from numbness. The same tale is told by the alchemist who helps the rebirth of the spiritual light from the darkness of physical nature, the body:

[80]

self-knowledge is the deliverance of the pneumatic body (spiritual matter!) from the corruption of the flesh. Tantric and Taoist speculation describes ways for the light to circulate inside the body so that a spirit-body may be born from the "true seed." Then fire brings to life this embryo, a higher being.[11] Studying the alchemists' operations, Jung concludes that their purpose was to produce a physical equivalent to the *substantia coelestis* (the heavenly substance), recognized by the spirit as the truth and as the image of the God innate to man. This substance was to be incorruptible, inert yet alive, and a universal remedy. The alchemist was looking for a symbol; the *substantia coelestis* was the symbol's chemical equivalent.[12] In other Hermetic symbolisms the various ideograms play the role of the alchemist's operations. The square surmounted by the cross is the pattern of materiality tamed, cleansed, and sublimated to such an extent that it becomes the indispensable support for the manifestation of the spirit. In fact, the ideogram is the last trace of materiality linking the spirit to the physical world; without it, the spirit would take off in the direction of absolute emancipation.[13]

There is no contradiction between the soul's aspiration to leave the body (matter) behind and join the One (or God) and the assumption that matter too is potentially spiritual and a sign of spirituality. Everything is possible for the initiate possessing divine powers because his knowledge includes the understanding of the unicity and potential divinity of existence. Once more we find positions *A* and *B* in close relationship as two aspects of the same doctrine. The unicity of existence and the consequent reciprocal influence and action of all parts of the universe on all other parts must, indeed, be assumed if the privileged spirit (magician, alchemist, or Theosophist) is to capture the full powers of knowledge, which is the equivalent of joining subject to object or abolishing both. Alexandre Koyré has argued that this assumption is typical of the Renaissance optimism of an expansionist human spirit that did not regard anything as impossible since everything was God, life, vital forces, and unlimited magic manipulation.[14] Yet, the concept of universal harmony and reciprocity of influences seems to be as old as esoteric speculation itself; one may even say that this speculation would run out of inspiration without this concept. Everywhere that we find alchemy we find related to it a mystical tradition: in China Taoism, in India Yoga and Tantrism, in Hellenistic Egypt Gnosticism, in Islamic countries Hermetic and esoteric mystical schools, in the Western Middle Ages and Renaissance Hermetism, Christian and sectarian mysticism, and Cabala.[15]

The unicity of existence, to be found among the Hellenistic philosophers of Alexandria and their medieval followers, is the guarantee that bodies and elements are mutually transmutable. This was announced as the Grand Principle of Hermes Trismegistus himself, namely, that "everything that is high is equal to what is low, and everything low is equal to what is high," a formula with considerable significance for Hermetism because it means that there is an absolute although hidden concordance between the lower and the higher worlds, the key of which lends to the magus incalculable powers. We saw how Hermes instructed his son, Tat, in the possibility for man to acquire divine intellect; in the fourth and fifth centuries, the Neoplatonist thinkers Jamblichus and Proclus were confident that whatever we find in the inferior world is also found in the superior world and in the Creator. The scholars of the Renaissance took this for granted, they, in fact, focused the bulk of their activity on the comprehension of this principle and its translation into acts. During the Renaissance, Cornelius Agrippa of Nettesheim was perhaps the farthest advanced on this road. He taught the doctrine of cosmic unity that permits us to ascend to the original world and to make use of the things above. Such is this concordance, according to Agrippa of Nettesheim (in *De occulta philosophia*), that "celestial things draw super-celestial things, and natural things supernatural things through the virtue running through all and the participation in it of all species."[16] This was also the core of Paracelsus's teaching: since we are all "products of nature" and "children of the same vital and magic forces," there is a precise relationship between the various organs of the human body and the "organs of the world," such as planets and constellations. Evidently, if the soul is influenced by the astral bodies, in turn it exerts a definite influence on the "world-soul." Paracelsus is of the same conviction as Agrippa, Bruno, Campanella, Pico, and as the Gnostic Valentinus, the Tantric sages, the Yogi, and so on. Various texts in the *corpus hermeticum* describe the magus who manipulates divine figures made with his own hands and who achieves thereby certain results among the superior forces—gods—who cannot help responding. We find these figures or statues in the Hermetic documents; one such is the golem of the Cabala. Paracelsus spells out that when the soul influences (manipulates) the world-soul, the latter "thinks and imagines" what was suggested and carries it out in our own lower world. This is how the human soul can command to the stars, can direct events, and even produce "new beings" (*creatur nachmachen*).

Parts of these operations take place in the visible world, other parts in the invisible world, but the magus obviously has access to both. Like Valentinus, Giordano Bruno made the imaginary Gnostic ascent, underwent the Hermetic initiation, and became divine. Similar is the transformation of the alchemist's matter. As we have seen, matter is alive; as a mineral it matures in the earth as the embryo grows in the maternal womb. In the alchemist's work, Caron and Hutin observe, matter even undergoes passion, death, and resurrection; in other words, it is treated like a god. Resurrection was meant to be the final result of transmutation.[17] The magus, it is clear, performs all these acts as a means of reconciling what is arbitrarily separated:

the visible and the invisible, the finite and the infinite, the human and the astral, man's soul and the world-soul, darkness and light, celestial things and supercelestial things, natural and supernatural. The Hermetics' English disciple, Robert Fludd, believed that the elixir of long life permits us to enter immortality while still in this world; the proof is that the immortalized is capable of corporifying his spirit through the spiritualization of his body. The mythical founder of the Rosicrucians, Christian Rosenkreutz, also had the revelation of universal unity that brings man into harmony with God, the heaven, and the earth. Let us note that the Rosicrucians regarded themselves as heirs to Brahmanic and Egyptian wisdom.

Paul Vulliaud has showed us in a most interesting study that the art of painting in the pre-Renaissance period and the Renaissance could also be a means of translating philosophical and theological language into the symbols of esoterism. The modern, nonscholarly eye no longer detects these symbols in the apparently natural colors and shapes of flowers, gems, alchemical instruments, magic tools, and animals or in the gestures and attitudes of the human figures represented in certain paintings. On the basis of the principle that all parts of the universe interact, these symbols, let me state again, were no mere symbols but potent instruments of transformation. The architect Averulino, a little before Leonardo's time, constructed the blueprint of a city on a "purely symbolic basis," believing that the "total picture of the city is the image of the universe."[18] Of the city he had planned, "Sforzinda," Averulino said that it was "beautiful, good, and perfect because of the course of nature" it apparently embodied, it was more than a city, full of buildings "made in the form and likeness of man."[19] A century and a half later the monk Campanella was to do the same (see Part Three). Their plans were more than images, they were talismans that, appropriately manipulated, like the statues of Hermes, could bring about desired changes in the upper as well as the lower world.

[84]

The Magic Way to Perfect Knowledge

The saving of the soul from the bodily prison and the purification of matter for the purposes of spiritualization represent attempts to deal with the totality of things as with one substance, all of it assimilated to the substance of the manipulator or knower whose knowledge is thus perfect because it is more than knowledge, it is *union*. In the extensive esoteric-hermetic literature of all ages the union was sought in the reconciliation of opposites (*coincidentia oppositorum*), the abolition of conflicts, and the final reduction of all things to a common substratum—a not impossible task if the unicity of existence—matter and spirit—is assumed. Much of this literature concentrates on the philosophical stone (*lapis philosophorum*) and the methods of its production. All alchemists and magi were involved in this crucial operation, and what they performed may be regarded as a second creation insofar as it aimed at correcting a hitherto imperfect world by the reintegration of the dispersed elements. Or, as Eliade writes, "the alchemist is the brotherly savior of Nature. He assists nature to fulfill her final goal, to attain her ideal —which is the perfection of her progeny, mineral, animal, or human—to her supreme ripening, which is absolute immortality and liberty."[20] This can be done in the alchemist's oven much more quickly than in the millions of years during which the metals "ripen" in the depth of the earth. Eliade speaks of the alchemist and the metallurgist's "demiurgic enthusiasm" as they perform faster than nature and interfere, in possession of a sure knowledge, in the processes of cosmic forces.

The philosophical stone is also described as the marriage of sulphur with mercury (representing the male and female principles), which gives rise to a *spiritual matter*. The latter is the common constituent at the same time as the stone of the Sage to which all else may be reduced. On the other hand, it must be emphasized that gold, the end-result of the alchemical operation, and the philosopher's stone itself are not the real objects of the search; they are valued only insofar as they are symbols of yet more hidden things. As it might be expected, in the mind

[85]

of alchemists the philosophical stone is equated with the perfect knowledge of God, and gold is the symbol of light, that is, ultimately also of God. In the *lapis* "evil must become the same as good," the medieval alchemist Basil Valentine is supposed to have held.[21] It is a reconciliation of contraries and of enemies, thus also of chaos; it is the *prima materia* sublimated.

The alchemist himself plays an uncommon role in these operations in which not only the interfusion of elements but also, at least symbolically, the destiny of mankind is controlled. A disciple of Paracelsus, a hundred years after the death of the disquieting magus, declared that alchemists are "holy men by virtue of their Deifick Spirit, having tasted the first fruits of the Resurrection in this life and had a foretaste of the Celestial Country."[22] C. G. Jung legitimately raises the question why the alchemists felt a disunity in themselves, although they were supposedly Christians. After all, the alchemical operation was to be valid also for them; it was a religious function requiring of the alchemist a pure, often ascetic life, "a foretaste of the Celestial Country." Jung assumes that the alchemists were Christians, but I think it is fairly well established—and I shall further argue for the point—that they, together with other esoterics, were either adepts of Gnosticism or Christians only inasmuch as they intended to improve the Christian religion with the help of what they regarded as an older, purer tradition, going back to Egypt and India. True, the *lapis philosophorum* is at times described (namely, by Jung himself) as a "parallel to the Christ figure"; yet, as again Jung observes, Christ may also be thought of as a dividing factor, sundering the spiritual man from the physical. "Since most of them were physicians," writes Jung of the alchemists, "they knew the transitoriness of human existence and were impatient to wait till Kingdom come for more endurable conditions better in accord with the message of salvation. . . . They wanted to bring about the *unio mentalis* [the mental union] with the body as the foreshadowed idea of God . . . and save the body from the original sin. To do this, they

[86]

wanted to extract the quintessence which would be the physical equivalent of heaven [the first four elements being the constituents of the earth], of the 'potential world,' called *caelum* [heaven]. . . . What was left over from the body was a *terra damnata* [accursed earth], while the quintessence corresponded to the pure, incorrupt, original stuff of the world, God's adequate instrument."[23]

The alchemist's work appears in the Jungian text as inspired by a "demiurgic enthusiasm" to change the human condition through an impatient unification of opposites. The Hermetic regarded the world as the fruit of dispersion and reflection, so he trained himself through purification and Gnostic ascent to deal adequately with symbols of integration and union in order to bring about a totality. This enterprise seems to have received a further impetus with the new scientific spirit of the Renaissance, which conceived even of the object of the Christian religion as a union between the infinite and the finite, of spirit and matter, in the Logos. The theme of the *coincidentia oppositorum* goes, however, well beyond Renaissance predilections.

My conclusion regarding positions *A* and *B*, as examined in Part One, was that both postulated a union between two terms —God and man—when *in fine* one of the terms was abolished or absorbed in the other. According to *A*, the "distant God" leaves man in mastery of his destiny, and according to *B*, man also remains the master since he will have become divine. In either case the opposite terms become *one*—the kind of situation we found referred to as *coincidentia oppositorum*.

It is fascinating to find the many ways this situation—obviously the ideal one from the Hermetic point of view—is approached, formulated, or described in esoteric and quasi-esoteric literature. The most obvious union of opposites is that of man and woman, then that of the male and female principles, the male element (sulphur) and the female element (mercury), the male color (red) and the female color (white), and so on. Alchemy conceived the Sponsus (Christ) and the Sponsa (church) as forming together the image of totality, uniting the spiritual and the material. Alchemists spoke also of the "marriage of metals," a very ancient idea. The Cabala uses sexual symbols to express the union of two complementary principles in God, the female person (*Shechina*) and the male (*Barouch Hou*). In the Orient too, the attributes of both sexes characterize those gods who presided at the creation of the world and at the reproduction of all beings. In Tibetan symbolism the jewel in the lotus corresponds to the union of the masculine and feminine forces, which represent also the spiritual and temporal elements. The essence of Tantrism is the union of male and female energies; in the Tao, *yang* is the male and *yin* the female element.

The ninth-century philosopher John Scotus Erigena regards the division of the sexes as part of the cosmic process. He belongs to those thinkers who hold that the first division took place in God, then continued throughout the world as its characteristic principle and affected the nature of man, which was divided into male and female. To attain God again, the reunion of substances will have to begin with man and woman. We see in this example that the union of opposites is not conceived merely as a reconciliation, but as an end too, a folding up of the process of creation, a *finis* written to the cosmic drama. Union of the sexes, then the union of all other beings, finally the union of all of these with God restores the primordial integrity of God, that is of the One. As always in Hermetic, Gnostic, and alchemistic speculation, man's discovery of his dividedness makes him aware of the loss of paradisiacal unity, not only as a temporary mutilation but as an imperfection of the very constitution of his being.[24] The ideal situation of the *union* is then pursued as the final state of absolute *knowledge*, and knowledge itself becomes union. All relative situations are transcended, and the unconditioned state thus recovered is the same as the primordial situation in which the division of the real into subject and object did not exist.

This is further symbolized by a series of ageless symbols. Original Man is often pictured as a *sphere*, that is, the combination of all four elements by means of a circular movement. The sphere can also take the shape of an *egg*, as when it signifies the resting place of metals before maturation, or the shape of the *athanor*, the alchemist's oven, in which the decisive fusions take place. Another major symbol of the Original Man or of union is the *androgyne*, pictured as a sexless body with two heads, one male and one female. It comprehends the male *activity*—called in Hermetic symbolism Jakin and characterized by red as its color, sulphur its elemental sign, and fixity its chief attribute—and the female *receptivity*—called Bohas and characterized by white as its color, mercury its sign, and volatility its chief attribute. The Hermetic initiate is often represented as an androgyne since he is supposed to combine virile energy and feminine sensitivity, a combination whose alchemical representation is "rebis" (*res bina*, double thing). Paul Vulliaud shows in his study that Leonardo and the painters of his school often included in their compositions the androgynous columbine, which was a medieval symbol of *union*. In Theosophy, the androgyne figure is the symbol of the union of divine and human nature, and hence of the soul purified in view of ascent to unity in God. The androgyne is thus the archetype of man, symbolizing the end of passion, the final reabsorption of creation. The German Romantics considered it as the perfect man of the future. Novalis's friend, the poet Ritter, used alchemical language, a sign that the androgyne figure came to the Romantic generation from medieval and Renaissance, as well as post-Renaissance (Rosicrucian, Freemason, and generally "spiritualist") sources.

Through androgyny or other forms of Hermetic union the manipulator gains access to magic knowledge and power in order to complete nature's work and to complete it in a shorter time than nature would be able to do it. Paracelsus was among those who assumed that nature has a certain direction not decipherable except by the true knower, and that this direction pointed toward the primordial—undivided—state, toward the reintegration of the heavenly elements in one unity. The task of the Hermetic was to help nature achieve this end. Thus the Hermetic Sage, a true follower of Hermes Trismegistus, acquires through hard work, self-purification and initiation a superhuman power that makes him the master of nature, of the visible and invisible world. As noted before, as late as the seventeenth century the Rosicrucians regarded themselves as the heirs to all the prestigious esoteric sages, the Brahmans, the Egyptian priests, the mystagogues of Eleusis, the magi of Persia, the Pythagoreans and the wise men of Arabia, the Neoplatonists, the Gnostics, the Albigensians, the Beggards, the Hussites. The Freemasons count their origins from the pharaoh Tutmes III, four millennia ago. Pico della Mirandola described the magus who can marry earth to heaven since "he was once, and can become again through his intellect, the reflection of the divine *mens*." And Pico has a profound significance in the history of Western man as the first to suggest that "man as a magus may use Magia and Cabala to act upon the world, to control destiny by science."[25] The Hermetic adept becomes indeed a beneficiary of redemption, and as such he benefits both by the highest reward for the Christian and by what powers magia puts at his disposal. Thus he can imitate God, liquidate old creation, and fashion a new creation. The Hermetic is supposed to help the growth of God in our obscured intellect where God is feeble.[26]

According to every criterion, the magus *is* a divine being. The heterodox tradition within medieval Christianity may have helped him reach this status, if not by direct influence, at least by creating the intellectual climate favorable to the success and authority of the Hermetic tradition. Let us reflect on the fact that during the Renaissance Pico della Mirandola, Reuchlin,

The Magic Way to Perfect Knowledge

Guillaume Postel, Agrippa of Nettesheim, and Paracelsus and later Fludd and even Spinoza[27] offered a favorable and intrigued reception to the Cabala, the *corpus hermeticum*, and numerous other esoteric documents. This literature, then, was considered as equal in importance with the ancient Greek. In the view of these humanists, the two literatures were equally significant, although the Hermetic writings had the advantage in a still Christian, or at least religious, world of raising ultimate questions regarding God, creation, the nature of evil, and so on. No doubt, then, that medieval heterodoxy had prepared the mind of Renaissance humanists for the candid discussion of man's divinity. "Mysticism fed by thirteenth-century translations of Proclus, Plotinus and the pseudo-Dionysius came to be one of the mainstreams of unorthodoxy," writes Leff. "The search for God in the soul, with its emphasis on inner experience, turned toward depreciating the sacraments and the mediation of priesthood, even where it did not lead to identification of the soul with God, as it did with the Free Spirit."[28] The question of mediation does not interest us here; what is evident is that "the search for God in the soul" among Christian mystics like Joachim de Fiore and Meister Eckhart was encouraged by the same Neoplatonic and Gnostic influences that were exerted also on the medieval Hermetic speculators. We have seen Eckhart's position: to be joined to God, man must renounce his separateness and renounce himself as creature. Empty the soul and let God enter so that he may be born in you—but God enters only the perfectly virtuous soul to speak the Word within it. Joachim de Fiore and a century later the Franciscan Peter John Olivi were criticised by the church for their conception, which would transfer to men in this world the faculties reserved for the saved ones in the next. They would cease to be *viatores* (travelers, pilgrims) and become *comprehensores*, that is, in Hermetic language, initiates, magicians.[29]

. . .

God and the Knowledge of Reality

In a brief and necessarily schematic description we have now before us the career of Hermetism as a *parallel tradition* to the Christian tradition for one millennium and a half. Later, in the eighteenth century, one of the outgrowths of Hermetism, namely, Freemasonry, was to pull the Hermetic line of thinking and symbolization in a secular direction, which was natural in a world losing contact with its sustaining myth, desacralized to the extent of finding no reality under its symbols. Even so, however, in the eighteenth century alchemy was still recognized among the Freemasons, and in France, for example, almost all prestigious alchemists were also Freemasons.

This secularization does not affect the truth of the statement that Hermetism, at every juncture of the system, presents itself to us as a way, fervently argued for, of a superior, privileged *knowledge*, a purely intellectual knowledge through the identity of the divine and the human. There is such a correspondence between "the high and the low" (Hermes' "grand principle"), between microcosm and macrocosm, the knower and the known, that *to know* is regarded as becoming identified internally with the object *known*. This is made possible thanks to the belief that God himself is and acts in the subject, and that the object itself is, in the last analysis, of the same substance (*vide* the unity of existence) as the self. Man, as Koyré writes apropos of the doctrine of Valentin Weigel, a German "spiritualist" of the seventeenth century, is understood as the center of the world containing everything that the world contains: he is at once divine, astral, and material. "He is able to know the worlds because they are in him."[30]

We shall see in the next chapter that these views, so characteristic of all branches of Hermetism, profoundly influenced German philosophy of the eighteenth and nineteenth centuries; Weigel himself may have foreshadowed Kant's epistemology. At any rate, we observe here that from the point of view of the

[92]

theory of knowledge, the Hermetics equate *knowledge* and *being*: we *know* to the extent that we *are*, and the fuller, the more total our being, the more complete is also our knowledge. True, only God has full being, therefore all knowledge; but insofar as we are essentially divine and manipulators of the divine, our knowledge is also full knowledge, indeed indistinguishable from that of God. The Judaic and Christian traditions also hold that man is a "co-creator" of God, but this on an ontologically lower scale, as viceroy or steward of created things. For the Hermetics this lower scale seems intolerable; they regard the stewardship of creation as a mandate to abolish creation, that is, to accelerate the process of maturation—of metals into gold, of matter into spirit, of man into God—and by overcoming time, to bring all of it into reabsorption in the One.

It does not occur to the Hermetic that being may be both unlimited (for example, eternal, or rather, outside time) and transcendent, and that man is constitutionally limited. He does not recognize being unless he has entirely absorbed it with his intellectual faculties and permeated it with his consciousness to the point of total coincidence. The ideal must, then, be the equivalence of being and consciousness, the divine man, both Being and Knowledge. Martin Buber analyzes admirably this position when he writes that the philosophizing mind is tempted to fuse the "conception of the Absolute as object of an adequate thought, with itself, the human spirit. In the course of this [speculative] process, the idea which was at first noetically contemplated, finally becomes the potentiality of the spirit itself that thinks it. . . . The subject, which appeared to be attached to being in order to perform for it the service of contemplation, asserts that it itself produced and produces being. Until finally, all that is over against us . . . all partnership of existence, is dissolved in free-floating subjectivity."[31]

This description is true of the Hermetic magician in the variety of his practices and performances. Manipulation of the "upper world" becomes *producing* the world, re-creating it, and not only the "lower world" but the "upper world" too—although the whole operation remains a mental one. Yet, it is an effective operation from the point of view of the philosopher who aspires at demiurgic powers. If "service to being" is exchanged for "mastery of being" through inner possession, then, by the intellect's natural propensity, the Ockhamist God's *potentia absoluta* is transferred—in the order of speculation—to man.

NOTES

1. C. G. Jung, *Mysterium Conjunctionis* (Princeton, N.J.: Princeton University Press, 1970), p. 109.

2. Paul Naudon, *Les Loges de Saint-Jean et la philosophie ésotérique de la connaissance* (Paris: Dervy-Livres, 1957), p. 8.

3. Buddha taught that there are sensations, pain, facts of conscience, and so forth but no *subject* who sees, suffers, or understands. Being is a process that destroys and creates itself at every moment.

4. Robert M. Grant, *Gnosticism and Early Christianity*, 2nd ed. (New York: Harper Torchbooks, 1966), p. 65.

5. Paul Arnold, *La Rose-Croix et ses rapports avec la Franc-maçonnerie* (Paris: Ed. G.-P. Maisonneuve & Larose, 1970), p. 106.

6. Maurice Caron and Serge Hutin, *Les Alchimistes* (Paris: Ed. du Seuil, 1970), p. 110. My translation.

7. Quoted in Frances A. Yates, *Giordano Bruno and the Hermetic Tradition* (New York: Vintage Book, 1969), p. 33. Yates remarks of this and other texts of the so-called Egyptian Revelation that they belong to the optimistic type of gnosis. See, for the distinction of "optimistic" and "pessimistic" types of gnosis, "The Inaccessible God."

8. This is exactly what Hegel held too. See "The Inaccessible God."

9. Quoted in Yates, *Giordano Bruno*, p. 198. Most texts of the Hermetic body of literature, like the *Poimander* or the *Asclepius* are impossible to date and attribute with any precision. They were known, however, by the time of the early Middle Ages.

10. Mircea Eliade, *Myths, Dreams, and Mysteries: The Encounter between Contemporary Faiths and Archaic Realities* (New York: Harper & Row, 1967), pp. 106–7.

11. Mircea Eliade, *The Two and the One* (New York: Harper & Row, 1969), p. 48.

12. Jung, *Mysterium Conjunctionis*, p. 525.

13. Oswald Wirth, *Le Symbolisme hermétique dans ses rapports avec l'alchimie et la franc-maçonnerie*, (Paris: Dervy-Livres, 1909), p. 42.

14. See Alexandre Koyré, *Revue d'histoire et de philosophie religieuses* (1933).

15. Mircea Eliade, *The Forge and the Crucible, The Origins and Structures of Alchemy*, (New York: Harper & Row, 1971), p. 183.

16. Quoted in Yates, *Giordano Bruno*, pp. 132–33.

17. Caron and Hutin, *Les Alchimistes*, p. 105.

18. Paul Vulliaud, *La Pensée ésoterique de Léonard da Vinci* (Paris: Odette Lieutier, 1945), p. 95.

19. Quoted in Eugenio Garin, *Science and Civic Life in the Italian Renaissance* (New York: Anchor Books, 1969).

20. Eliade, *Forge and the Crucible*, p. 52.

21. Basil Valentine may not have existed at all, or the name may be a pseudonym. It means powerful (*valens*) king (*basileus*).

22. Quoted in Eliade, *Forge and the Crucible*, p. 166.

23. Jung, *Mysterium Conjunctionis*, pp. 541–43.

24. Eliade finds in the Indian fakir's well-known rope trick—in which he climbs a rope hanging rigid in the air before it is cut down—a reference to the fall of man. The rope symbolizes the unity of heaven and earth, a unity suddenly interrupted by the fall, which brings about an ontological change in the structure of the world. Man becomes mortal, separated into body and soul. The soul (and some pious men) will be allowed to ascend to heaven. *The Two and the One* (New York: Harper Torchbooks, 1969), p. 167.

25. Yates, *Giordano Bruno*, p. 116.

26. Wirth, *Symbolisme hermétique*, p. 111.

27. In a letter to Jarrig Jollis dated 27 March 1667, Spinoza speaks of an experiment in gold making he had verified and in the course of which the philosophical stone was used. Benedict de Spinoza, *Selected Letters* in *Chief Works*, 2 vols., trans. R. H. Elwes (New York: Dover Publications, 1955), 2.

28. Gordon Leff, *Heresy in the Later Middle Ages: The Relation of Heterodoxy to Dissent, c. 1250–1450*, 2 vols. (New York: Barnes & Noble Books, 1967), 1: 30–31.

29. In the nineteenth and twentieth centuries the belief in man becoming God has hardly diminished. Henri de Lubac quotes Philarète Chasles as saying that Buddhism, like Gnosticism before it, multiplies divine incarnation in man and makes possible unification with the "eternal substance." Maurice Magre (in *Pourquoi je suis bouddhiste*) hopes to enlighten the "barbarians of the West" in the same way as the Rosicrucians, the German Masonic sects, and Helen Blavatsky's Theosophists obtained the wisdom. Magre's message: there is no other wisdom but that we discover in ourselves

and no other God but the one we bear inside. Quoted in Henri de Lubac, *La Rencontre du Bouddhisme et de l'Occident* (Paris: Aubier-Montaigne, 1952), p. 219.

30. Alexandre Koyré, *Cahiers de la revue d'histoire et de philosophie religieuses* (1930). My translation.

31. Martin Buber, *Eclipse of God: Studies in the Relation between Religion and Philosophy* (New York: Harper & Row, Publishers, 1970), p. 124.

THE PHILOSOPHER'S MAGIC QUEST

E<small>MPLOYING</small> the preceding chapter-long examination of Hermetism and its various branches as a basis, we may now ascertain the parallel that exists between the esoteric line of thought and modern philosophy. The essence of Hermetism can be summarized in the following basic tenets, which are, of course, accompanied by pertinent symbols and carried out through certain operations.

The Hermetic believes that his mind is part of the divine *mens*, and that therefore he should be the rightful beneficiary of *true knowledge*. Ordinary, worldly knowledge is disqualified because it is characterized by reflection, that is, by the mirroring of an imperfect world. True knowledge is not acquired by ordinary mental processes, it is the result of a *union* of opposites and ultimately a union with the One. The process leading to union is the *maturation* (spontaneous or artificially accelerated) of elements, of male and female, even, as Oswald Wirth says, of God within our intellect. Maturation itself is promoted with the help of *magical transformers* like the alchemist's salt, the philosopher's stone, the Hermetic's talisman, or the *materia spiritualis*, that is, half-spiritual, half-material instruments symbolizing in themselves and thus prefiguring the projected union.

[97]

God and the Knowledge of Reality

At first impression it is hard to conceive how philosophy, an enterprise without materials, symbols, instruments, and without experiments to carry out, can follow a similar line of procedure. Philosophy's methods are purely speculative; its field is constituted by the fields of human knowledge and experience; and unlike alchemy, its powers do not include the transformation either of substances or of what we may call the constitution of being. Philosophy appears to me as a permanent quest of reality that, for man, is unending; it is not a method of changing the heterogeneities of the universe into a homogeneity, a way of transmuting the being of things into a new being.

Yet, let us make the following considerations, to be substantiated in the course of this and the next chapter.

Mircea Eliade speaks of the metallurgist and alchemist's "demiurgic enthusiasm" for intervention in the processes of nature. Something of this kind may be stated of the philosophical speculation to be examined here. This philosophy too assumes the actual or potential homogeneity of the universe (monism) so that its manipulation (maturation) may take for granted the equivalence of the "high" and the "low," of reason and history. The experiments promoting the formation, first, of the *materia spiritualis*, then of the spiritualization of all matter take place, instead of the *athanor*, in another privileged laboratory, the philosopher's *mens*, which is of the same substance as the One. This mental reconciliation of opposites (subject and object) leads to the supreme knowledge conceived as a *union* and at the same time, it leads to the end of the maturation process, history. The *conjunctio* of high and low is then the convergent maturation of reason (knowledge) and history (the object of knowledge). Those who performed the operation possess something that mortal men never obtain, something that religions promise only as a reward in the "Celestial Country." With a medieval expression, we may say that the philosopher ceased being a *viator* and became a *comprehensor*.

The most notable thing about this comparison between Hermetic speculation and modern philosophy is the fact that all the operations of the philosopher are *mental* operations. They take place in the *subject*—not in the sense in which cognitive processes are, of course, mental ones, but in the sense that the subject regards his ideas as *agents* shaping the real world. The real world must be then inside the subject in order to be shaped. Ideas do shape the extramental world. Before and while digging a hole in my garden and planting a tree, I must think and visualize the process and the result in my mind. But even if I build the pyramid of Kufu, I still only *accompany* (mentally) the structure of the given world; I do not modify this structure.

The subjectivist philosopher is convinced he does more: he is convinced he modifies the constitution of being. His increased "true knowledge" signifies a general increase of mankind's and the world's maturity; it also modifies radically the relationship between the object-world and the perceiving mind; it brings about an absolute change, a transmutation in man's morality, intellectual powers, and political insights; it brings about a change of being.

I am assuming that these transformations do *not* take place, and that the subjectivist philosopher, like the alchemist, only *shuffles the symbols* of transformation, symbols he has mentally fashioned somewhat the way Hermes Trismegistus fashioned his "statues." No matter how well he refines and manipulates the symbols, they have no point of contact with reality. Neither do the subjectivist philosopher's mental moves; he makes only imaginary ascents, and the models he constructs are impotent to influence the real world. Yet, he is not discouraged in his search of the philosophical stone, the power of his own mind. Since he assumes a secret correspondence between himself as microcosm and the macrocosm that is the One, he *knows* that everything is possible in proportion as the *mens* is refined and more subtle symbols are found. Since the magus is divine, the world now spiritualized and internalized in his mind changes at the subject's touch.

Magic may be generally defined as a shortcut to what the performer wants to achieve: the full and unmediated[1] *cosmic* powers (the "higher sphere" or "macrocosm" of Hermetism) brought to exert their impact on the lower order or "lower sphere." This is true of the various Hermetic doctrines examined in the previous chapter. The basic assumption of all of them is that there are, throughout the unicity of existence, correspondences of animal, vegetal, mineral, human, and astral orders, so that the adept is able to set into the desired motion any part of the universe by performing certain operations in his own privileged sphere.

The most serious obstacle to the unicity of existence and the correspondences derived from it is the factor of time. In the natural order, hence in man's experience, time is not compressible. It measures all processes of maturation; it separates project from realization; it is the gap not bridgeable by impatience. The magician is, of course, the privileged human able to bridge a gap in time, between the now and the future, that is, to abolish time altogether. He can do this, however, in privileged experiments only, as in re-presentations of archaic myths or in the alchemical operations of fusion. For this reason, the magician, whether the alchemist or the archaic metallurgist, was regarded as sacred in his community: he knew how to reconnect the community with its ancestors; he knew the secrets of fire and of the fusion of metals, of their maturation in the wombs of mountains, and so on. Yet, all the magician could do was to accelerate the maturation process; he could not make it permanent or cosmic.

What is true of metals is true of humans also. The *lapis philosophalis* was able to effect a union of opposites, but not of all opposites, *hic et nunc*. If the androgyne represented the union of male and female principles, of the aggressive sulphur and the receptive mercury, that is, of the two fountainheads of passion and conflict, it was, together with others, the symbol of an ideal state, not an accomplished state. Hence, this side of magic and alchemy we find man incomplete, unfinished and limited; in short, we find him in a creaturely state. This is, however, not an exclusively Hermetic lament. The philosopher may also deplore man's finiteness, his creatureliness, and with a "demiurgic enthusiasm" he may attempt to bring about the maturation of man, of mankind. In other words, the philosopher too may become a "magician."

In Part One we made it clear that in many instances it is difficult to distinguish among philosophers, mystics, and magicians, although a different universe of discourse, speculative methods, and terminology classify them in separate categories. Yet, all three types of speculation may have affinities with positions *A* and *B*; the label *philosopher* is no safeguard against its bearer's adhering to positions shared by mystics and magicians. The philosopher may be as impatient as the alchemist. The latter's aim is to produce the *materia spiritualis* that will help him to transmute base metals into gold; the former's objective in some cases is to discover the secret of the spiritualization of man so as to transform him into an omniscient being, into God. (Of Hegel, for example, Eric Voegelin uses the term *sorcerer*, a significant reference to a major modern thinker in the West.) Some philosophical systems, then, may actually perform a *metabasis eis to allo genos*, the passage from one kind of discourse to another, a performance rather analogous to the alchemical transmutation of elements. The alchemist justifies his operation by reference to the unicity of existence; the philosopher has no such justification. What he does is to perform a mental operation without impact on reality, a mental operation in which time (history) is supposed to bring about an ontological change that the intellect cannot effectuate. The philosopher assumes that the phases of history measure, at the same time, the phases of the growth of the mind (reason) too. The danger, the intellectual danger, is obvious. It is the conclusion that to each one of our historical (political) desiderata there corresponds an appropriately higher form of intelligence, insight, and mature judgment: to the *ideal* polity also the *perfect* cognition.

It is thus evident that what I have described as the characteristic form of thought of Hermetism is not limited to esoteric speculation; it is often manifest in philosophical speculation also. We recognized its presence in classical Greek philosophical tradition, in Neoplatonism, in some early church fathers like Origen and Tertullian, then in philosophers such as John Scotus Erigena, mystics such as Meister Eckhart, thinkers such as Nicholas of Cusa. In this long speculative tradition—with which Hermetism at times merged, of which it remained at times an attentive companion—it was generally assumed that existence, marked by the multiplicity of beings, the preponderance of matter, the stumbling block of temporality, and the humiliation of sexuality[2] is a product of the fall. Since this could not be the last word about man, it was then further assumed—by Origen, later by John Scotus Erigena—that the work of necessary and salutary purification would be achieved through renewed cycles of fall and redemption, a doctrine imported from the Orient (metempsychosis), but to which the early Greek Orphic tradition and the Pythagoreans also adhered. The best souls in each new cycle shed part of their creatureliness that was still attached to them and acquired or reacquired more of the divine perfection that was their true nature.

We have seen some of the avatars of this myth as part of position *B*. It accompanied the Christian concept of creation and redemption throughout the Middle Ages, became particularly strong with the Renaissance, and penetrated the territories that went later over to the side of the Reformation. We saw its spread and underground (?) popularity in Italy in the late fifteenth and the sixteenth centuries: the humanists Marsilio Ficino and Pico della Mirandola treated as equivalent the Greek philosophical tradition and the Cabala as well as Hermetic magic, and they produced a *mélange* of philosophy, esoteric gnosis, Judaism, and Christianity. They attempted a synthesis, writes Frances Yates, of all philosophies on a mystical basis, in search of a new gnosis. Two generations later Giordano Bruno was to give a new twist to this synthesis by calling Moses and Jesus "great magi." While Bruno was in England, he brought "magical hermetism to the discontented [Elisabethan] intelligentsia and a new outlet for the secret yearnings of other secretly dissatisfied elements of society."[3] This influence, according to Yates, survived Bruno's sojourn in England, and even his death in 1600 by burning in Rome; in Shakespeare's *The Tempest* she recognizes Bruno's benevolent magus in the character of Prospero, creator of the ideal state after the defeat of the earthly Caliban. And were Thomas More's Utopians, Yates further asks, not really the *prisci theologi*, the original "Egyptian sages" allegedly the teachers of Moses, the entire Hebrew tradition, and thus of the Bible and of Jesus? If so, then More's *Utopia* is not the playful satire that various critics have seen in it, but a piece of nostalgic and at the same time hopeful literature about the possibility of building the ideal commonwealth with the help of a more authentic wisdom than that preached by Christ and the apostles.[4]

The lines of philosophical and of esoteric speculation intermingled even more thoroughly on German soil (as well as in the Netherlands and Switzerland). Luther was denounced during his lifetime for having set up a new orthodoxy, a new church with new and mercilessly enforced dogmas, rites, and attitudes. Such criticisms and attacks had been leveled almost ceaselessly against the medieval church also by a great variety of "spiritualist" movements and sects, a few of which have been mentioned in earlier chapters. But the reformed communities were even more impatient than the medieval movements of Fraticelli, Amaurians, Brethren of the Yellow Cross, and others, and Luther's authority was also far from solidly established. Thus the German, Dutch, Swiss, and other "spiritualists" managed to take off on their own and to elaborate new metaphysical concepts, although still dressed in the terms of religious discourse. Their influence on the great nineteenth-century German theologians and philosophers, including Kant, Fichte, Hegel, and Schelling, has been demonstrated by modern scholarship.

The German "spiritualists" and their confreres in the sixteenth and seventeenth centuries (Schwenckfeld, Valentin Weigel, Sebastian Franck, Jacob Boehme himself, men influenced by Paracelsus and the esoteric-alchemist tradition) exacerbated and sharpened some of the main themes of Renaissance and Reformation syncretism. Another, Dirk Camphuysen, stressed the antagonism between religion and church, between Christianity and its organized forms, faith and the holding of ecclesiastical office. A similar incompatibility was found between heart and reason, of which only the first represented faith, while the second, identified with theological disputations, was rejected. Maybe the radical utopianism of the Polish philosopher Leszek Kolakowski is responsible for the unsolvable conflict he sees between "reified" institutional ties and personal ties within the religious community—between "Paul, the young Luther, Kierkegaard" and the organized church[5]—but there is little doubt that the post-Reformation intellectual climate in German-speaking territories did promote a "spiritualist" version of philosophical issues. It is another matter that a century later Protestant nonconformism was quieted down forcibly in both Germany and England (English and Dutch nonconformists emigrated to America), and that the Rosicrucians, for example, like other bearers of Renaissance Hermetism, went underground, transforming "what was once an outlook associated with dominant philosophies into a preoccupation of secret societies."[6] That the Rosicrucians, nevertheless, did not give up the fight is shown by the movement's first document (published in Cassel in 1614), which promised that "after a time there will be a general reformation both of divine and human things." The document's title expresses quite a mouthful, too: *Allgemeine und General Reformation der gantzen weiten Welt . . . an alle Gelehrte und Haupten Europas geschrieben* (The Complete and General Reformation of the Whole Wide World . . . Written to All Scholars and Leaders of Europe). Hardly any wonder that these ideas prepared much of German idealism. They did so in two ways: one was the secularization of the spiritualist discourse, the "humanization" of what for the spiritualists was still the realm of theology; the other was the elaboration of an epistemology consonant with the ideal of knowledge in the sense of *union* with the One, the main theme of a tradition that was quite long by that time. Nietzsche remarked ironically that German philosophy was the product of "sons of Protestant pastors," meaning that it was a secularized theology; Karl Barth hardly disagreed when he wrote that by the nineteenth century the problem had become "how to make religion, revelation, and the relationship with God something which could also be understood as a necessary predicate of man, or at any rate, how to demonstrate that man had a potentiality, a capacity, for these things."[7] By these "things" Barth chiefly meant "the ascent of humanity [culminating in] man's apotheosis" for which German thought from Luther through Schleiermacher to Feuerbach and Strauss had prepared the way. Feuerbach himself was quite justified to claim the theologian's role in a theology whose object was no longer God but man. "God," he wrote, "is nothing but the means by which man realizes his own blessedness."[8]

Consider now the following situation. On the one hand, it cannot be said that modern philosophy evolved directly from the esoteric speculation of the past many centuries; on the other

[105]

hand, I have listed so many similarities between the Hermetic line of thought and the philosophical discourse—and more will follow—that at the beginning of this chapter I was able to draw two parallels showing the influences and the analogous endeavors. Shall the conclusion be that modern philosophical enterprise is part of the Hermetic tradition?

It is perhaps unnecessary to argue for such a conclusion. A common source of Hermetism and modern philosophy, a source deeply encased in the human mind, is the adoption by both of positions *A* and *B* as formulated in Part One. Whether the Hermetic or the philosophical line is followed, the common premise is man's divine self-assertion to which there belongs a theory of knowledge affirming capabilities that transcend the human condition. This would explain the tendency of both Hermetism and modern subjectivist epistemology to see the source of true knowledge in the fusion of subject and object, just as man and God fuse in the Hermetic sage and in the modern philosopher. Both are loath to operate with *distinguos* by which the knower and his object are regarded as separate entities, and by which God and man are irrevocably separated into two vastly unequal and by no means consubstantial entities.

These considerations go a long way toward explaining why subjectivist (immanentist) philosophy has proved so voracious in modern times. Although formally it claims no exclusivity in representing philosophical thought, its ambition is so intense that it necessarily occupies an ever larger place in contemporary speculation. Many philosophers are unable to resist the attraction of such a doctrine, particularly since the (nonmaterialist) alternative is regarded by them as an intolerable scandal, intellectually and ideologically: namely, the mediating figure of a personal yet transcendent God. As noted earlier, the epistemological consequences of this alternative (position *C*) imply that only a limited knowledge is available to man, whereas the epistemological consequence of man's apotheosis (to use Barth's phrase) is knowledge realized as union of the subject and the object. By the eighteenth and nineteenth centuries Christianity, and with it the "anthropomorphic" God, was anyway completely discredited; it was regarded by modern philosophy as it had been by Renaissance humanism: in comparison with combined Indian, Egyptian, and Plotinian gnosis a rickety system of superstitions, taboos, irrational restrictions, and antiscientific obscurantism. Who would have paid attention to what Christianity had to say about the conditions and limits of cognition when itself was regarded as obstructing the improvement of the intellect and standing in the way of progress?

Much of the philosophical debate centers around the concept of man's *maturation*. This was the great quest of the Hermetic tradition, and it has also been that of premodern and modern philosophy. We ascertained the smooth transfer of this quest from the former to the latter, and I explained this continuity by the fact that the notion of man's maturation follows from the premise, common to Hermetism and modern philosophy, that man's patrimony includes total being and total knowledge, full intelligibility by full being. The human being thus matures from the state of creatureliness toward fullness, oneness, and divinity.

At the core of this concept we discern a fundamental assumption, again common to the esoteric tradition and exoteric speculation. The assumption is that the function of reason is not to ascertain the equation "adequatio rei et intellectus," that is, cognition in the ordinary sense, in which thing and thought reliably fit together, but to transform the world in the process of comprehending it. If this is so, then our human task is to develop in us the kind of absolute intellect—the divine *Nous*—that will correspond also to absolute being. The doctrines we have examined, from Gnosticism and astrology to much of modern philosophy, have all argued that in various proportions the human intellect is mixed with the divine mind; the point at which these doctrines may diverge is whether the two already constitute one single entity or whether they will do so only at some future time. We examined the question in the second section of Part One where we found the quite natural preponderance of doctrines that describe the way to union; in the first section of Part Two we found that the way can be the ritual of initiation or the process of maturation. On the way to union, or completed being, knowledge also grows, whether it must be extricated from *amnesis*, alchemically produced like the fifth essence (*quintessentia*), drawn down from the higher spheres by magic, or displayed as the result of the gradual discarding of creatureliness.

The main theme today is, of course, the latter, because it best harmonizes with Judaic and Christian concepts of messianism and salvation, still the cornerstones of Western intellectual-spiritual tradition. Knowledge as *anamnesis* (recovery of a previous state, of memory) may be regarded by most philosophers as too Platonic, hence too static to be popular, and whatever survived of it in modern, half-esoteric, half-philosophical speculation has anyway merged with the concept of transmigration of souls that mature not as individual souls but through the avatars in a multitude of bodies and states. Knowledge as the *coincidentia oppositorum* or by magic was discredited in its alchemical and other forms by modern science. But modern philosophy is able to favor the notion that knowledge, and with it *being*, grows by the shedding of human limitations and the progressive emergence of a better intellect encased in better moral and historical forms. This notion is not only not hindered by modern science, it is promoted by evolutionary theories in the realm of biology and morals. The popularity of writings by Teilhard de Chardin shows best the mutual support lent each other by belief in an emerging Super-*Nous* (noosphere) and a scientific conception committed to the idea of historical evolution. Thus an epistemology has come to be favored according to which knowledge is at an imperfect stage corresponding to the phase of creatureliness, itself the source of human limitations. As knowledge grows, so will the divine substance in man, cracking the carapace of all other limitations too. This theory necessarily divides history into phases, each phase being a kind of self-contained framework within which the levels of knowledge, morality, historic meaning, and general maturation correspond. That the level of knowledge at each phase is the privileged yardstick of maturation for the philosopher is hardly surprising. In each of the doctrines we studied the *pneuma* is the essence of the elect who is in contact with the *gnosis*, which, as we know, is not a knowledge subject to amplification by the dialectical and discursive methods, but a divine substance spreading like light in the darkness.

In the twelfth century Joachim de Fiore, whose story merges with that of esoterism, divided sacred history in three ages. The first, that of the Old Testament, was the age of domination and fear; it was followed by the "age of grace," that of the New Testament. And some sixty years after Abbot Joachim's death, around the middle of the thirteenth century, history, according to his vision, was supposed to turn into the third, final age of "mental perfection and love" (*tertius status in plenitudine intellectus*), beyond the scope of the New Testament and dominated by the "monks" whose society would coincide with the entire earth. Are these "monks" still creatures in the ordinary meaning of the word, are they *prisci theologi* with the original knowledge restored, or are they in some other manner of a higher status (reference to "mental perfection")? At any rate, Joachim's texts imply complete newness; the state of the world will be changed, and man will begin to be other: all-knowing, free, contemplative, and loving. A late spiritualist, Caspar Schwenckfeld of the seventeenth century, also speaks of "creature" as a being outside God and in whom "God is absent, an impure and profane being." A creature is imperfect *ex defini-*

tione, since he is finite and limited. Salvation, according to Schwenckfeld, is not deliverance from sin, but divinization (*theosis*), God's ultimate design for man. We may surmise that Joachim's "monks" were beneficiaries of this design.

Contrary to natural theology, Joachim's or Schwenckfeld's view asserts that there is no valid way for the creature to apprehend the world, and that a growth in being, a rise from creatureliness, is necessary in order to have real knowledge. Man is, therefore, not a mere creature, at least potentially. He is, as Hegel writes, the incarnate Logos, and as such, the enemy of Being: "He is the negative being who *is* only insofar as he overcomes Being." For Hegel, Being is overcome in the guise of the object, because the object, as the type of otherness (alterity) is opposed to the self. The God of Christians (and of Jews) is the par excellence *other*, the God-object, so that the self can achieve absolute status only if he asserts himself vis-à-vis God.

The thought of the contemporary Hegelian Ernst Bloch is similar. There is a distance, a temporary dichotomy, between man's present appearance and his nonpresent essence,[9] which is expressed by Bloch in the famous formula "S is not yet P," that is, no subject has, as yet, its adequate predicate, the world has not yet found itself. This, writes Bloch, is the case at the beginning of philosophy; but philosophy, in his view, is the demiurgic effort to change the world, to realize utopia. "S is not yet P" means that we are at the beginning of both philosophy and history (we are, as Bloch puts it, the *thesis*, waiting for completion or synthesis), and we shall remain so until Utopia and with it the "unalienated subject," the divine self, emerges. His program is to "transmute all the evil of this world and of creatureliness into a luminous Jerusalem."[10] As Jürgen Moltmann points out, Bloch's reading of the Bible does not begin with the creation, but with the watchword "Eritis sicut Deus" ("You will be like God"), and it ends not with God who has become human, but with man who has become divine.[11]

The Philosopher's Magic Quest

In order to liquidate creatureliness, the philosopher proceeds with the abolition of man's limitations, time-boundedness, ordinary ways of cognition, and his concept of philosophy as a quest. Finite things are not real, declared Hegel's friend, Schelling in the introduction to *The Ages of the World*, only the absolute is. Hence there can be no communication from the latter to the former because things are groundless, having fallen from the absolute. A similar "phantomatization" is performed on the concept of time by Hegel: time too is unreal insofar as it marks "the fate of the Spirit" that has not yet found its fulfillment in itself.[12] We have noted in numerous passages that in the Plotinian view the soul does not reason unless as a prisoner of the body, because reasoning is the symptom of a diminution of intelligence that is no longer self-sufficient. Reasoning, wrote Plotinus, grasps things in succession. But there is no succession in what is simple, in which case an "intellectual contact" is sufficient. Indeed, "those who have been in contact with the One, know that no thinking [noesis] should be attributed to it." This was also the fundamental point in the philosophy of Henri Bergson and Edouard Le Roy, namely, that discursive knowledge cuts up, fragments, and enumerates its object, and thereby falsifies it; real knowledge is derived through intuition, the coalescence of the self with the essence of the object, with what is "vital" and "real" in it.

Existentialism is indebted to the same viewpoint with its excessive distrust of concepts and of discourse. Antirationalists, observes Albert Dondeyne, "speak as if the concept did nothing but rigidify our infinitely mobile apprehension of reality and shut us off from the concrete."[13] The return to experience is understood neither in the sense of scientific verification nor in the sense of inductive reasoning, but as the only way of getting to reality, the only way because of its immediate resonance in the self.

What summarizes all these epistemological attempts to liquidate conceptual knowledge, time-boundedness, and the rational use of the mind is the conviction that these are crutches for man as a creature, that is, as long as he needs them, but that he may progressively discard them as he leaves his inferior state. Kant spoke of man leaving behind his age of minority, which was the "inability to use his intelligence without being directed by somebody else." He cried out, "Sapere aude!" ("Let us dare to know").[14] More subtly, Le Roy understood that the problem of epistemology is ultimately linked to the God-problem, and he tried to find his own formulation somewhere between "the two opposite conceptions: the transcendent and the immanent God, both of which are false because static. A dynamic reconciliation is possible since we, human beings, are not fulfilled and closed natures," but indefinitely open to an undisclosed (open-ended) evolution.[15]

Philosophy itself is *on the way* to Being (*das Sein des Seienden*), writes Heidegger, or rather, what philosophy is on the way to will be revealed as Being. It describes a process of growth that is a "conversation" in the course of which not only reason, sentiment, and will, but an infinity of existential aspects of man—including those still to emerge—enter the multifaceted and open-ended dialogue with Being. The modalities of cognition become historical modalities in view of approaching Being ever closer, so that ultimately it is not the object of cognition that determines the knowledge I have of it, but it is *my* biography, *my* growth in history, that makes the arbitrary decision about what can be accepted as knowledge.

Attention is thus focused on the fascinating parallel lines along which the two modern philosophical endeavors are running: the increasing "openness" of man as he rises toward higher states of being, and his gradual acquisition of knowledge toward the ultimate coalescence with the object. What adds to this fascination is what has been called the dialectical play between *being* and *nothingness*: full being is equivalent to nonbeing, as full knowledge is equivalent to union, that is, to the absorption in the One where knowledge is abolished. The existence of the extramental world, and with it ordinary knowledge directed at it and cognizing it, remains a stumbling block, an embarrassing obstacle for the mind impatiently longing after the stillness of *bei sich sein*, homecoming; the philosopher, therefore, in quest of the absolute solution, sees and seeks the final ontological reconciliation in mutual absorption, in the nothingness pregnant with being, or vice versa. "Not to exist, not to have become—this is the real basic definition of the *ens perfectissimum*," the perfect Being, writes Ernst Bloch. This is also the ideal of cosmic religions without any clear idea of creation, since creation implies a distinction between God and creature, consequently a relationship that is not a fusion.

We are here, one might say, at the heart of the matter. The "absolute solution" involves, to be sure, the abolition (or fusion) of separateness and conflict, of subject and object. It is clear, however, that the subject has an edge over the object because the "inner man" remains conscious even after the object-world has been evacuated from his consciousness. The expectation of the One fills him. Meanwhile, the extramental world is regarded as phantomatic, as not having full existence. Only the noetic *I* has existence, and the only worthy object of his *noesis* is *noesis* itself, or, as Maritain puts it referring to idealists and phenomenologists, they do not begin their speculation by the act of knowing things, but by an act of knowing knowledge ("un acte de connaissance de la connaissance").[16]

It is obvious that if things have natures and human beings have other than divine natures (actually or *in potentia*), the subject is forced to take cognizance of objects, to share the world with them, and to accept the most intimate thing of the material world, namely, his own body with its limitations that are, at the same time, the subject's own limitations also.[17] The subjectivist epistemology, however, does not accept what

[113]

Maritain calls "les choses et leur puissance regulatrice de notre pensée" (the extramental things and their power to direct our thought), because if things have an existence independent of the mind, then fusion with them becomes as impossible as their spiritualization, which is another way of saying absorption in the noetic continuum of the One. More than that, the Judeo-Christian-Aristotelian conceptual framework of our thought sees the existence of things in their createdness, so that the reality of objects presupposes also the reality of a supreme transcendental creator. This is not the case, incidentally, in oriental philosophies where the so-called aesthetic component does not have to be rooted in ontological reality; it is a social product making life easier to bear. This is true of the "ethical component" also, from which it is not, in fact, separable. Western man, on the other hand, cannot help asking questions about the *quidditas*, the "whatness," of things; he is not satisfied with the answer that things are appearances and that therefore social convenience is the only legitimate arrangement for dealing with them.

Briefly, the aim of the epistemology here described is to introduce the extramental world in the subject, or at least to reduce its reality until its residual existence may fuse with the subject. The subject is then enabled to study itself, its own laws and categories, its moods and reactions before the stirrings of the "inner man." Kant was still concerned with the dependence of knowledge on the categories of the mind like spaciality, causality, temporality; Heidegger found an endless number of existential modalities that constitute the subject: anguish, presence of death, contingence, freedom, and so on. These modalities transcend the self, or, more precisely, in their dynamic self-projection they endlessly reconstitute new selves, together with new worlds depending on the selves. True, this is no longer the Cartesian subjectivity without opening on the outside world; yet its consequences are not essentially different since Heideggerian subjectivity endows man with powers to create the reality of the world, including his own reality.

Kant's justification for this demiurgic operation is the thesis that "understanding does not derive its laws (a priori) from, but prescribes them to, nature."[18] Man's mind is autonomous in intellectual cognition, in spite of (or because of?) the justified supposition of an extramental world. In a famous passage Kant both denies and asserts the idealist thesis as applicable to his own system: "Idealism consists in the assertion that there are none but thinking beings, all other things, which we think are perceived in intuition, being nothing but representations in the thinking beings, to which no object external to them in fact corresponds. I, on the contrary, say that things as objects of our senses existing outside us are given, but we know nothing of what they may be in themselves, knowing only their appearances, that is, the representations which they cause in us by affecting our senses."[19] Like Heidegger, Kant too found that his "transcendental philosophy" justified man's going beyond himself, since he is autonomous both in regard to intellectual and moral judgment and prescribes its laws to nature. Knowledge, consequently, does not have to be verified, it refers to objects a priori, nondemonstrable a posteriori. God and the *Ding-an-sich* lose simultaneously their relevance to man, and autonomous man becomes totally relevant.[20]

The *dépassement*, the rise of man toward a "higher man" is also Hegel's theme, and there too the process implies the voracious absorption of the extramental world, described usually as "reconciliation": of ego and nonego, of the finite and the infinite, of things within and without. We have seen that Hegel considered consciousness as the seedbed of revelation, so that individual reason understands itself as also the reason of God; as such, it is not opposed to God's intelligence. Hegel corrected the paganism of the Enlightenment, which saw a dichotomy between divine and human intelligence. If God stands in op-

position to reason, this opposition is provisional and will be re-
solved through man's "homecoming," the last act of the grand
dialectical world-process; God *in actu* reabsorbs reason again.
Because God, according to Hegel's *Philosophy of Religion*, is
this: "to distinguish oneself from oneself, to be subject to oneself, but to be completely identical with oneself in this distinction." Thus, for Hegel, the fusion of subject and object takes
place in God, *is* God, although the process of the fusion can be
called history. Since God is action, ceaseless action, truth is the
ceaseless completion of the reconciliation of opposites. The flow,
like the alchemical operation, is life and truth itself; error as
well as sin consist in stopping at one of the moments of the
flux and in regarding this moment as something stable, permanent—making a concept of it. Concepts may be necessary
stages of the flux, but they must be passed through (transcended) toward even higher forms of the dialectical movement.

It has been assumed, wrote Kant in the preface to his *Critique
of Pure Reason*, that our knowledge must conform to objects.
Yet, no necessary knowledge has so far resulted from this assumption. We must now try if we do not succeed better in the
tasks of metaphysics by supposing that "objects must conform
to our knowledge." The first way, the one Kant thus disqualified,
was regarded as *static*, as knowledge *in aeternum* of things
that remain always identical to themselves and about which all
propositions are true or false according to the so-called Aristotelian logic with its principle of identity. True or false; there is
no third possibility, *tertium non datur*. The second way, on the
other hand, is regarded as *dynamic* because through it the
world adjusts to the changing meaning-requirements of our restless mind. Thus, what is not in accord with the mind (subject)
is neither true nor false; it is meaningless or has many meanings;
it is *my* representation, *my* will, *my* quest for meaning (relevance) that creates the world, which is then exclusively mine.

[116]

This is basically what Schelling asserted in his *Philosophy and Religion*: "If the perceived world exists only in the mind of those contemplating it, then the return of the souls to their origin and their detachment from the concrete mean the dissolution of the perceived world and its disappearance in the world of minds. In proportion as the soul comes nearer its center, it progresses toward this objective."[21] This, in turn, recalls Fichte. He went beyond Kant, holding that the phenomena themselves, like the categories of the mind, proceed from the self, so that our science measures genuinely all things. For Kant, phenomena were still at least "bubbles," "mere representations" with which metaphysics had hitherto deceived itself; for Fichte, the mental world was all, and the mind itself was declared to be the proper domain of investigation for the mind.

Thus arises *subjective evidence* as the measure of all cognition in the absence of *being*, which is either denied or held unknowable since what mediates being to the subject—namely, the extramental world—is also declared to be "bubbles," "illusions," "phantoms," or "mental constructs." Subjective evidence, after having been a Cartesian requirement, became Husserl's target in the twentieth century. Like Descartes, the phenomenologists too propose to build a radically pure philosophy with no preconceptions unfounded in reason. To do this, they must evacuate (again like Descartes) from the mind all certainties about the extramental world so as to constitute and grasp a *world-for-me*, inseparable from me. From this apparent interaction (which is nothing else than a new way of "absorbing" the world of objects) rises rationality that the self creates *in actu* and that nails him to the world. But if reason is precisely that faculty of man by which he becomes aware of the outside world, formulates judgments about it, and recognizes its distance from him (I spoke not of *coincidentia rei et intellectus*, complete overlapping of thing and thought, but of *adequatio rei et intellectus*, reliable fitting), then action that is intelligent

presupposes reason instead of producing it. However, do phenomenologists need reason in order to reach reality? Does intuition (phenomenological reduction) not replace reason when
it cuts through the cultural, linguistic, utilitarian, and other sedi-
ments and strikes against the "original perceptive layer"? (The
term is Alphonse de Waehlens'.) When, instead of perceiving
this book, I perceive myself-perceiving-this-book, I do not
grasp a reality but only the *process* of grasping reality. I am
again, Husserlian intentionality notwithstanding, inside my subjectivity, and my evidence does not include the concurrence of
the extramental world. Husserl himself says that "pure *cogi-
tatio*" is "as little interpretation as possible, and as pure an intuition as possible. In fact, we will hark back to the speech of
the mystic when they describe the intellectual seeing which is
supposed not to be a discursive knowledge."[22]

It is claimed that Husserl tried to break out of the iron circle
of subjectivity in which philosophical speculation had found itself locked since Descartes. There are indeed attempts in this
direction. The distinction of appearance and reality is not derived from experience, the phenomenologists say, but from
Plato. What *is* also *appears*; the phenomena are real, not in the
sense of Kant and certainly not of Fichte, but in the sense that
they fill out the real and nothing hides behind them. Yet, Husserl's assurances about the reality of the real soon tend to evap-
orate. First, the epistemological problem is presented as awe-
inspiring and forbidding: "With the awakening of reflection
about the relation of cognition to its object abysmal difficulties
arise. Cognition . . . suddenly emerges as a mystery."[23] "How
can we be certain of the correspondence between cognition and
the object cognized? How can knowledge transcend itself and
reach its object reliably?"[24] No wonder the task is not executed
in the desired direction. Phenomenology, refusing to investigate
its object as composed of the ego and of the world, sets out to
grasp it as an "absolute datum" in purely "immanent seeing."

The consequence, as Husserl admits, is not the investigation of human cognition, but of cognition in general, "apart from any existential assumptions either of the empirical ego or of a real world."[25] Does this operation (eidetic reduction) yield up the so ardently desired "pure self"? But the question must at once be "What is a 'pure self' if it has nothing in common with the only self of which we are aware, what the phenomenologist calls 'empirical self' or self-as-I-the-person in my human and objectual environment?" Besides any other consideration this poverty of the pure self is also regrettable as we are told that, since Plato, representations have slowly substituted for the "richness of things the definition of their essence."[26] And Robberechts, the author of this statement, declares once more that things and beings are *present*, they are not *re-presented*.

Where are then these "things and beings," where are they in the Husserlian epistemology? Where does their richness hide when the "empirical ego," the receiver and transmitter of this richness, is, as the phenomenologists insist, "bracketed"? If to know things absolutely is to know their essences, then, according to Husserl, the essence must be discoverable in appearances, in the phenomena.[27] But, as we have found, the reduction to phenomenality does not grasp the thing, only the process of reduction, and what it finally does grasp and calls objectivity is "subjective through and through."[28] "To be is to be given to consciousness . . . in such a way as to manifest the impossibility of being given otherwise. . . . Phenomenology is a doctrine of essences, and it simply ignores the question of the extra-mental realization of essences—it is concerned with what things are, *not* with whether they are."[29]

Husserl's critic is thus obliged to oscillate with him between a realist and an idealist position, to deepen the search for an ever-elusive object, while the subject too remains ungraspable. One should not be surprised to find Robberechts, a devoted Husserlian, exclaim at the end of his study that for phenomenology there is neither a pure subject nor a pure object, that, in fact, there is no subject and object at all as separate entities. "The best," he says, "would be to erase these words from our vocabulary."[30]

There is a longish passage in Jacques Maritain's quasi-memoirs, *Le Paysan de la Garonne*, where he recapitulates his philosophical acquaintances, the line of distinguished thinkers from Descartes, through Berkeley, Spinoza, Hume, Kant, Hegel, Auguste Comte, to the logical positivists, Husserl, Heidegger, Ricoeur, and Sartre. "Their contribution to the history of thought is immense, and they rendered great services to philosophy. In particular, they obliged philosophers to pay more attention to the theory of knowledge and the critique of its methods. We must study them with a burning interest for the way their brain works and with lively curiosity for the mystery of their reasoning. . . . There is only one thing I contest absolutely in their regard, but that point I contest absolutely: that they are philosophers. They are *ideosophers*. . . . There is nothing pejorative in this appellation, it merely indicates another quest than the philosophical quest."[31] Maritain does not spell out exactly what he means by *ideosopher* (it is, in my view, not an adequate term), but he summarizes his charges against the thinkers in question—and asks his readers not to regard his iconoclasm as the dotage of an "old fool"—in this way: they begin with thought only (*la seule pensée*) and they never move on to the reality of things and of the world. "In one way or another they reabsorb the world in thought."[32]

This is what I have been arguing here also, trying to understand the epistemological processes by which idealists, phenomenologists, existentialists, Bergsonians, and others arrive at their conclusions. I have concluded that these thinkers do not really interest themselves in the problem of knowledge, but in the problem of union, or fusion between object and subject, the speculative *lapis philosophorum.* This aspiration, notwithstanding Husserl's earlier quoted comparison, is not that of the genuine mystic who remains aware of the distinction between self and its object, God; it is the aspiration of the "monist" mystic and of the Hermetic practitioner who bypass experience and the laborious formation of concepts in favor of symbols and the manipulation of symbols. For them, as well as for the subjectivist philosopher, *experience* is radically altered by their rejection of the extramental world; and they suspect the *concept* too because it signifies a "stopping and staying" at arbitrarily chosen moments of the Hegelian "ceaseless completion of the circle." Thus the concept can be obtained only at the end of the circle when everything, the flux of experience, has stopped. The concept is God, Hegel teaches, inasmuch as it is the dictum and the contradictum, the reconciliation of the subjective-finite and the objective-infinite. Bergson too rejects the concept on the ground that it is the product of the mechanizing utilitarian mind, and he makes exclusive place for the ceaseless flow of life and for experience that accompanies the flow and is immersed in it. He therefore does not speak of concept but of *truth*—which, however, *is not*, only *becomes* through the freedom of the mind. Nothing is, everything becomes; and in the process of becoming (*devenir*) the contraries being and nonbeing, good and evil, merge in one identity.

"The development of the mind," wrote Hegel, "lies in the fact that its going forth and separation constitutes its coming to itself. This being-at-home-with-self [*bei sich sein*] or coming-to-self of mind may be described as its complete and highest end: it is this alone that it desires and nothing else. Everything that from eternity has happened in heaven and earth, the life of God and all the deeds of time simply are the struggles for mind to know itself, to make itself objective to itself, be for itself, and finally unite itself to itself: It is alienated and divided but only so as to be able thus to find itself and return to itself. Only in this manner does mind attain its freedom, for that is free which is not referred to or is not dependent on another."[33] The whole spirit and program of modern subjectivism is summed up in this passage, the culminating point of which is that the mind invents and shapes its own testing ground; it excretes, for the purpose of self-completion, the objectual world. At no time—throughout the "life of God" and "men's deeds"— is the mind *dependent* on that world, or is it in a give-and-take relationship with it. The mind is free because it is self-contained. Thus it cannot be said to be intent on knowledge, since it feels at home and feels autonomous when it rules experience completely and need not stop at concepts that, in the normal processes of cognition, order that experience by being parts of it.[34]

The question then arises: if subjectivist epistemology is not interested in knowledge, *what* constitutes its field of interest?

NOTES

1. The magician is not, strictly speaking, a mediator; he belongs to the cosmos, with which he is in occult commerce.
2. See the Gnostics' invectives against the soiled processes of conception and birth.
3. Frances A. Yates, *Giordano Bruno and the Hermetic Tradition* (New York: Vintage Books, 1969), p. 233.
4. See Thomas Molnar, *Utopia, the Perennial Heresy* (New York: Sheed & Ward, Inc., 1967), p. 141.
5. Leszek Kolakowski, *Chrétiens sans Eglise* (Paris: Gallimard, 1969), pp. 804–5.
6. Yates, *Giordano Bruno*, p. 407.
7. Karl Barth, *Protestant Thought from Rousseau to Ritschl* (New York: Simon and Schuster, A Clarion Book, 1969), p. 358.
8. Ludwig Feuerbach, "Comments upon some Remarkable Statements by Luther" in L. Feuerbach, *The Essence of Faith according to Luther*, (New York: Harper & Row, 1967), p. 126.
9. Ernst Bloch, *Das Prinzip Hoffnung* in *Man on his Own* (New York: Herder & Herder, 1970), p. 12.

The Philosopher's Magic Quest

10. Ernst Bloch, *Thomas Münzer, Théologien de la révolution*, Les Lettres Nouvelles (Paris: Julliard, 1964), p. 79.

11. Jürgen Moltmann, Introduction to Ernst Bloch, *Man on His Own*, p. 19.

12. We noted, with C. H. Puech, the Gnostics' hostility to time as a sign of the fall.

13. Albert Dondeyne, *Contemporary European Thought and Christian Faith*, Ed E. Neuwelaerts, Louvain. (Duquesne Univ. Press, 1963), p. 102.

14. Immanuel Kant, *Réponse à la question: Qu'est-ce que "les lumières"?* in Kant, *La Philosophie de l'histoire*, Ed. Gonthier by Ed. Montaigne, 1947, p. 46.

15. Edouard Le Roy, *Revue de métaphysique et de morale* (1907).

16. Jacques Maritain, *Les Degrés du savoir* (Paris: Desclée, De Brouwer & Cie, 1939), p. 208. My translation.

17. Generally rejecting both a disincarnate idealism and a coarse materialism, modern philosophers insist on giving the body and the material world their due. This stance is, however, more for ideological than for philosophical purposes. By considering that matter finds itself in a transitional stage toward spiritualization, modern philosophers accept a kind of hedonism but reject the limitations implied in our physical-intellectual conditon.

18. Immanuel Kant, *Prolegomena to Any Future Metaphysics* (New York: The Bobbs-Merrill Co., 1950), p. 67.

19. Ibid., p. 36. It will be noted that Nicholas of Cusa argued in like manner for the *theologia negativa*, God's absolute unknowableness. Kant's knowledge of the extramental world is, similarly, a "docta ignorantia."

20. Rousas J. Rushdoony, *The One and the Many* (New Jersey: The Craig Press, 1971), p. 302.

21. Claude Tresmontant, "Notes sur la présence de la Gnose et du Néoplatonisme dans la pensée occidentale," appendix to *La Métaphysique du Christianisme*, (Paris: Editions du Seuil, 1961), p. 734.

22. Edmund Husserl, *The Idea of Phenomenology* (The Hague: M. Nijhoff, 1964), p. 50.

23. Ibid., p. 14.

24. Ibid., p. 15.

25. Ibid., p. 60.

26. Ludovic Robberechts, *Husserl* (Paris: Editions Universitaires, 1964), p. 71.

27. Edmund Husserl, *Philosophy as Rigorous Science* (New York: Harper and Row, 1965), p. 45.

28. Husserl, *Idea of Phenomenology*, p. 51.

29. Ibid., p. 59.

30. Robberechts, *Husserl*, p. 93.

31. Jacques Maritain, *Le Paysan de la Garonne* (Paris: Editions Desclée de Brouwer, 1966), pp. 151, 152. My translation.

[123]

32. Ibid., p. 150.

33. Georg W. Hegel, "Lessons on the History of Philosophy," in G. W. Hegel, *On Art, Religion, Philosophy*, (New York: Harper & Row, 1970), p. 230.

34. This is what Plato seems to say in the *Parmenides* (132 D): the ideas stand as models not outside the flux of events but in the world of nature. Concrete changing things are modeled after structures that can be grasped by the mind.

THE PHILOSOPHER'S ABSOLUTE BEING AND ABSOLUTE KNOWLEDGE

THERE seems to be a clear answer to the question raised at the end of the preceding chapter: subjectivist epistemology, consequently the bulk of modern philosophy, is interested in locating *the end of the world process* because then knowledge will be perfect and, at the same time, the process of man's maturation will be terminated. Once more, let me state that modern philosophy is not alone in question here; it is only a phase in the long tradition encompassing thinkers, mystics, and esoteric magicians. The exaltation of the spirit (*pneuma*) leads these speculative minds to the conclusion that since the world is ontologically flawed, imperfect, the process of perfecting it must consist in changing its ontological status, beginning with the spirit's self-assertion as an absolute. Common-sense knowledge, addressing itself to hyleic (material) existence, shares the superficiality (profaneness, nonseriousness, immaturity) of matter, so that the philosopher's task is to raise the object-world, the profane world, to a higher level where it becomes worthy of pneumatic contemplation.

The phenomenological search for the "pure self"; Hegel's search for the last concept, which is God; the Sartrian obsession with the fusion of *en-soi* ("in-itself") and *pour-soi* ("for itself"); the Bergsonian universe, which is a "machine creating gods"; Ernst Bloch's inscription above his ideal city ("socialist society")—"the end of the object with the liberated subject, the end of the subject with the un-alienated object"[1]—all these quests show a basic lack of interest in the profane, extramental world, and a turning toward the *end* that is at once an ontological novelty, a new creation, and an ideal state of *noesis*. In the eyes of some Greek philosophers who belong to a very respectable tradition—Heraclitus, Empedocles, Plato—the soul was of a divine race, too noble for this world, so that it began to live only after its escape from the body. "While confined within the body, it has its separate existence: it has no concern with the everyday business of perception and sensation; it is active in the higher mode of knowledge, in ecstatic inspiration."[2] As we have seen, it is this tradition, culminating in Plotinus, that lasted longest in the ancient world. The rejection of time by the various Gnosticisms (later by alchemy) went together with the rejection of whatever is immersed in time, namely the non-pneumatic existence, the quest for other things than union with the One, the inauthentic life of Heideggerian description.[3] The only serious objective is the soul's liberation; daily worries must be left to the nonserious; although, as Claude Tresmontant remarks, the domain qualified by Plotinus as "nonserious" was precisely the preoccupation of the Hebrew prophets and of Jesus Christ, according to the promise that "God will dry the tears of their eyes."[4]

It follows from these considerations that knowledge is sought through *initiation* into a higher order, a definitive ontological reality. The Upanishads lead the wise man to overcome the illusion of personal existence as well as the moral demands resulting from it. The Brahmanic God is all light; it rejects the body and is knowable only to the Brahmans. Heraclitus deals contemptuously with the perpetual process of *want* and *satisfaction*, expecting the day when the fire will overcome everything and God will be utterly by himself, all in all. The individual souls will then be united with it, because isolation (from God) has neither importance nor value. When the Hegelian *I* becomes assured of the certainty of the spirit within itself, then it turns into the God fully revealing himself "in the middle of those who know themselves as pure knowledge." The term used is not *knower* but *knowledge*; it is the more appropriate since, as Eric Voegelin comments, consciousness as "absolute knowledge" is finally alone with itself.[5]

Knowledge, then, depends on the ontological status of the knower, the subject, whose ambition is to realize the highest ontological status for himself and the world. This is the core of subjectivist philosophy. It is often assumed that subjectivist doctrines are richly different from each other since each interprets the world from a unique viewpoint. The case is quite other: the only divergence among these doctrines concerns the method of initiation to knowledge and the manner of maturation toward the desired ontological status. The result is the same: the construction of a *new reality* that will be reflected in the *new knower*'s mind as an absolute knowledge. *Initiation* itself is, therefore, not a mere coming face to face with a secret gnosis; it is the creation of a new reality (by verbal-magic manipulation), an ontological ascent. In the ordinary operations of the intellect, in the process of going from nonknowledge to knowledge, the subject seeks the correct reasoning about two or more terms whose quiddity, "whatness," is independent of him.[6] In the operations favored by subjective epistemology, the subject assumes his own, potentially perfect knowledge, and insists on manipulating the extramental world until its quiddity changes, until it conforms to his inner light.

The subjectivist kind of knowledge opens a wide vista of distinguishing between those who know and those who do not, the initiated and the profane. The mundane man, the sinner, the alienated, has no knowledge, not because he has deficient mental equipment, but because he belongs to the ontologically lower status. In contrast, the initiated, the mature, integral, and reconciled man possesses knowledge because he has discarded the status of creature. Ernst Bloch remarks of Joachim de Fiore that he transformed the "soul's travel guide to God" into a movement of history itself: with the transcendence of the kingdom of the law (Old Testament) and the kingdom of grace (New Testament), the *plenitudo intellectus*, the fullness of the intellect, was attained—not in the beyond, but this side of the last things, *eschaton*, in history. For Meister Eckhart too, the movement of the world process is the same as mankind's union in knowledge. "In medieval millenarianism," notes Ernst Bloch, "the age of the Holy Spirit is no longer that of the commitment and the promise. The Paraclete lays down reality in which inwardness has become outwardness of mind. He becomes the utopia of the Son of man, who is not utopian any more because his kingdom is present. . . . The kingdom is outwardness, not only inwardness . . . it is the order of a subjectivity to which objectivity is no longer something extraneous."[7]

The coalescence of subject and object, the "inward turning of outwardness," and the spiritualization of the extramental world as a *plenitudo intellectus* are ways of describing the objective of knowledge in subjective epistemology. Making use of St. Theresa's expression "soul castle," Bloch describes it as the new ontological reality in which the "dualisms coalesce" and the separation of *I* and *not-I* is abolished. "It [dualism] fades in the mystical union. . . . The castle no longer has a partition between *I* and *not-I*, subject and object, subject and substance. The castle is built without otherness."[8]

Insofar as philosophy pursues knowledge, it comes to an end when there is no more to know, when the object has been abolished. But the "object" was not only the extramental world of surrounding things, it was also, and mainly, the events in time, the actions of men, in short, history. The abolition of "outwardness" is also the cessation of history. "There will be no longer any difference between the world of thought and the world of reality," writes Schelling. "There will be one world . . . the age-old unrest of the human spirit comes to rest. . . . Where man takes finally possession of the true organism of his knowing, where, these parts of knowing until now separated receive the universal mediation, healing like a balm the wounds inflicted by the struggling human spirit on itself."[9] This is no mere romantic view of the individual as incomplete, a fragment of a whole, nostalgic for his missed and mystic home, *Heimat*. Or, if it is a romantic view, then the romantic mood apparently reappears quite frequently in history; it accompanies mankind as a jealous reminder of its incompleteness. At any rate, the world of thought and the world of reality celebrate their union in Hegel's synthesis, which is, logically, the end of history itself. Indeed, let us note the importance that the expression "history of philosophy" receives in Hegel's system. For him the history of philosophy is not a branch of philosophy, the story of speculative systems that can continue forever, retold by many chroniclers from their various points of view. For Hegel the history of philosophy is the privileged story of the spirit, its biography which is *one*, and it cannot be told except as he himself did, closing it at the same time. In this perspective, philosophy, as the biography of the spirit, is the biography of history also; and history, as part of the dialectical process, becomes a mode of cognition. In consequence, history and philosophy are terminated simultaneously since, as Schelling put it, "philosophy can only face the whole" and the philosopher, like the physician,

God and the Knowledge of Reality

"seeks to heal with slow gentle hands the deep wounds of [an incomplete] human consciousness." These quasi-hermetic images clearly signify that man's not yet perfect spirit is "wounded," and that the philosopher's task is to heal the wound, to "restore consciousness in its integrity."

Each subjectivist epistemology thus seriously envisages the end of the quest for knowledge. The encounter of the pure self with the pure object, mediated via subjective evidence or realized in the "soul castle" where the dualisms fade, describes this termination. Well known is Hegel's suggestion that philosophy give up its name as love of knowledge and become real knowledge (*wirkliches Wissen*). It is the end of the search for truth needed only in the long aeon of mankind's imperfect state. During this time, world history was the dazzling display of the spirit in its many forms, all amounting to its efforts to acquire the knowledge of itself. In contrast, perfect knowledge is a way of saying that history is also terminated, because the spirit has completely saturated itself and turned with all its substance into consciousness or subject. No new historical forms are forthcoming, and there is nothing more to know.

Yet, the human mind is unable to conceive the end, the end of knowledge and of history. The philosopher or seer claiming to have grasped the end continues constructing mentally a new aeon, beyond the end. The Gnostics and the Neoplatonists had no such problem: situated inside the religious world-view, the end for them was reabsorption in God. The modern subjectivists, however, regard God merely as a convenient hypostasis of the first aeon, to be superseded by the human essence immanent in history; *volens-nolens*, history, in some form, must then go on, *after* a period of transition, an ontological-epistemological mutation. The mutation may take three increasingly spiritualized ages as for Joachim de Fiore and for Hegel, or

[130]

three secularized ages as for Vico and for Comte; the significant thing is that the modern mind no longer deals with God conceived as the end of history, but with God absorbed as a human ideal in the human essence. The human essence, however, requires an *unfolding*, a structuralization in time, a history. Thus philosophy, asked to terminate the first aeon, is subsequently expected to serve as the revelation of the new aeon. In other words, without explicitly admitting it, the philosopher who "closes" history, must open a new history; yet, unable in fact to take the ontological leap, he takes it speculatively, not unlike the magic performer or shaman who reconnects his community with its model through the symbolic flight.

The philosopher "constructs" the new world with the help of the only things he knows, the old material, but stripped of its context and arbitrarily selected. Spinoza assures us that the complete knowledge of all laws of nature delivers into our hands the complete knowledge of God, thus the ability to become autonomous, no longer exposed to the caprice of fortune, to the incalculability of history; Husserl expects the same from the intersubjectivity of evidences;[10] Comte from the age of positive science; Marx from the classless society in which philosophy, first materialized in the proletariat, then in history, abolishes itself; Sartre from the age of abundance in which individual consciousnesses, no longer in conflict for scarce products, cease regarding each other as hostile and the *en-soi* as impenetrable.

An uncomfortable problem may be raised by pointing out that the subjectivist philosopher who still belongs to the first aeon, who has not, therefore, undergone the ontological transformation, nevertheless claims to have a new epistemological insight. There is an incongruity here that arises only because knowledge, for these thinkers, is tied to the ontological status. Let us, however, bear in mind what I have said about esoteric operators and their shortcuts toward, or ascent to, the magic realm, their ability to bring into fusion disparate elements and to quicken the maturation process of body and mind. The subjectivist philosopher performs speculatively the same operations: only instead of ascending to the realm of magic manipulation (the "gnostic ascent," as Frances Yates calls it), he takes the leap into the incomparable forward, the new aeon; instead of fusing elements in the alchemist's *athanor* or combining the male and female principles in the androgyne, he prepares the coalescence of subject and object (through the techniques we have examined); and instead of accelerating the process of maturation of mineral substances, he acts on history's substance by saturating it with the spirit so that time, compressed and emptied of nonserious events, is abolished.

Thus the problem just raised ceases being uncomfortable, provided the philosopher no longer claims the philosopher's status and accepts that of the alchemist or of the Hermetic. The substance on which he performs his operations is history, or better, the human condition, the stuff of existence, the constitution of being. Ludovic Robberechts, Husserl's commentator, writes, that because history progresses, reason does also; the two mutually favor and promote one another. Reason only seems to be speculative: in reality it emerges from *praxis* and immediately returns to it.[11] In a famous formula, Hegel put it this way: "Whatever is rational is real, and whatever is real is rational." The philosopher's relation to this complex world becomes the Heideggerian attentiveness to Being, or: revelation, unveiling, bringing the world to meaning, to light. For Hegel, the philosopher must help the ultimate gestation of the spirit, its passage to outwardness. "The goal of world history," he wrote, "is the development of the Spirit until it forms a new nature, a world adequate to itself. . . . The new reality will be created by the concept of the Spirit, and it will possess in this objectification the consciousness of its freedom and its subjective rationality. . . . The work of the Spirit aims at its own realization and at the consciousness of this realization."[12]

Absolute Being and Absolute Knowledge

On 13 October 1806, when Napoleon entered Iena at the head of the French occupying forces, the thirty-six-year-old Hegel wrote in a letter: "I saw the Emperor, that soul of world-wide significance, riding on parade through the city. It is indeed a wonderful sensation to see such an individual who here, concentrated in one point, sitting on a horse, encompasses the world and dominates it." Is Napoleon the ontologically transformed man, no longer man but god, "concentrated in one point" and containing in himself the deity? If he is not, then it is Hegel himself who outdoes the emperor by comprising in his own consciousness both Napoleon and his world-historical significance. Napoleon is the noble metal, but Hegel is the alchemist.

Hegel's position in modern philosophy is like a mountain peak that has on all its slopes outcrops of various speculative positions similarly suggestive of the ontological transformation. Thus one cannot say that the Hegelian culmination means the end of this tradition. To simplify matters somewhat, we might say that from Spinoza to Hegel (naturally, with notable exceptions, Leibniz, Reid, and others) nature and nature's extention toward precision, science, were used to describe and measure man's ascent to absoluteness. After Hegel, when the left-wing Hegelians have pierced his "secret"—namely, that his God is an unnecessary postulate—the march in the direction of the absolute took new forms: science still remained a privileged highway (materialism and Marxism have been the most important travelers on it), but a new mystic way, of the monistic kind, was also cut as parallel to it. Representative travelers on the second highway are Bergson, Laberthonnière, Le Roy, Blondel, Bloch, Teilhard de Chardin, Heidegger, Bultmann, Karl Rahner, and numerous others, characteristically many of them recruited from theology.

There is no reason to study here the thought of all these men in detail. A general overview will suffice. Before and after Hegel, they all argue for the intellectual, moral, and ontological as-

[133]

cent to absolutization. The more we recognize nature's perfection, goodness, and beauty, wrote Herder in *Ideas in View of a Philosophy of History of Mankind*, the more her living frame will mold us after the model of the Godhead. This idea of ascent is not the same as the progress preached by the *philosophes* of the Enlightenment, whose objective, from Diderot to St. Just, was the virtuous society. To Herder, and to others, progress is a process of identification with the divinity: they are not interested in setting up perfect institutions; they regard all institutions as the results of deplorable sidetrackings of the mind at arbitrary points of reification, departures from the flux of an exalted Nature. Institutions should be abolished since they remind mankind of its fragmentedness. Science is supposed to take their place, not as a reasoned exploration of the universe but as a new outlook—in Husserl's words, "a universal critique of life and its goals, of all forms and systems of culture . . . a critique of mankind itself and of the values guiding it."[13] The aim of the new outlook is to elevate mankind through universal scientific reason and thus to transform it into a radically new humanity capable of an absolute responsibility to itself on the basis of absolute theoretical insights.

It is somewhat ironic that, as Quentin Lauer, Husserl's commentator remarks, Husserl had no time to devote to this enterprise and left it to his disciples. Ironic but also characteristic of his program: man's limits are such that such programs must remain only visions. They are honorable, to be sure, but since they are by necessity left as a heritage to subsequent generations, the directions they take cannot be remotely controlled. They fall out of the philosopher's hands. Hence Husserl's insistence that his science is not of the ordinary sort but a "progress of being towards absoluteness. Since, however, such progress is meaningless in terms of this or that isolated subject, it is *humanity* which progresses, subjects in communication, whether socially or historically."[14] Do we have any kind of guarantee that what subjective evidence could not achieve since Descartes, namely, a knowledge on which a coalesced mankind may build its destiny, will be achieved by Husserl's intersubjective evidence, that is, the multiplication of myriad quasi-mystical instances of correct seeing after *reduction* to the transcendental ego? In his *Logical Investigations* Husserl answered that one genuine "essential intuition" cannot contradict another. Who does not see that we are back at the Cartesian position?

The Cartesian position, at least in its tentative stage where Descartes left it, concerned itself with the subject as an intellect. The ontological transmutation, however, includes the whole man, nature, the cosmos itself. It opens literally on a new creation in which there are no longer distinctions, separations, partitions, otherness. Nature, wrote Herder in his *Ideas*, sheds her envelope and builds the spiritual edifice. Our burgeoning humanity expands under its truly human form, that is, its divine form. Karl Marx dated this transformation from the day private property would be abolished. In the first of his *Manuscripts of 1844* he speaks of nature as "man's non-organic body," to which man will return from alienation. This is not the place to discuss Marx's materialization of Hegel's *Geist* (spirit), only to note that it explains why Marx viewed the process of man's fusion with nature from the side of nature, so to speak, instead of the side of the spirit. Although Hegel described the avatars of the spirit and Marx those of matter, their respective conclusions were by no means in contradiction. *After* the ontological mutation the problem of mind versus matter, subject versus object, does not arise; the two coalesce in the absoluteness of man. As Ernst Bloch puts it, "it takes an open subject and its open world to reabsorb the anticipations of outright perfection in the way the subject has projected them out of itself."[15] At the end, the liberated subject readmits the various god-forms it has created, from the astral-mythical and harvest gods to Jesus Christ, and it reveals the veritable identity of these trial-projections: man.

[135]

God and the Knowledge of Reality

According to the logic of their various systems, Marx, Bloch, Bergson, or Teilhard de Chardin expect the transmutation to occur at different moments when certain conditions are fullfilled. Hegel's system is probably unique, as is his hubris. The date Joachim de Fiore predicted was 1260; Cardanus, a sixteenth-century mathematician, thought that the year 1800 would usher in a great mutation in Christ's religion. Lessing did not agree that a date be fixed, but he saw the mutation as a consequence of the "education which the human race has undergone and is undergoing still," an education based on reason, itself the revelation of history. The idea, in a cruder form, was shared by Samuel Reimarus, whose writings Lessing later edited and published; both men believed in a purely natural religion that would bring into the open all the human possibilities. The difference between them was only that Reimarus hoped that the relentless criticism of revealed religion (biblical criticism, *avant la lettre*) would open the doors for the timelessly valid natural religion, whereas the more sinuous Lessing opted for the Freemasons' tactics (late in life he joined this society). "The Freemason," he wrote, "quietly waits for the sun to begin to shine and lets the lamps burn as they are willing and able to burn. To put out the lamps [to combat the churches] or to relight or replace them—this is not the Freemason's concern."[16]

It is time now to sum up Part Two in the light of the conclusions of Part One where we briefly touched upon the consequences for epistemology of the God-problem as posed by *A* and *B*. It was argued in Part One that a certain type of philosopher, which I did not then identify, uses the speculative quest as a search for forms of unmediated knowledge. We saw that the preconditions of such a knowledge are the postulation of an unlimited subject and of an extramental world absorbable by it (acosmism) either from the beginning or at the end of a certain process. This, in turn, requires that the unlimited subject be identified with a divine soul, a fragment of the world-soul, and that the fragment rejoin the whole via the gnostic ascent. I further argued that all this mental construct rests on the acceptance, as a premise or as a consequence, of a view of God as *distant*, authorizing the individual soul to organize the knowable world on its own, or in *union* with the soul, in which case too the latter is appointed as supreme knower and organizer. A remark by Jacques Maritain cuts to the entrails of this position when he writes that "if things really exist, it is inevitable to postulate God's existence also."[17] The observation is directed at various idealist and subjectivist thinkers who regard the extramental world as unreal and regard themselves authorized to take the creator's place. On the other hand, to postulate a God independent of man (transcendent), yet concerned enough (personal) to furnish the universe with other things and beings also—a position outlined in Part One, and to be further discussed in Part Four—such a God stands guarantor to the reality of what he creates.

The subjectivist philosopher cannot, therefore, reach knowledge as he defines it, unless he takes the place of the divinity. He has for this the double assurance of his inner light and of the process of maturation he claims to detect in the outside world and in history. Schelling and Hegel, for example, believed they were building on the foundation stone laid by Kant, who had set into motion the process of liberation. The system of alienation in which mankind had lived was marked by the reign of the object, the nonself (otherness, alienation, separation, *Trennung*), of the external forms of God and religion. This alienating system was coming to an end, the young Schelling wrote to the young Hegel on 14 February 1795; man gets everyday nearer the Absolute, that is, of God and immortality ("daher nur praktische Annäherung zum Absoluten, und daher Unsterblichkeit").[18]

Yet, it is significant that these apparently exalted worshipers of the subject regard the process toward the immortal absolute not

[137]

as a mere subjective ascent, but a collective one, involving all mankind. This belief is, of course, inscribed in the theories, from Joachim de Fiore to Hegel and beyond, of subsequent and increasingly free ages; a further stimulus was provided by the French Revolution, which, as we shall see in the following chapter, created great excitement in German academic and theological faculties. But let us bear in mind that Gnostic logic also took it for granted that in order for creation to be reabsorbed and for the tranquillity of pre-creation to be restored, all men (all *pneuma*) must return to God so as to reestablish original unity. In the Gnostic view, God, deprived of part of his substance, can be rendered integral again—can be *saved*—only if his scattered fragments, the *pneuma* imprisoned in bodies, are reunited.

This view was easily secularized. It was kept before Western eyes by the Stoics and, more importantly, by the concept of Christ's mystical body, which, "brought down to earth," was to serve the solidarity of men. As soon as this togetherness is achieved, God will have been born. Bruno Bauer's critique of his Hegelian confreres is in this respect quite trenchant. The other "young Hegelians," Bauer believed, misunderstood their master's concept of God: God is not a particular consciousness, the world-soul's manifestation in man; God is an infinite number of spirits throughout time, until in one of them—Hegel—the world substance becomes conscious of itself. Another of Hegel's disciples, Ludwig Feuerbach, came to a similar conclusion: God was the quintessence of all perfections and realities scattered among the human species and manifesting themselves in the course of world history.

Whether on the level of the individual or of the collectivity, the process of self-divinization raises the inner man to the absolute and transforms not only his cognition but also his moral and political status. When he says "I know," God knows in him, or better, God knows himself in him. When he asserts his moral will, he is the supreme legislator of the "religion within"; he is, as

Absolute Being and Absolute Knowledge

Kant calls him, the "interpreter of the God within us." (*The Conflict of the Faculties*, 1798.) When he says "I am free," he is a creator; "creation is no mystery, we experience it in ourselves when we act freely," Bergson wrote.[19] His political will also creates absolutes; "A cherished idea of Professor Kant", wrote the *Gotaische Zeitung* on 11 February, 1784, "is that the final objective of the human species is the realization of the most perfect political constitution."[20] The fact that the inner man exalts the incomparable beauty and uniqueness of his soul means that he stands alone in the universe as the supreme measure of goodness. Is it a mere figure of style when Rousseau in his *Rêveries d'un promeneur solitaire* engages in this strange monologue: "What does one enjoy in such a moment of loneliness? One enjoys nothing exterior to oneself, nothing except oneself and one's own existence; while it lasts one is self-sufficient like God. The feeling of existing, stripped of all other emotions. . . ." Karl Barth is not wrong in arguing that what Rousseau discovered was *himself*, and that he reached the conclusion, informed by his inner light, that the new world was good: nature is man himself, liberated from the external world. Rousseau did not merely express the Romantic mood; this is attested by Hegel's words, a generation later, in the *Life of Jesus*: "All that is beautiful in human nature we have deposited *in das fremde Individuum* [that is, in God], keeping for us only the ugly things. . . . But we shall again take possession [*es uns wieder aneigen*] and learn to respect ourselves." For Hegel, as for Herder (and for Schwenckfeld before them), Jesus was the *schöne Seele* (the beautiful soul) who attempted the reconciliation between human and divine, the reabsorption into the former of what had been "transported out of it" into the latter.

The God "within" is, thus, the explicit denial of the transcendent and personal God and the affirmation of man as God. Herder (in *Letters Concerning the Study of Theology*) showed that Jesus, since he could not be a "divine phantom," had to be a "human Christ" on earth for imitation and perfection. The more practical mind of Auguste Comte found that the time had come for the establishment of a truly universal religion for the elite but that the search for such a religion could be satisfied by any supernatural belief. Christianity and Islam could fill the role during the second, the "metaphysical," age, although only at the price of having to combat and suppress successive outbursts of discontent. Comte was now the prophet of the third, the "scientific," age, in which the system of belief was to reconcile all social conflicts and to become the expression of social cohesion.[21]

Hegel's critique of religion went naturally much further, since his dialectical method allowed him to find in the Hebrew and Christian God an intolerant and jealous master, robbing his worshipers of their own hidden divinity. Thus religion had to be the supreme exaltation of man who finds the absolute within himself. As he wrote to Schelling in 1795, "there is no other world above the senses than the world of the absolute self. And the absolute self is God." How modern Schelling and Hegel's synthesis seems when they define religion as an "active personal participation in an act taking place in us and through us."[22] It is perhaps the first time that the traditional God is excluded without any reservation from the definition of religion—not by two atheist-materialists, let us note—but by men who considered themselves believers, indeed good Lutherans, to the end.[23]

Let us pause for a brief summary of the preceding two chapters. Our points of reference are the conclusions reached in Part One where we examined positions *A* and *B* and explained why these two positions are found in opposition to *C*.

Ample proof has been provided for my original statement that the God-problem, whether philosophers speak about it as such or not, remains a central preoccupation of their systems. The human problematics is of such a nature that if God is eliminated from our discourse, the void left must be filled by another absolute possessing the same or similar attributes. There is, perhaps surprisingly, only one candidate to fill the void—man himself, temptingly similar to God since he possesses the spirit as thought, as intellect. (Hegel, Bergson, and others never tire emphasizing it.)

The inescapability of man's self-absolutization as an alternative to the transcendent and personal God may not be evident to every generation. In so-called ages of faith, the notion of the union of God and the soul—position *B*—can create the illusion that God is the "dominant partner," that he dwells in man's conscience and speaks through his mouth. This supposed equilibrium of partnership is, however, broken in ages of weak faith when the God figure fades and the balance shifts in man's favor. The soul itself is then regarded as divine, a conviction translated into epistemological terms as meaning that man knows the world *in* himself. This took place, for example, at the time of Meister Eckhart and William Ockham, again in the period between Jacob Boehme and the German *Aufklärung*.

The way to restore knowledge as a valid relationship between subject and object as separate entities passes through the deabsolutization of the soul. When the soul realizes its creatureliness, its nonidentity with God, a crucial distinction has been made because the self has grasped itself as limited and the extramental world as real. While the epistemology of subjectivism is based on the union of God and soul, the epistemology derived from position *C* is based on this distinction, in fact a series of distinctions. And knowledge begins, of course, with distinctions: between the I and the not-I, the separations in space, the sequences in time. Later the metaphysical distinctions are also grasped: between the self and the extramental world, God and the world, the self and God. The most sophisticated of these distinctions tells us that knowledge is mediated, in spite of the self's *evidence* that he contains all that is.

It is the absence of these *distinguos* that opens the way toward an intellectual hubris, lack of measure. If we take for too

God and the Knowledge of Reality

long and too intensively for granted that God is in ourselves, the long familiarity makes his image fade. Somehow we want to go then even beyond God, beyond ourselves as God—not merely legislating in an ordered universe that has preceded us, but creating a universe according to an inner order; the extramental world drowned long ago in the flux. Thus it happens that reason, long abused, becomes unhinged for lack of experience on which to exercise itself. The "doors of perception" open up wide and the subject is lost in self-contemplation, or, what amounts to the same, it stares ahead into nothingness. Let us not be misled by such expressions as "total hope" and "mystery sense" in the following passage by Ernst Bloch; they illustrate the unhinged mind's perspectives: "The greatest paradox in the religious sphere is the elimination of the deity itself so that religious mindfulness and total hope may have an open space ahead. . . . The place marked by the former God is not nothing: it is what is still undefined and undefinitive, what is really possible in a mystery sense."[24]

NOTES

1. Ernst Bloch, *A Philosophy of the Future* (New York: Herder & Herder, 1970), p. 77.

2. Erwin Rohde, *Psyche, The Cult of Souls and Belief in Immortality among the Greeks* (New York: Harper & Row, 1966), p. 384.

3. The spirit, argues Hegel in his *Phenomenology*, appears in time only until it grasps the pure concept of itself; then time will be abolished.

4. It is to be noted again that the genuine mystics, like the prophets, did not despise the "nonserious" dimensions of life; they helped in concrete and institutional ways to remedy and relieve the daily concerns of their fellow men.

5. Eric Voegelin, "On Hegel: A Study in Sorcery," *Studium Generale* 24 (1971): 347. Voegelin makes this comment in reference to Chapter 8 of Hegel's *Phenomenology*. In an ironic vein, he concludes: "Since these chapters were written by Hegel, and presumably he was not unconscious when he wrote them, we must conclude that in 1807 Hegel became God."

[142]

6. St. Thomas refused to distinguish between the intellect of the regenerated man and the intellect of the nonregenerated man. Moral differences between men do not bring about a corresponding epistemological difference.

7. Ernst Bloch, *Man on His Own* (New York: Herder & Herder, 1970), pp. 200, 210.

8. Ibid., p. 228.

9. F. W. J. von Schelling, *The Ages of the World* (New York: Columbia University Press, 1942), p. 91.

10. Edmund Husserl, *The Crisis of European Man* (New York: Harper Torchbook, 1965). Husserl sees reason as no longer the same as the faculty of reasoning, of induction and conclusion, but as the principal shaping force of human becoming. To him, reason has been only a phase in man's cosmic evolution, and its role is to help build the happiness of an autonomous man kind.

11. Ludovic Robberechts, *Husserl* (Paris: Editions Universitaires, 1964), p. 50.

12. Georg W. Hegel, *La Raison dans l'histoire*, transl. from German by Kostas Papaioannou. (Paris: Union Générale d'Editions, 1965), p. 296. My translation.

13. Husserl, *Crisis of European Man*, p. 169.

14. Edmund Husserl, *Philosophy as Rigorous Science* (New York: Harper Torchbooks, 1965), p. 56.

15. Bloch, *Man on His Own*, p. 210.

16. Quoted in Karl Barth, *Protestant Thought from Rousseau to Ritschl*, (New York: Simon and Schuster, A Clarion Book, 1969), p. 129.

17. Jacques Maritain, *Les Degrés du savoir* (Paris: Desclée, De Brouwer & Cie, 1939), p. 212. My translation.

18. Quoted in Paul Asveld, *La Pensée religieuse du jeune Hegel* (Publications Universitaires de Louvain, 1953), p. 93.

19. Henri Bergson, *Evolution créatrice*. My translation.

20. Kant's works, notes Barth, "are so demanding that behind the cold deliberateness of his style few are able to detect the hidden enthusiasm, which is greater than can be found in any number of frankly enthusiastic proclamations." Barth, *Protestant Thought*, p. 197. Did Heine not say of Kant that he was a more dangerous revolutionary than Robespierre?

21. Auguste Comte, *Catéchisme positiviste* (Paris: Garnier-Flammarion, 1966), pp. 32–33.

22. Quoted in Asveld, *Pensée religieuse du jeune Hegel*, p. 99.

23. Yet, let us not forget that Hegel and Schelling do belong to a tradition and that they are therefore not the first "atheist believers"; we have seen that more than a century earlier Schwenckfeld regarded salvation as a *theosis*. Like Herder later, Schwenckfeld searched for a human, finite Christ so that man should not have to be considered outside the divinity.

24. Bloch, *Man on His Own*, pp. 160, 161.

[143]

Part Three

THE IDEAL SOCIETY
AS THE FRAMEWORK
FOR ABSOLUTE
KNOWLEDGE

WHAT happens to the world and to history after philosophy has delivered its last message and has ceased to exist? Far from being meaningless, this question is, rather, at the center of modern subjectivist philosophy, for the following reason: the aim of this philosophy is to achieve a quasi-mystical union between the absolutized subject and the object-world and its history, a union Hegel calls absolute knowledge (*wirkliches Wissen*), and which is also the Gnostics' supreme aspiration. In this perspective, philosophy consists of the restoration of a broken unity, the healing of all separateness. Hegel is, of course, a very subtle thinker: while the spirit (*Geist*) is the original totality and is, as such, self-sufficient, in its desire to know itself it somehow allowed the totality to break up and unravel (according to the dialectical process). The breakup that was the origin of all separation is also, however, a sin, because, as Hegel holds, sin is division (*Ent-*

[147]

God and the Knowledge of Reality

zweiung) into subjective and objective, hence the cause of reflection, reasoning, judgment.[1] If now philosophy puts an end to *Entzweiung*, reason will be automatically abolished (reabsorbed in the *Geist*) in the reestablished oneness. Even the need to philosophize disappears since systematic speculation was motivated by the search for unity. The world will go on and men will continue using their intellectual faculties; but this posthistorical world will also be postphilosophical or a-philosophical, it will lack a sustaining principle, the *Geist's* curiosity to know itself. The *Geist* will, indeed, be at home, *bei sich*; the "enigma of history," as Marx was to put it, will have been solved. The rest will be uncomplicated because the citizen will be both free in, and a part of, the state.

Thus culminates Hegel's system, the paradigm of subjectivist philosophy in that it forges an iron link between the life of reason and the flow, the *déroulement* of history. Without going deeper into the details of the Hegelian philosophy of history, let us see its dramatic developments working up to the last phase. The Christian ideal of the "religious man" and the atheism of the "intellectual" (Hegel meant primarily the French *philosophes*) ended in an impasse because both separated the divine and the human, both dealt with only a half of totality; hence, they were unable to transform the world otherwise than verbally. In 1789, however, some active men stepped on the stage who transformed the bourgeois world into one of genuine citizens by "creatively negating" the Christian and atheist ideal, in other words—and as Marx was to say somewhat more crudely—by bringing it down from heaven to earth. What happened in the concrete world reflected itself in the mind: the bourgeois ideologies became useless together with their generators, the unfree bourgeois, and the ideologies yielded to true philosophy, that is, to the Hegelian science as represented by his *Encyclopaedia of Philosophical Sciences* and his *Phenomenology of the Spirit*. What Christianity and the *Aufklärung* failed to accomplish, Hegel per-

[148]

formed speculatively: the reunification of the human and the divine in the unity of reconciled consciousnesses.[2]

History thus stopped because man was now satisfied (*befriedigt*), unsurpassable, self-comprehending. With Napoleon, who is the revealed God (*der erscheinende Gott*), two—always parallel—lines, the historical and the philosophical, have run their appointed course, finally converging: the absolute spirit was restored in the fullness of consciousness (*Bewusstsein*) and self-consciousness (*Selbst-bewusstsein*), and the potentially universal and homogeneous world-state came into existence.[3] Alexandre Kojève, whose lectures on the *Phenomenology* I am following on these pages, concludes his analysis of Chapter 6 by asking if Hegel, the prophet to the God-Napoleon, was not actually expecting to be invited by the emperor to Paris to become the court-sage of the Universal State. No doubt that there is in this supposition enough material for an intriguing theatrical play (as in Plato's visit to the Syracusan tyrant), but we may perhaps suggest that Hegel was almost as content with his later role as virtual state philosopher of the Prussian kingdom, successor, in his mind, to the Napoleonic empire. At any rate, the important point here is to note that the logic of Hegelian (and of subjectivist) philosophy leads it to require an *aboutissement* in history too, in the form of a society that does not merely satisfy certain philosophical propositions but actually embodies these propositions. It follows that the course of history is regarded by the subjectivist philosopher as consisting of a number of *phases*, each "higher" than the preceding one in terms of historical maturity and philosophical truth-content. The end is signaled when ontological perfection and epistemological perfection (absolute knowledge) are achieved.

It would be incorrect to attribute these thoughts exclusively to subjectivist philosophers as if others were not equally tempted by them. I have said that often in the history of thought philosophy was regarded as dealing with "serious" matters, not with

God and the Knowledge of Reality

"mundane" ones. And, indeed, what can be more serious than entrusting speculation with the promotion of ontological perfection? Plato, in the *Republic*, the *Laws*, in *Gorgias*, and elsewhere, made it quite clear that the philosopher thinks only of the salvation of his soul and finds the state, founded on passion and deception, hopelessly corrupt; if *he* were the statesman, the state would turn to serious matters, not to the building of ships and harbors and walls, but to justice. (It is, of course, understood that practical matters would also be taken care of, but that for the performance of these tasks the highest virtue is sufficient, and particular virtues would be rarely, if at all, needed.) But the decisive difference between Plato and Hegel is that for the first, philosophical speculation, the process of thinking, can never be aimed at the transformation of what thought is about, that is, of reality, of the constitution of being; only the soul, that is, man, can change (turn around, *periagogé*), develop a different view of reality, by deepening his understanding of it, by turning from error to truth. For Hegel, on the other hand, reality itself changes, it gradually becomes what the philosopher, as the privileged representative of the *Geist*, wants it to become, or better, what he understands as being in the nature of reality to become. Plato's human conversion is a *metanoia*, a change of mind and attitude with regard to existence prompted by contact with it and reflection on it; Hegel's change is a *metastasis* that assumes that starting from subjective criteria and will (voluntarism), reality itself undergoes the foreseen and willed transformations.

In Part Two I showed that the subjectivist philosopher aims at the transformation of reality into a *second reality* of which he is the artisan and the demiurge. Speaking of Hegel, Eric Voegelin notes that in order to fulfill this purpose, the image of the future must be modified from unknown (the conventionally stated essence of futurity) to known, and the modification justified scientifically.[4] But, of course, the ultimate justification is the philosopher himself who, from "imaginator" becomes the "inaugurator" (Voegelin's terms) of the new age. Hegel performed this magic transference in front of his students in a lecture at Jena on 18 September 1806: "We find ourselves in an important epoch, in a ferment; the *Geist*, with a sudden jerk, has moved to advance beyond its previous configuration and to assume a new one. The whole mass of hitherto accepted conceptions [*Vorstellungen*] and concepts, the bonds of the world, have been dissolved and collapsed like a dream image. A new epiphany of the *Geist* is preparing itself."[5]

This is obviously more than a mere statement of perceptible but limited historical change, and the religious terminology is not inadvertently used: Napoleon was the revealed God, Hegel the prophet who revealed him, and the world-historical empire had the appearance of an eschatological event. In the Jena lecture Hegel did not teach either philosophy or history, he inaugurated the last age toward which—the universal goal that the sage had located—history and philosophy had been moving. And Hegel is no exception in this respect; with less or no underpinning taken from history, other modern thinkers also couch their ideal in eschatological language so as to give it—not in mundane history but in a history of cosmic proportions—the finality of a new age that is also a new society. The "how" of this new society is hardly ever spelled out, and when it is, the terms are emotional, enthusiastic, abstract, and utopian; but the "what" is all the more intense, and we may often deduce from it at least the general features of the social-political forms envisaged as an ideal.

Bergson, for example, identifies God with "moral reality," and this with the "foundation of being" (the *Grunt* of the German spiritualists). As morality is in permanent ascent toward betterment and perfection, so is God, or, putting it differently, the world is approaching the ideal that is mirrored in an increasingly better, more spiritual and saintly, society. The phases of growth are not here historically identified, but since God is a reality constantly transcended by his own renewed reality, Bergson provides us with an abstract scheme, while Hegel is documenting history, even though he passes it through the sieve of an extremely personal interpretation.

Ernst Bloch is another example when he squarely announces that the history of philosophy is a preparation of utopia. His utopia is best described as an inconclusive world, "substantially still undetermined, but unmistakably wonderful," hence open to reabsorb what the subject, when it was still closed to his own potential divinity, had projected out of himself. Despite a different accent in his religious language, where a certain reverence for the numinous is detectable, Bloch speaks in essentially Hegelian terms, although, like Bergson, he does not articulate his utopia. He does say, however, that "world history is an experiment . . . aimed toward a possible just and proper world . . . toward an omega instant as was always intended in philosophical anticipation: true being, substance, full identity of appearance and essence. . . . A possible governing reference point of the historical where-to . . . locatable in the utopian field." And farther on he adds: "The meaning of human history already from the start is the building of the commonwealth of freedom."[6]

Even if we consider that for Bloch the commonwealth of freedom is not a necessarily locatable place now or in the future, and that future itself is for him not so much a temporal category as the "principle of hope," the impact of his logic leads to an ideal society where subject and object, both finally "open," coincide. The fully open subject-object relationship, he writes, remains logically a frontier notion and metaphysically a frontier ideal;[7] yet, all considered, what separates the ideal from the concrete when growth toward a perfect state is taken for granted? Will there be an unexpected obstacle on the way? Will perfection itself never be reached? Bloch does not mention any such thing. Thus it remains that the subjectivist philosopher, one way or another, must conclude that the ideal subject-object relationship requires as its framework an ideal society where this requirement is fulfilled; the ideal society consists, in fact, of this relationship. It is a philosophical *sequitur*, whether the philosopher in question follows it to the end or only approximates it in the ideal commonwealth of his own theoretical construction.

In his early work on the sixteenth-century German revolution-ary-reformer Thomas Münzer, Bloch was more explicit. His hero claims a soon-to-reach divine status for all who believe[8] in a "luminous Jerusalem" where the *status creaturae* will be abolished in the framework of a universal mystical republic without rulers and laws. The expression "Christian community"[9] means here not the church structured according to hierarchy and sacramental functions and bolstered by tradition, but a community of the elect with the inner light guiding their steps in the leap from the old into the new world where "even God disappears." Bloch here takes up the themes of medieval and Renaissance chiliasm and church criticism, which we shall consider later on.

The disappearance of God is a central issue to Bloch's thought. Certain passages of *Das Prinzip Hoffnung* on this issue are fasci-nating, because they restate, in the middle of the twentieth cen-tury, supposedly forgotten controversies between medieval ortho-dox thinkers and heretics in a language not so dissimilar from theirs. For this reason Bloch's thesis puts the problem of episte-mology, community, and God in an excellent perspective, which ranks in importance almost with Hegel's. Many other modern thinkers, perhaps too embarrassed to incorporate the God-prob-lem in their systems, tend to blur the issue. Like Hegel, Bloch conceives a universe that is evolutive, and, as indicated earlier, he too thinks that both history and philosophy are on the way to utopia, the reconciliation of opposites, the healing of separations. His difference from Hegel is that in his philosophy not the *Geist* but belief in God measures the phases of maturation: from the oriental cosmogonies to Christianity and beyond. As we have done with Hegel's analysis of the penultimate phase of history (that is, prior to 1789), let us now join Bloch's argumentation at the moment when the impersonal and static God of the myths yields to Yahweh who, in turn, is also "dropped as a creator and remains solely as a goal."[10] Then a new God (Christ) arises, "one hitherto unheard of, who sheds his own blood for his children, a God who is the incarnate Word, capable of suffering the fate of death in its full earthly sense, not merely in the ceremonial of the Attis legend."[11] The evolution from the god-figures of the astral myths points, according to Bloch, to an increasingly humanized God, not, of course, because of the Christian concept of God-man, but because the higher mankind steps to its final utopian openness the more clearly it sees itself, its own humanity, in the God-figure it still projects. Thus in Christianity the founder (Christ) no longer points beyond himself to an imaginary hypostasis; he absorbs God into his own humanity and "becomes the glad tidings itself."[12] He calls upon the community gathered around him "to serve as the goal's building material and its city,"[13] that is, to build the par excellence human community now taking God's place. "God becomes the kingdom of God, and the kingdom of God ceases to contain a God"[14] is Bloch's *raccourci* of history, divine and human. The religious heteronomy and its materialized hypostasis dissolve completely in the theology of the community—but of a community that has passed beyond the threshold of the creature as he used to be, anthropologically and sociologically.[15]

I have said that the urge for a utopian solution is neither an emotional issue nor simply a matter of equalitarian preferences, but a requirement with roots in epistemological imperatives. In view of restoring knowledge (the self-knowledge of the *Geist*), Hegel proceeded to unify what was dual and divided, ultimately sealing the unity in the Napoleonic world-empire grasped in the synthesis of the *Phenomenology*. In order to reconcile subject and object and abolish the "walls of partition," Ernst Bloch proceeded to have all hypostases absorbed in the utopian community. More examples will be adduced later. But it is clear already that the community that these philosophers try to construct has a pattern that reproduces in a different medium, as it were, the *cheminement* (the progression) of knowledge according to their epistemology.

Here again the best we may do is to study the elaboration of this pattern throughout medieval, Renaissance, and post-Renaissance times, when epistemological propositions had to be disguised so as to avoid the penalties likely to be visited on their authors by lay and ecclesiastical authorities. Paradoxically, the result was that the patterns—which on the surface were nothing more than descriptions of the ideal community and could pass as products of idle but still Christian minds—were clearer in their true, that is, epistemological, significance than what today's savants produce as utopias almost as an afterthought. The reason is that the modern philosopher, fearing no Inquisition, is able to elaborate his "utopia" without being obliged to use such a utopia as the image of an epistemological, hence speculative, position, translatable into a doctrinal position. He proposes his utopia more carelessly, almost gratuitously, one might say, or simply because utopian thinking has become a fashion. Whereas earlier philosophers, churchmen or laymen, constructed their utopias with an ulterior motive, as a disguise for something more fundamental, an illustration of a speculative mode.

These reflections are eminently valid for the later Middle Ages. No sophisticated scholar need be told today how diverse was intellectual life under the general sponsorship of the medieval church in the field of theology, philosophy, and political thinking. We might distinguish for our purposes two trends of thought, the chiliastic movements and the critique of the ecclesiastical structure. The two trends are not to be confused, of course, yet we may take them here as one because of their combined impact and their similar epistemological premises.

Ostensibly, both were directed against institutionalized mediation between Christians and their God. The church's position on the matter can be summed up in a passage of Thomas Aquinas's *Sententiae*: "God always respected the natural law he imposed on all beings, namely that they should join his unity and perfection through mediating influences." Opposed to this position, tacitly or explicitly, were the Joachists, the Franciscan Fraticelli, Ockham and all those, up to Luther, whom he influenced, the various millenarists mentioned in earlier chapters, and later, in the sixteenth century, certain Spanish mystics and the German spiritualists of the sixteenth and seventeenth centuries. Their arguments may be presented in the following manner: the Roman Church conducted well the affairs of Christendom until Pope Silvester I accepted the so-called donation of Constantine (or as the Franciscans said, until their own order was given protection by the papacy), but after that Rome ceased to be God's church. God's church was now being restored by the critics themselves, for which reason they were persecuted by the false Church of Rome. The Franciscan Peter John Olivi and his disciple, Ubertino de Casale, maintained that Rome had turned against their order and that therefore it would have to yield, in short course, to the New Jerusalem, just as the synagogue had yielded thirteen centuries earlier to the church.

The division into ages (synagogue, church, New Jerusalem) shows a Joachite preoccupation with a graduated *sanctification of history* from the Old Testament through the Age of the Son to that of the Holy Spirit. Since the third age is not yet, Joachim deduced from the relationship between the already known first two ages the pattern of history by which he could prognosticate what was still to come in the future third age. It was this transition from the second to the third age that had such a stirring relevance for the thirteenth-century mystics, sects, and movements. Joachim did not go beyond allegory and metaphor in describing the new order, but there is no doubt, remarks Leff, that he envisaged it as one of spiritual renewal in which the spirit would triumph over the letter. This is indicated by Joachim's frequent reference to the displacement of the outward "figures" of the sacraments in favor of their inner spiritual import.

This displacement presupposes a decisive change of maturity in the faithful, a point of view also held by Ockham, who argued in a similar vein that at the beginning of Christianity a clergy (institutionalized mediators) was necessary for the layman's salvation but that at present (the fourteenth century) the laity was as well instructed as the priests and prelates, hence the need for clergy had decreased, if not altogether ceased. We find the same reasoning on many subsequent occasions; as the papacy went into eclipse (Avignon period, schism, Reformation), the criticism leveled at the ecclesiastical structure, while not lessening, was paralleled by the criticism of profane institutions also. The basic preoccupation remains the same: the mind hastening toward reunion with God has only contempt for creatureliness, and this contempt manifests itself in the stand taken against institutions as well as against mediated knowledge. It is then assumed that institutions, that is, the whole historical order, are obstacles in the way of direct knowledge, the epistemological order, so that if the perfect society were to be brought into existence, cognition in it would also be perfect. Within the church this position was advocated by some radical mystics, from Tauler in the fourteenth century to Angelus Silesius in the seventeenth, who rejected cognition as an inferior form of knowledge directed at inferior beings, and who emphasized the superiority of *seeing* (Tauler's "thinking divinely") as a way for the soul to rise above the region of lower causes. Leszek Kolakowski argues in his *Chrétiens sans Eglise* that this attitude was an attempt to secure the independence of religious values from organized ecclesiastical life. The mystics, according to Kolakowski, expressed their feeling of despair over the intolerable situation of men condemned by their finiteness, their *status creaturae*.[16]

These motivations, I repeat once more, are true for the monist mystics whose way of thinking I have described earlier and for

[157]

the ones Kolakowski mentions, the Franciscan illuminati in Spain who were converted from Judaism, such as Francisco Ortiz, Bernardino Tovar, Juan de Cazalla, and Pedro Alcazar.[17] Ortiz held, for example, that Jesus Christ was more perfectly present in the soul of the just man than in the sacraments, and Alcazar believed that the love of God in man is God himself. Kolakowski comments that these men elaborated a model of religiosity that was irreconcilable with the principle of ecclesiastical organization. What he ignores, however, is that the monist type is not the only type of mysticism and that it is, in fact, rejected by the true mystic. St. Paul, St. Bernard, and St. Theresa, for example, not only did not try to elaborate their mysticism independent of the church, but they integrated it easily and naturally with the life of the church's institutions and sacraments. In the fourteenth century Ruysbroeck denounced as heretical those mystics who saw in individual man a higher nature as well, both creaturely and beyond the status creaturae. In contrast to the monist mystics, he taught that the true mystic does not turn away from the things of the senses but accepts them as they are.

We find the attitude Kolakowski describes in a variety of situations where unmediated knowledge of God and the abhorrence for institutions go hand in hand. For people with this attitude, "worldly governments, being of purely human institution, have no mandate to exercise authority. . . . Always the enthusiast hankers after a theocracy in which the anomalies of the present situation will be done away, and the righteous bear rule openly."[18] The Lollards found a contradiction in Christians bearing office in the commonwealth. In 1640 the Anabaptists declared to the House of Lords that the king could make no perfect laws because he was not a perfect man. The Ranters, English illuminati of the same period, asserted that they were God, not subject to human laws. Some of them—Coppe, Clarkson, and others—declared that they had been "wholly and lastingly absorbed into the divine unity," having passed beyond good and evil and thereby risen above the normal human condition. They called themselves angels, and held firmly that the "rebirth of the world into innocence also implies a radical transformation of society."[19]

Is the theocracy of which Ronald Knox speaks a form of government, a structured society even if, as the Ranters wanted it, "radically transformed"? It seems that we deal here with more than challenge to church authority: to the principle of organized community, whether ecclesiastic or lay. Most heretic movements discarded impatiently any and all institutions, claiming that such institutions were not only unnecessary but, in contrast with their own perfection, sinful and wicked as well. (Thus in contrast to the "true apostles" and the "anointed," the church was the "Whore of Babylon.") It is another matter that, as Kolakowski's main thesis has it, heretics and nonconformists, once separated from the body of their church, always reestablish a new, structured church that will, in turn, have its own heretics, and so on, indefinitely. The point is that the gap between the institutionalized and the unmediated does not cease acting as a stimulus to the enthusiast who can only be satisfied with the establishment of a theocracy, the rule of the elect—which is not supposed to be a *rule* at all, but rather a general ascent of the whole community to the highest ontological and epistemological status.

At the beginning of the ascent this status is not shared by the whole community, only by its leaders, who bear various and often picturesque names and titles. We have seen that Hegel was convinced that he himself belonged to the category of the sage in whose mind and works the synthesis of world and thought was effected. In the writings of the Renaissance magi the authors themselves had made the Gnostic ascent, but they were only the precursors of others, a new priesthood to be followed through the sacred gates by the entire community. Agrippa of Nettesheim believed in an approaching theocracy governed by priests possessing the secrets of magia with which they would hold society together. These secrets (the meaning of the magical rites) composed the *religion of the mind* (later to be called *natural religion*), the worship of the One, perceived by the initiated who rise to the divine *mens*. So it was with Giordano Bruno. As the Venetian Inquisition found out from the reports of Bruno's host, Mocenigo, Bruno held that in their own time the state of the world was at the lowest ebb of corruption, but that it was on the way to an incomparably better state thanks to the restoration of the "Egyptian religion" of Hermes Trismegistus. This was a marvellous magical creed, destroyed earlier by the Christians who replaced the Egyptian priests' "natural religion with the worship of dead things." According to Mocenigo's testimony, Bruno himself expected to be a *capitano* in the new community—a strange foreshadowing of Hegel's own expectations to become the philosophical leader of the universal empire!

Thomas Campanella, a Calabrian like Joachim, a Dominican like Bruno, proposed a more complete system of the ontologically perfect community than either Bruno or Agrippa. Like these two, he was convinced of his powers to communicate with the cosmos and to lead a universal magico-religious reform.[20] The *Civitas Solis* (*The City of the Sun*, 1602), as mentioned earlier, conveyed in its layout, situated on the *axis mundi*, the secrets of securing the influence of the benevolent forces of the universe. At the center a dome represented the correspondence of heaven and earth, and the seven sections into which the city was divided were arranged concentrically around the dome so as to represent the seven planets. It is clear that the dome was a detailed model of the world and that the cult of the world was celebrated inside. The seven sectors of the city held representations of all knowledge, and in the outermost wall there were the images of supreme lawgivers and inventors: Moses, Osiris, Jupiter, Mercury, Muhammad, and others. Thus the City of the Sun was an immense urban and architectural synthesis, a "complete reflection of the world as governed by the laws of natural magic in dependence on the stars."[21] In every respect it was the *final* city, the mystics' "luminous Jerusalem," the alchemists' *ecclesia spiritualis* (spiritual church) where all were brotherly, intelligent, and healthy. The Sun Priest himself combined spiritual and temporal rule, assisted by three collaborators, Power, Wisdom, and Love.[22] Let us note that in this manner the Sun Priest was accorded the privilege denied to the Roman pope, namely the possession of the "two swords," and that he was also assumed to embody the supreme wisdom, love, and power over against the human limitations of the pope as stressed by Marsilius of Padua and William Ockham. But the City of the Sun is not to be measured with the yardstick of reality, it is an ontologically different community, the result of the *coincidentia oppositorum* incorporated in its central temple. Frances Yates has remarked the similarity of Campanella's plan with the equally magical city of Adocentyn, which is mentioned in the Hermetic work *Picatrix*. There too the number seven appears as an organizational principle; the center is occupied by a castle with, on top, a rotunda with seven constantly changing colors that daily illuminated the city differently in the course of a week.

Campanella's ideas were transplanted into German soil by his collaborator, Johann Arndt, who was in turn teacher of Valentin Andreae. The latter's work, *Description of the Christianopolitan Republic*, followed in some respects the *Civitas Solis*, but by this time a huge literature was anyway available from which to choose various descriptions.[23] Future society must be an incarnation of integral Christianity, at the very opposite of the present society, which is in the throes of evil, of error, and of lie. Andreae's work goes beyond Campanella's: the Christianopolitans are not ruled by a Sun Priest, but directly by God who is the Great Metaphysician elected by the people. His assistants are Force, Wisdom, and Love, like those of the Sun Priest. Needless to add, in all these religious utopias (as well as in the nonreligious ones) the citizens have been purged of selfishness; they own no property, and they live in all respects according to the tenets of integral

[161]

communism. It is enough to read any representative sample of this literature to realize that the citizen of utopia is not an ordinary human being, but one stripped of common human frailties and existing in a kind of rarefied atmosphere.[24] Living under the unmediated rule of the divine being (or of his ontologically promoted representatives who are, thus, not mediators in the earthly sense), the utopian citizens lack passions and ambitions. Let us remember that in Hegel's world-state there is no *history* any longer; men have ceased to be bearers of aspirations because all that the *Geist* ever wanted to achieve through them is now given. They go about their daily business; but otherwise are merely *befriedigt* (satisfied), possessing a *happy consciousness*. In fact, the Hegelian-Marxist Alexandre Kojève concluded that not only the philosopher is not obliged, under the circumstances of wisdom concretized, to continue searching for wisdom, but that boredom would be the utopians' inevitable lot.

Utopia is, then, the description and the symbol, one might say the *map*, of the perfect ontological status. On a descriptive level it is the equivalent of the philosopher's effort to achieve perfect knowledge by eliminating passion from his heart and conflict from his intellect—the alchemist's objective. We have noted that the chiliast, the negator of institutions, the utopian, deny authority—prompted less by democratic convictions than by impatience to reach God or some equivalent perfection (for example, in a theocracy). In the religious sphere, then, Christ is denied preeminence, except as a very good man; the pope is denied preeminence among bishops; bishops over priests; priests over laymen; finally lay authorities over citizens generally. The fourteenth-century critic of the church, Marsilius of Padua, observed that Peter had no right to the keys and that the pope is subject to the *congregatio fidelium*, the council composed of all faithful —but in which, quite naturally since a vacuum has been created, a specific weight is adjudged to the emperor. It is instructive to find Ockham attacking John XXII, the pope who was firmest against the anarchy preached by the Brethren of the Free Spirit and the Spiritual Franciscans, and supporting the cause of Louis of Bavaria, the emperor.

On the level of the body politic these efforts were to lead to the democratic system of representation, itself challenged in our days as not sufficiently disinstitutionalized. From the philosopher's point of view the motives were different and the political developments were only a by-product. The philosopher aspired at total knowledge and unencumbered ways leading to it. This, in turn, demanded self-purification and a religion not of external forms, but of the mind, a religion of total intelligibility, a natural religion corresponding, on the communal level, to a collective self-purification. Decisive steps were made in this direction in the late Middle Ages when Ockham's fideism and Eckhart's mysticism compelled people to conclude to a rationally unknowable and distant God in whom we may only *believe* but whom we cannot reach by *reason*. Once the Christian God was removed from the intellect's scope, the philosopher abandoned the upward way, the *voie ascendante*, of Plato and Plotinus and redirected his passion for knowledge toward a horizontal objective—but with a religious intensity. Perfect knowledge was now expected to be found not in God but in an ideal community, a utopian construct. If God was infinite, so was utopia furnished with institutions derived only from nature, therefore neither limitative nor coercive. Infinite also in the sense that all of man's capacities and dispositions—as texts from Pico della Mirandola to Herbert Marcuse illustrate it —would find unobstructed scope in it. This is also what Ernst Bloch has in mind when referring to utopia's "openness" and "indefiniteness," "something substantially still undetermined but unmistakably wonderful." In brief, utopia's members would be supremely *befriedigt* and blessed with the *plenitudo intellectus* (the fullness of intellect), since their community, as Campanella and Andreae's constructs show it, would itself incarnate knowledge.

The objectives of the *Aufklärung* (the German Enlightenment) were not different, namely, the design and construction of an ideal community where all the dispositions of man and his thirst for knowledge are given full satisfaction. We remember Ockham's view that in an age of insufficient knowledge people needed a clergy but that with instruction spreading (in our days the word *information* is usually added to such statements) this need disappeared. Kant was to argue the same way in his work *Religion within the Limits of Pure Reason*, which deals with what I have earlier called the religion of the mind. Positive revelation has no longer any meaning for enlightened mankind, Kant writes. The church's faith was perhaps necessary earlier in order to bring all men to the moral view.[25] Now, however, the philosopher's task is to make the church's faith superfluous: through education men may be brought to live without a religious faith, while the philosopher makes new contributions toward the approaching pure religion of reason in which God will be all in everything.

Kant envisages then the gradual impact of practiced free thought on people's sentiments so that they will experience an increase of their aptitudes to behave freely and change the foundations of government.[26] There is here a whole conscious strategy to reach this goal, although, as Karl Barth remarked, Kant's works are so demanding that most readers remain unaware of the "cold deliberateness" with which he pursued his "enthusiasm" for the new world. The foundation stone of the strategy, as expressed in Kant's entire lifework, is the hope to place reason on such a firm basis that it may serve the main objective: the formulation of a natural religion as the organizing principle of the new community of men. Three stages may be distinguished in this strategy: first, the removal from the religious purview of all those elements that hinder the universal union of all religions into one single church. For this purpose Christianity must be stripped of superstitions, miracles, revelation, atonement, grace, and hierarchy. The second step is to assign to morality, independent of religion, the role of principle of the ecclesiastical union; finally, the unanimity of all men must be achieved by pointing out that with the removal of the nonessential features of religion, a firm ethical entity remains in which a pure and rational catholicity may hold the reigns of government.

Once the main roadblocks (faith and hierarchy) are eliminated, there will be no obstacle left before the public use of individual reason. By this Kant understood the philosophers' books and the reading public studying these books with an emancipated mind.[27] We recognize the pattern suggested by the Renaissance magi and taken up, more elaborately, by Hegel a little later. Bruno's *capitano*, Campanella's Sun Priest, Andreae's metaphysician-God, Hegel's all-comprehending sage, and the *duces* and emperor-figures of Joachites and others are varieties of the type to which Kant's savant can now be added.[28]

After having examined the relationship of religion and reason so as to formulate the religion *of* reason, Kant turned to the study of the French Revolution, again in the light of reason. Impressed by the capacity of reason shown in various manifestations in history—science, art, morality, and religion—Kant began investigating whether reason had the further capacity of *achieving* these things, that is, of organizing a world along new principles. The question he asked was whether reason would remain merely a faculty of the mind or bring about an intermental world based on reason. His question was, in effect, twofold. Does man, led by reason, possess the capacity of becoming truly human, that is, moral and virtuous? Is the idea of a perfect republic governed by principles of justice impossible merely because it has not yet been tried? It is obvious that these questions are not addressed to the mankind that Kant knew, but to an ontologically perfected mankind yet to be created.

Kant himself was ambiguous on the matter, and Karl Barth's

view is that he actually contradicted himself between the advocacy of a religion of reason and the advocacy of a church led by God. We should, I think, disagree with Barth, although it is a fact that Kant retained enough of his Lutheranism to remain cautious, an attitude condemned by his younger deist contemporaries. And there was also the Königsberg philosopher's fear of censorship, eventually of the loss of his chair. True, he had vowed never to write and publish what he did not believe to be true, but he preferred to confide his innermost thoughts to his notes which were published in 1920 only. Therein we find a much more radical Kant, one for whom man's inner moral autonomy is justified by the God within him. Two passages from the somewhat disjointed notes—Kant was obviously searching for the correct and definitive formulation of his thought—show that he too believed in an ontologically promoted man, a complete self-legislator. "The proposition: There is a God, says nothing more than: There is in the human morally self-determining Reason a highest principle which determines itself, and finds itself compelled unremittingly to act in accordance with such a principle. God can only be sought in us." And: "God must be represented not as a substance outside me, but as the highest moral principle in me. . . . The Idea of that which human reason itself makes out of the World-All is the active representation of God. Not as a special personality, substance outside me, but as a thought in me."[29]

At any rate, reason in Kant's view as expressed in his published works, namely in his *Critique of Practical Reason*, does not deny God or other objects of worship; it merely refuses to include them in the maxims for thought and action. Reason knows its limits, all it needs (all that man needs) is courage ("Sapere aude!") within these limits. Fully and courageously used, reason would make the nature of man completely aware of itself—as it was just then in revolutionary France. *Why not* a perfect republic, Kant was asking; perhaps reason is able to lead us to things within the scope of nature, although never yet experienced?

[166]

The Framework for Absolute Knowledge

In a letter written in 1793 to a Berlin editor, he refused to share his correspondent's abhorrence before the turn the Revolution was taking, reaffirming his faith in the kind of social theories Rousseau and the Abbé de St. Pierre were proposing. The *ought to happen*, he argued, can be made to happen—if only governments are willing to act with this conviction in mind, "making things possible by this very action."[30] Thus the cautious Kant, always governed by reason, adopted the view that the virtuous and perfect republic cannot be realized through gradual reform but must be effected through a revolution in man's disposition. He can become "a new man by a kind of rebirth, as it were a new creation." Granted, he writes in *The Conflict of the Faculties*, that the revolution in France accumulates miseries and horrors, the kind that a sensible man would not plan at any price; but this is unimportant, the revolution finds in the minds of uninvolved spectators a *sympathy* (Kant's italics), a spiritual participation bordering on enthusiasm. This proves that the moral disposition of mankind inclines in this direction. After many failures, Kant felt that reason would emerge victorious.

The meaning of this was that in Kant's conception mankind was approaching a society of world-citizens and of permanent peace. The perfection of nations (perfect republics of the first period) was to spill over their borders "to people's external relations until a cosmopolitan society is established."[31] At times, Kant thought of this as a "sweet dream," but he kept reaffirming that it is nonetheless a possibility, even a duty for all to work for. "I maintain," he wrote in 1798, "that I am able to predict such a state for the human race, judging by the signs of our age. . . . Its progress toward this goal will never again be entirely imperilled."[32] In 1784 had appeared his essay "Idea for a Universal History from a Cosmopolitan Point of View," containing nine propositions. Proposition 8 summarized in advance the thesis that Kant insisted on seeing confirmed by events a decade later. "One may consider the history of the human race as the realization of

[167]

God and the Knowledge of Reality

Nature's hidden design to produce a perfect political constitution on the domestic plane, and also on the external [cosmopolitan] plane. This is the only way nature can develop all the dispositions with which it had endowed mankind." And he commented this proposition before engaging the discussion: "philosophy too can have its own millenarism."[33]

All this sounds quite conclusive of Kant's belief that reason is both a midwife for the unborn human world-society and its human product inasmuch as it guarantees that the new creature remains rational, moral, and virtuous. Yet, other, younger figures of the *Aufklärung*, Lessing, Herder, Goethe, Hegel, were not entirely satisfied because their illustrious predecessor still spoke of a human nature and saw in it certain inherent evil features. Was it not evident that for Kant, insofar as reason was the dominant characteristic of human nature, reason too contained evil, at least in the sense that it could not, by itself, satisfy its own moral requirements? For his young critics, more typical than Kant of the *Aufklärung*, the concepts of religion, reason, morality, human nature, mankind, and revolution had to be arranged in an order different from that elaborated by Kant. Above all, they insisted on the religious discourse, not as believers but, on the contrary, as subtle liquidators of religion. Herder saw its roots in moral sentiments (like Godwin and Shaftesbury in England), while Lessing wished to put it in the center of a well-planned strategy whose final outcome would be the victory of natural religion. Yet others, like Hegel, saw in the rehabilitation of the religious discourse a convenient antithesis to the *philosophes'* atheism, the two leading to the synthesis of the disalienated man; Goethe and Schiller regarded religion as part of man's aesthetic apotheosis.

Characteristically, Lessing in *The Education of the Human Race* looks back to the time of Joachim de Fiore and other medieval chiliasts, and while he finds their efforts toward a natural religion praiseworthy, he regards them as premature. Thus Lessing too regards history as a long preparation of his own times, a process of maturation bearing fruit *hic et nunc*. Perhaps, writes he, some enthusiasts of the thirteenth and fourteenth centuries had caught a glimmer of the new eternal gospel, erring only in predicting its arrival so near to their own time. Their "three ages of the world" were not such empty speculation that we may not learn from it that the new covenant must become as antiquated as the old. What caused their failure was that their contemporaries were still children "without enlightenment, without preparation, not yet worthy of the third age that they had predicted."[34]

Lessing saw this immaturity as the cause of the medieval chiliasts' impatience and short-lived enthusiasm. He himself, fully aware of his own decisive role in changing the course of mankind, decided to be patient, to let, as stated in an earlier quoted Masonic phrase, "the lamps [of revealed religion] burn as long as they can," which could not be now too long. On 2 February 1774 he wrote to his brother Karl, who had not understood why he undertook studies in theology instead of writing plays: "We are one in our conviction that our old religious system is false." The strategy, he went on, is to fight the liberal theologians so as to prepare the radical overthrow of the old religion. "Orthodoxy is patently absurd, and should be upheld in order to hasten its destruction." Then in another letter to his brother, written 20 March 1777, he said, "I only prefer the old orthodox theology (at bottom, tolerant) to the new (at bottom, intolerant) because the former is in manifest conflict with human reason, whereas the latter might easily take one in. I make agreement with my obvious enemies in order to be able to be the better on my guard against my secret adversaries."[35]

This was an obviously subtle strategy, reminiscent of this century's ideological in-fighting. Yet, a year later, in 1778, censorship was imposed on Lessing. But not even this contretemps could daunt his determination. On 11 August 1778, we learn from another letter to Karl, he was preparing "to play the theologians a still more annoying trick" than the pamphlets, letters, and answers to attacks he had been publishing; he was to put his theology into a play, *Nathan the Wise*. The well-known message of this play is that no one religion has the truth in its possession and, indeed, that the exact nature of this truth is unimportant. Lessing's life-concern was to help abolish all distinctions of religion, class, race, and nation, so that mankind, organized hitherto in separate states, might fuse in a freemasonry of the spirit. This is what he explains in a posthumously published fragment, "On the Origin of Revealed Religion." Mankind must agree on a minimal content of natural religion, he suggests, one God, only ideas worthy of him, and actions in harmony with these ideas. But since men's capacity of commitment even to this minimum differs from one to another, these differences should be prevented from affecting adversely (conflictually) people's social connections. This can be achieved by uniting people around certain ideas, provided these ideas are few in number and common to all positive religions. Then only will the core, natural religion, shine forth as evident and become the public religion.

This can be described as a pragmatic approach, the kind Hegel was to castigate as representing "bourgeois ideologies," mere verbal attempts to mask the absence of a real community. From a certain point of view this was correct because Kant and Lessing may have seemed to represent a regression if compared to the Renaissance magi; Agrippa, Campanella, Andreae regarded full knowledge and the modified ontological status as *embodied* in the perfect community, the kind of community that the alchemists called *ecclesia spiritualis* and, according to Jung, considered their true aim. The thinkers of the *Aufklärung* seemed to show less temerity; they approached the issue of the ideal community with a certain amount of hesitation. For this, however, their official social status must be held responsible. While the Renaissance magi, the Rosicrucians, the spiritualists, and the Freemasons labored largely in secret (Valentin Weigel, for example, was a minister all his adult life, and his community which he served faithfully learned only after his death about the ideas he harbored and the manuscripts he prepared), Kant worked in the limelight as a salaried professor and Lessing as a state librarian. This position imposed on the latter the necessity to be patient; his chair in Königsberg imposed on Kant a generally prudent attitude to the extent that once or twice he was obliged to retract some of his ideas. In his own admission he decided not to write everything he meant to, but at least not to write anything of which he was not convinced.

With Hegel we return to the intellectual freedom enjoyed by the earlier "underground" of alchemists and Paracelsian sages, since his teaching benefited by the postrevolutionary philosophical ferment (in the eighteen thirties and forties Hegel's works were in the center of discussion by Russian intellectuals) and also by the ambiguity of his doctrine, which apparently flattered the new Prussian state instead of putting its authorities on their guard. After all, some students of Hegel regard him even today as a nationalist thinker, who justified the nation-state as the highest expression of historical evolution, and fail to see in him the founder of a utopia and utopian religion with unceasing revolutionary potential. The reason is, I think, the impressive elaborateness, the first since St. Augustine's, of a *system* embracing history, philosophy, politics, anthropology, economics, psychology, and other branches of learning, pulled together in a sweeping phenomenological analysis in which the buildup itself may overshadow the final synthesis. Yet, it is the synthesis that crowns the edifice and has had the decisive impact on contemporary speculation. In Hegel's own mind the system was justified by history. As Kojève puts it, imagine Hegel sitting at his table and writing his *Phenomenology* while listening to the cannonade of the battle of Jena. *That moment* and the fact of writing *that book* were as important as the contents of the book—which now reached out, as it were, from the pages demanding the status of ontological truth.

God and the Knowledge of Reality

In other words, we see once again that the philosopher does not intend to establish a timeless truth that follows not from his mind but from the nature of reality and that translates the constitution of being into the language of cognition, itself a bridge linking the knower to reality. Rather, the philosopher claims to have accompanied the *growth of truth* through its phases, and he then announces its full maturity at the phase coinciding with his own and brought about by his own labors as a creator. Until he has reached, ontologically and speculatively, the last phase, the last *Gestalt*, he considers all previous phases and "truths" as preparatory, so that all previous judgments about them were necessarily imperfect since the object of these judgments was itself not yet fully real. Only the philosopher's own judgment has a privileged relationship with reality and is, consequently, correct because from where *he* stands the entire growth of reality and its phases can be encompassed in one true statement.

Now this one true statement—for Hegel, his *Phenomenology*—is equivalent, in historical-ontological terms (for in the terminal phase history has become ontological reality, and this reality has become fully expressed in history), to the last world-society, man's last supreme creation. In the bourgeois world everything culminated in private interests, but the French Revolution swept all this away. In the new and last world the complete Being came to realization and history came to an end. And still, in spite of Hegel's considerable powers of imagination (the "master-slave" relationship reads like a fascinating novel), he cannot overcome the nature itself of his discourse: the "last world" appears in his writing less described socio-politically than adumbrated in a quasi-religious language. This kind of embarrassment is evident in modern philosophers from the Renaissance on. As authors, they are able to create elaborate frameworks within which ideal societies emerge and scenarios for the citizens are set. But when they must put their new citizens into lifelike motion so as to follow their scenarios, the authors, like broken mechanisms, fail to carry on their speculation. Their ideal societies remain static, like motion pictures suddenly made motionless; only philosophical and quasi-religious discourse can translate the preoccupations of their new citizens.

This is quite understandable, since their new citizens are not human, having been created without regard for the constitution of being. All we learn about them from Hegel is that the divine values in them will now be revealed as society itself becomes harmonious. The meaning of *harmony* becomes clearer if we reflect that two consciousnesses (for example, the master's and the slave's) mirrored in each other induce the misery of both until they become aware of their unity. Then, the separation having ceased, they become *befriedigt*.[36] In Hegel's religious discourse this translates as the necessity for the Christian to realize his total individuality (the synthesis of the universal and the particular), that is, to become what he always believed god was, Christ, the God-man.[37] Thus the great substitution, the alchemical-speculative operation, has been performed; the universal, transcendent God who before had merely *recognized* man (as a slave—in both Judaism and Christianity) is now replaced by a universal that is immanent in the world and is called the worldly kingdom, the state. To use the Blochian language, God the hypostasis is now reabsorbed, and the total man, the "tiding-become-man," realizes himself in the human community that is as perfect as God was imagined as being.[38] More prosaically, Hegel taught that in the final world, beyond the revolution and beyond Christianity, German philosophy would take the place of all religious systems and that his own absolute science, itself the end of all philosophizing, was called upon to replace, once and for all, religion for mankind. There is nothing beyond, the definitive *Befriedigung* (contentment) renders all escape toward a *Jenseits* (a "beyond") pointless. An "empirical process" will go on indefinitely, but, as we noted before, without principle and therefore also without phases: man will no longer be stimulated to build "new worlds";

the Hegelian one is to be the last. Hegel's state is the point of arrival for the spirit incarnated now in the dyad formed by Napoleon and Hegel, and through them in the reunited consciousness of the perfect man: *befriedigt* that he *is* and that he *knows* he is.

If escape to a new *beyond* is now a pointless desire, we must assume that the Hegelian motor-force of man—the *Begierde* (greed; will to be and to overcome; ambition to prevail; and so on), which is also a wish to continue, to project into the future—has been arrested. We recognize here the promise of the great religions: man turning to God in whom he finds peace; the lion and the lamb reconciled; the desires of the Buddhist sage extinguished; and so on. Most religions, however, place this accomplishment in a heavenly abode, beyond, and external to, history. Otherwise, we are unable to imagine this end beyond the end, happening *after* history, yet with human beings as we know them as its actors.

What is remarkable about the thinkers we have examined is that they disregard the rules of man's condition, promote him to a higher status, and create speculatively a new condition embodied in a collectivity. This condition is not the Platonic paradigm as exposed in the *Republic*, the just yet earthly state, regimented so as to be durable. It is the result of a noetic process and, at the same time, it is the map of that process, the mind's way of *coming home*, a capturing (immanentization) of all universal (divine) powers in a last and definitive form. In the *corpus hermeticum* it took the shape of the city of Adocentyn; throughout the Middle Ages it was the spiritual church, as opposed to the mundane, organized, and institutionalized ecclesiastical community; at the Renaissance it was incarnated in the "Egyptian religion" of Hermes Trismegistus, which was to replace the decaying and corrupt Catholic Church. In *The City of the Sun* and

The Framework for Absolute Knowledge

in *Description of the Christianopolitan Republic* the supreme metaphysician was to take charge of the symbolically all-comprising community, which no longer had to *seek* knowledge because it *was* knowledge, and its signs, that is, idols possessing occult powers, were to be painted and sculpted according to the appropriate arrangement in a replica of universality (cosmos).

In Kant and Lessing's ideal world-community based on natural religion, the Sun Priest and the Great Metaphysician of Campanella and Andreae yielded to natural religion greatly simplified and rendered prosaic since the time that the exuberant minds of the Renaissance magi had put their imagination and their hand to it. In the Protestant mentalities of the German *Enlightenment* philosophers (sons of pastors, Nietzsche reminded us), natural religion consisted of only a few easy tenets, a kind of "digest" of scripture arranged after the convenience of reason. So that again the requirements of a reason reconciled with itself and in the role of a lawgiver were programming the community. This enabled Kant, reputedly so cautious in tiptoeing in the labyrinth of the cognitive process, to make predictions about the coming cosmopolitan society and world peace, receding violence, the increase of lawfulness, and the republican constitution that "can never be aggressive." In other words, Kant's cosmopolitan republic, like the other models before and after, is also an end to history; as Barth observes, faced with the accidental historical aspects of civilization, Kant sought what was essential and necessary about it.[39] But this is exactly the program of all the ideal communities mentioned, from the Adocentyn to Hegel's empire: the search, in the name of a noetic ideal, for the essential and necessary through the exclusion of the accidental.

Let us not be misled by the words *essential, necessary*, and *accidental*. In the sciences, *essential* and *necessary* are terms that can be defined and applied, for example, to a theory that gathers all necessary phenomena and, through the criteria it observes, excludes those that are not essential for the formulation of a stated law. Further, factors that can be labeled *accidental* sometimes contribute to the progress of science; accidental factors may be revealed through research as necessary, thus becoming essential parts of a new theory. In human affairs such as history, however, the meaning of these terms is merely speculative, not definable; it is impossible to ascertain what was essential, what was necessary, or what was accidental. Was it the length of Cleopatra's nose? Was it Caesar's genius? Was it passion over reason? What some thinkers call "the end of history" can be purchased only at the price of an arbitrary exclusion of human incalculability, of Pascal's "esprit de finesse," of man as he is. If reason is the sole "essential," then the philosopher's system based on it runs the risk of theorizing in a vacuum and setting up a utopian community embodying all that is to know. The citizens are turned into programmed figures on the philosopher's noetic map.

The world has moved on ever since Hegel, crowning all earlier attempts, had proclaimed its ultimate *Befriedigung*, but his speculative design has retained a surprising amount of favor among philosophers: it constitutes a privileged phase in the history of immanentist-subjectivist systems so that much, if not most, of contemporary speculation is its tributary. Hegelianism is a kind of modern, up-dated hermetism, and so the epistemological ideas of its adepts come to fruition in the perfect *noesis* embodied in the perfect community. Its difference from earlier, similar operations is that they spoke of a community of faithful ascending to spiritual purity, whereas Hegelian and post-Hegelian speculation replaces the *sacred* with the *socio-political* dimension. One may argue, naturally, with the Saint-Simonians, the Marxists, Ernst Bloch, and numerous others that all spiritual communities in the past chose images and concepts of a "vertical" ascent from fear of persecution in case their "horizontal" preoccupations (revolutionary ideals) become too obvious.

[176]

The Framework for Absolute Knowledge

This controversy is not in our purview, and I shall add to it only the remark that theoretical constructs—mythical, philosophical, and other—always contain a large part of the contingent, of elements taken from surrounding reality. At any rate, "utopias," either before or after Hegel, are prompted by immanentist and noetic ideals as well as by certain conclusions derived from the author's interpretation of events in his lifetime. Since Hegel, however, "utopias" have become perhaps more numerous and without a doubt more "horizontal." First, because no religion stands now in the way calling authoritatively to the philosophers' attention the transcendent and personal God who limits man's knowledge as well as his community-building (political) powers.[40] Second, because historicism, itself the product of immanentist-subjectivist speculation, considers history as the ultimate reality: to outline and perpetuate its last configuration appears now as the worthiest—and quasi-religious—enterprise, transcending in seriousness all earlier efforts.

Thinkers of the nineteenth and twentieth centuries have taken it for granted that the chief objective of their philosophy—and often of their science too—was to build the ideal community, expected to materialize as soon as their system was adopted or, indeed, gave the signal. This is a strange decapitation of history, and it is, at the same time, a testimony that the immanentist mode of thinking destroys reason's understanding of reality, and, within the constitution of being, also the understanding of its own limits. Most of these thinkers fell victim to a "coarsening" of the myth (the Swiss historian Jacob Burckhardt called them "terrible simplifiers") that used to demand—at the hands of Hermetics, Gnostics, magi, and Hegel—a careful, speculative elaboration of the link between the requirements of epistemology and the utopian framework within which it reaches maturity. Such an elaboration is now less frequently attempted; philosophers assume now more easily than before that man's faculties and dispositions will be collectively promoted in the perfect community, whereas the pre-Hegelian position was that the soul's maturation will produce the perfect community. There is an important problem of emphasis here for which this book's thesis accounts very well. Before Hegel, philosophers stressed the maturation of the soul since it was supposed to be the privileged abode of God. In our days this aspect is neglected; man is regarded as being well on the way to absolutization, hence unquestionably able to produce the ideal community. The social bias of these times absorbs, perhaps only temporarily, more attention than the issue of God's maturation in the soul. No question, however, that the contemporary philosophers also regard the conditions of *knowledge* and the conditions of *community* intimately linked and that they too find intellectual and political maturation an indivisible issue.

A few illustrations will suffice to establish this point. In the system of the Comte de Saint-Simon, Hegel's French contemporary, the religious, political, and cognitive elaborations run on parallel lines. The "new Christianity" will be run by scientists, artists, and industrialists whose leadership is not questioned by the happy masses whose well-being will be the former's chief concern.[41] Well-being consists of the liquidation of conflicts (an "Academy of Sentiments" will channel the instincts and emotions!), and the supreme rule will be embodied in a "pope of science." Domestic and world peace, rendered permanent, will permit the construction of a "gigantic computer fed by the data of a language common to physical and social phenomena." Thus people will learn the laws of universal social attraction (Newton's laws applied to social affinities), which lead to the possession of the "science of freedom."[42]

An even more thorough systematizer, Saint-Simon's one-time secretary, Auguste Comte, also finds after analyzing the historical past that now is the time to construct the ideal cohesive society. His key is "positive knowledge," and at the summit of his "universal religion" we find the new "positive priests" or sociologists in possession of universal and general truths. Mankind's maturation through the theological age and the metaphysical age to the positivist and scientific age proceeds with the force of a universal law. "In sum, humanity takes the place of God—without forgetting the latter's past services."[43]

Karl Marx's thought ran on similar lines.[44] The proletarian condition—and, generally, mankind's divided condition (into classes)—has epistemological consequences because detached from nature through wage-work and the fetishism of the merchandise, the proletariat does not *know* its condition, does not possess the consciousness of its class. Thus the classless society is not merely a reconciliation of nature and the (collective) human being, it is also a final and Hegelian *bei sich sein*: matter regaining its integrity through mankind's harmonious existence in material well-being.

If we switch now from the *socialist* line of thought to that of *philosophy*, we find that the latter's contemporary exponents believe also in a logical connection between their theory of knowledge (immanentist-subjectivist) and an ideal society on which this theory opens. In *The Crisis of European Man* Husserl shows himself a partisan of the world's necessary transformation in the direction of maturation. As we remember, he expects eidetic reduction to be the last word about the structure of reality, and he trusts that an evidently reliable intersubjectivity will result from all men practising it. This is the *basic evidence* that, however, has more than only a cognitive value; it is also the basis for the rational construction of an autonomous mankind. Out of eidetic evidence Husserl sees a unity emerge, in which all men cooperate so that the values of this unity will be the radically reshaped values of the present. Once again, *knowledge,* the process of cognition according to a new formula, *transforms* the object of cognition, transforms what it knows. Man's intellectual substance is supposed to participate in some mysterious way in the substance of the world: its maturation promotes also the world's perfection. In ages preoccupied with religion and eternal salvation, the idea of the world's perfection finds speculative expression in an *ecclesia spiritualis*; in ages preoccupied with social organization and collective promotion this idea is channeled into an ideal earthly community where material well-being goes together with the mundane equivalent of the beatific vision: the appropriate social attitudes based on the complete grasp of mankind's (thisworldly) objectives.

This is what confers on Husserl and others the right to proclaim the emergence of a new society from what they know, strictly speaking, only as a presumably more accurate method of cognition. This right is taken also by Bergson. Not that Bergson, Le Roy, or their somewhat lateral disciple, Teilhard de Chardin, worked out a model society with the help of material from political, economic, institutional, or other discourse. They too are primarily preoccupied with locating the *substance* or the force that suffuses intellect and world (Hegel's *Geist*, the alchemist's *materia prima*, and so on) so as to be able to accompany it on its course of maturation. They make no predictions about the shape of things to come in the historical order, but, transcending history, they make unverifiable statements about the activity of that mysterious substance as it affects the maturation of mankind and of the cosmos. This is how the world becomes a "machine producing gods," for Bergson, and this is how we are supposed to realize that, as Teilhard de Chardin says in *The Future of Man*, "there is in progress, within us and around us, a continual heightening of consciousness in the Universe." True, it may not be possible directly to draw from this phrase and others like it the concrete structures for a proposed community of human beings; but the essential thing about ideal societies or utopias is precisely that their members are noetically and ontologically of a different order than the humans we know, and that the higher ontological status is derived from a noetic promotion. Accordingly, Teilhard de Chardin speaks of mankind finally learning their "business as men" in increasingly higher degrees of "hominization" and moral and

[180]

intellectual maturity. If he does not outline a community like Campanella's or Andreae's, it is that even their exalted picture would seem too static for him; but his "human sense" now emerging is "the consciousness gained by Terrestrial Thought that it constitutes an organized Whole, gifted with growth, capable of and responsible for a particular Future." Teilhard, like the other immanentists, proceeds by distinguishing ages in history, although they are, in truth, phases of ontological maturation toward the Noosphere. As for other immanentists, for him too the decisive moment of change is *now*, ending and beginning a world: "interhuman affinities are coming definitively into play in our era. It is an irresistible and accelerated movement which welds together peoples and individuals, under our very eyes, despite some revolts, in a higher intoxication. It is the formation, actually in progress, of the organized human block, powerful and autonomous—taking Humanity as a whole."[45]

Husserl and Bergson, even Teilhard in his own way, are systematic thinkers. It is more difficult to discern the immanentist pattern of thought in Nietzsche's ambiguities because most of his statements, no matter how categorical, may be countered by an opposite statement somewhere else in his brilliant but equivocal and fragmented work. The main line is, however, not in question: Nietzsche belonged too—in fact, he belonged eminently—to the class of thinkers called "preparatory" of a new age, a new mankind. Next to Hegel, he was perhaps *the* philosopher who conceived his own role as that of a new creator, and he gave free and frequent expression to this belief. The year 1888 was particularly rich in such expressions in his letters.[46] To Franz Overbeck on 18 October, "I fear I am the one who will blow up the history of men into two halves"; to Peter Gast on 9 December, commenting on his new work, *Ecce Homo*, "It will literally make history explode"; to George Brandes on 20 November, "I am fate itself." At greater length in a letter to Helen Zimmern in November of that year, apropos of the transvaluation of all values,

God and the Knowledge of Reality

Nietzsche forecasts a crisis that the world has never seen, a fantastic collision of consciences, a collective decision against Everything (capitalized in the text) that had so far been believed, demanded, and sanctified. As he writes in *Ecce Homo*, the new values will be born out of mankind's supreme self-concentration, "a high noon at which men will cast their glance backward and forward."[47]

What will men see, looking forward and following the prophet Zarathustra-Nietzsche? On this point again, there are no ambiguities. We are at the threshold of a new era, writes Nietzsche, which for us, immoralists (or extra-moralists) ushers in the unintentional, the irrational, the nonconscious act.[48] *This* is the decisive value because all that is conscious is superficial, less than skin-deep, and it hides the essential. Like the German mystics and like Hegel, Nietzsche saw the source of evil in individuation, and he passionately called for the "restoration of unity," the "unity of all beings." (*The Birth of Tragedy*, # 10.)

How will the restoration be brought about? Nietzsche put his hope in a new positivism, beyond good and evil, at war with the religions of suffering, that is, Judaism and Christianity. His candidate is Buddhism, whose theory of knowledge, called by Nietzsche correctly "a strict phenomenalism" (*Antechrist*, # 20), makes of it the only positivistic religion in history. *Per absurdum*, it is the religion of joy since it has no concept of sin. We do not expect Nietzsche to develop a systematic theory of cognition, but the above as well as many other hints suffice. The new man will be noetically different from the old by returning to the (Dionysian) primordial unity, that is, by giving up the Socratic belief that reason, guided by causality, may reach being and morally guide it. (*The Birth of Tragedy*, # 15.)

Does Nietzsche point to a new and ideal society? If not directly, it is because his temperament skillfully mixes nihilism and utopianism, so that the critic can never catch him at either pole of the restless shuttle. While he scorns individualism, he also laughs at the "socialist imbeciles who see in the herdman the man of the future, the little animal with equal rights forming an emancipated society." (*Beyond Good and Evil*, # 203.) While he finds in Buddha's teaching a religion for aristocratic souls, he also warns Europe against the threat of a new Buddhism descending on it. (*Ibid.*, # 202.) Yet, these equivocations cannot hide the onus of the whole: the expectation that out of the smashing of history a new man, disdainful of forms, will arise.

Existentialism also follows the pattern outlined on these pages. The existentialist thinkers react to what they call the reification of man, a risk allegedly run when freedom is alienated to stable situations, socio-political forms, to the moral law, indeed, to any *essence*. The only injunction recognized by existentialists is that man must constantly renew himself and live with the awareness that *he* is and the *world* is a perpetual *remise en question*, a *not-yet*. Just as Ernst Bloch, asked to summarize his philosophy, responded with the formula that the subject is not yet wholly its predicate ("S is not yet P"), Heidegger describes the present world as that of no-more gods and not-yet gods, an in-between waiting for the unveiling of Being. But, of course, for existentialists man is always in an in-between, a period of progressive maturation. Thus man is defined by his temporality or historicity, and each phase is marked by a more authentic unveiling of Being, hence by a more authentic man who receives the revelation. What for the atheist Heidegger are the successive revelations of Being, become for his Christian disciples successive messages of God as interpreted by men of consecutive periods. Thus for Rudolf Bultmann "the man who understands his historicity, that is who understands himself as someone future, ever future, has to know that his genuine self can only be offered to him as a gift by the future. He is not allowed to look around for guarantees, not even those of a moral law, which might lighten his responsibility."[49] And: "it belongs to the historicity of man that he gains his essence in his decisions."[50]

God and the Knowledge of Reality

The growth-process is here even more radically presented than by Hegel, who at least stressed continuity also. Bultmann, as well as his disciple, Gogarten, believes that *historical* thinking has now superseded *metaphysical* thinking, and that the switch from the first to the second age occurred two thousand years ago when Christ had rid us forever of the "old Adam" and opened our way to the future. Like Hegel, like Heidegger, he believes in an infinite series of renewed self-revelations of the numinous being, revelations whose meaning (*Bedeutung*) is what Being, or God, wishes to say to me through changing symbols: yesterday the cross, tomorrow something else, in an ascending line of deepened truth. Hecker correctly called all these offspring of Hegel "preparatory" philosophers, racing forward to an anticipated and open future.

For Jean-Paul Sartre too, existence is perpetual openness to the future, itself measured by freely reached decisions. It is a denial of the past and of the past self, and a permanent self-invention, a positing of new values rooted and at once uprooted in our "dreadful freedom." This process has no end, and Sartre rejects even a climate of tolerance as a possibly inhibiting factor for absolute freedom. "The meaning of existence is never fixed," writes Simone de Beauvoir, "it must be constantly conquered."[51]

We should not be misled by the seemingly endless openness to the future of existentialist and Bergsonian (Teilhardian) thought. It would appear, at first, that the successive revelations, the openended evolution of the *élan vital*, and the fragmentation of individual decisions exclude the possibility for this thought to be trapped in the abrupt stabilization of an ideal society.

It is not so. Heidegger's encounter with national socialism is well known; it is believed, however, that his attitude and his texts of 1933 are detachable from his philosophical concepts. A reading of his proclamations and speeches as Rector of the University of Freiburg in the light of what we know of his philosophy shows the link between the two. Heidegger saw in Hitler—as Hegel had seen in Napoleon—an incarnate reality, the highest expression of

The Framework for Absolute Knowledge

a revolution that "totally reorders" the German national existence. "The Führer is, and is alone, German reality, present and to come."[52] The Germans of 1933 are compared to the Greeks for whom knowledge (science, *Wissenschaft*) was not "a reassuring way of understanding essences" (*Wesenheiten*), but "the inner determinant of their total existence as a state and as a race" (*völklich-staatliches Dasein*), "the force which grasps and embraces all of existence." We are now before a "great metamorphosis," since God is dead and man can give himself the freedom by which he will live in the true community (*Volksgemeinschaft*).[53]

If there is a fundamental thesis in Teilhard de Chardin's system, it is that sin, fall, redemption, and other such concepts are not acts of individuals—even less of an original couple—but cosmic events, avatars of the universe that proceeds from nonconsciousness (materiality) to full consciousness (in super-mankind). Therefore, those actors of the cosmic drama who at any given time are more in line with evolution's central thrust, find themselves in a better position than the rest. They advance toward more consciousness, that is toward a higher form of human "centration" at Point Omega. We find then that Teilhard de Chardin welcomes such *world-events* as concentration camps, the bomb on Hiroshima, and the two world wars as being in the line of increasing centration, although possibly as miscarried attempts. In his *Notes for Progress*, he predicated the second coming on the coalescence of individual men in one whole and of individual consciousnesses in one "cosmic conscience."[54] The vision of future as totalization—the highest mental form in the most advanced community of men—inevitably discerns in the milieu contemporary to the author the seeds of the most robust stem, the elect of the future: Joachim de Fiore saw them in the monks, Hegel in the revolutionaries of 1789, Teilhard in Mussolini and his movement. "Fascism opens its arms to the future," he wrote in 1937. "In the solid organization it dreams of, more care is given than you find anywhere else to maintain and make good use of the elite. . . . Fascism quite possibly represents a successful blueprint for the world of tomorrow. It may even be a necessary phase during which men have to learn their business as men."⁵⁵

For Sartre, the Marxist social system represents the logical outcome of existentialism, and he holds this so completely that he accepts now the modest role of an "ideologue" within what he considers the (Marxian) final philosophy. This acceptance was prompted by Sartre's sudden illumination (I think the term is appropriate) that what he had taken to be the impenetrable *en-soi* ("in-itself") was in fact the condition of economic scarcity in the world. Man's anguish is thus not caused by incompleteness, by the impossible reconciliation of the self and its object, but by prevailing misery. It follows that with the satisfaction of needs —that is, in the Marxist society—the ontological and epistemological conflicts will be solved too. In oneness with nature (Marx) men will discover the reality of their *praxis*, their free and positive conduct (existentialism of Sartre's first period). Freedom will no longer be a threat of looking into nothingness, but the free acceptance of one's self and of the others in a community of abundance.

What we have followed in this chapter is the course that the philosopher is compelled to pursue from a certain epistemological option to the creation of an ideal society or utopia. His vision of knowledge as a state of being has a series of consequences: first, the thesis that rational knowledge is a loss of innocence, a sin, which can be healed only when man realizes the privileged (divine) presence in his soul; second, the thesis that the maturation of God in the soul is paralleled by the world's ascent to a higher ontological perfection; and third, the thesis that the two processes must end in a community that *is* knowledge and beyond which there is no search either for knowledge or for being.

Concerning the second of these theses let me add that I find there the usual parting of the ways between the (monist) mystic and the philosopher. The mystic usually stops at the phase where he grasps God in his soul: he does not draw any further inference about the world's maturation. As Rudolf Otto has shown, two typical mystics, Meister Eckhart in the West and Sankara in the East, remained within the limits of ontological and epistemological speculation, and indicated no interest in mundane affairs since, precisely, such affairs constituted the sphere from which they meant to escape. This is what Otto calls the "inward way" where one looks "not upon the world but only into the self."[56] The philosopher, on the other hand, shows a great, even decisive, interest in the network that the divinely inhabited souls of men are able to build, that is, in the community where the absolute knowledge grasped by the philosopher materializes. We may then agree with Ernst Bloch's notion that the history of philosophy is the history of the march toward utopia —provided we add the all-important qualification: the history of *immanentist-subjectivist* philosophy.

As we have surveyed the utopias proposed in the history of immanentist thought, we have found the philosopher impatient of creatureliness and contemptuous of the constitution of being. Characteristic of the immanentist systems is their insistence on the *now* as the privileged moment of ontological transformation, hence of the building of utopia as the seal of the transformation. Thus the immanentist-subjectivist systems appear before us as collective and earthly doctrines of salvation and the philosopher as a demiurgos on the threshold of the promised land. The promised land takes various forms—some more and others less explicitly drawn by the philosophers—but one can say regarding all of them that they are generated by a sense of urgency and crisis. Is this crisis-approach to reality a genuine concern of the philosopher—or of the demiurge whom today we call an ideologue? This is the question that I set out to answer in Part Four.

God and the Knowledge of Reality

NOTES

1. As Groos remarks (*Der deutsche Idealismus und das Christentum*), the monist Hegel cannot accept creation, preferring the idea of a divine fall. Creation becomes evil, while sin becomes creative. Note how close this reasoning is to the Gnostic concept of fall and ascent.

2. "The return of the Idea to itself through man had become with Hegel an accomplished fact. Since his philosophy had proven 'that this Idea . . . reveals itself in the World, and that in that World nothing else is revealed than this' (introd. to the *Philosophy of History*), not only had Hegel's question about the ultimate design of the world received its answer, but also the world itself had achieved its ultimate design." Etienne Gilson, *Unity of Philosophical Experience* (New York: Charles Scribner's Sons, 1965), p. 278.

3. To the objection that the Napoleonic state was limited in space and time, Hegel answered that it comprised the historically active part of the world and that it was to be continued by the Prussian state.

4. Eric Voegelin, "On Hegel: A Study in Sorcery," *Studium Generale* 24 (1971): 337. In contemporary lingo the Hegelian "absolute science" is translated as "futurology."

5. Georg W. Hegel, *Aus Jenenser Vorlesungen*, quoted in Alexandre Koyré, "Note sur la langue et la terminologie Hegeliennes," *Revue Philosophique*, (1931).

6. Ernst Bloch, *A Philosophy of the Future* (New York: Herder & Herder, 1970), pp. 112, 139.

7. Ibid., p. 36.

8. Ernst Bloch, *Thomas Münzer*, Les Lettres Nouvelles (Paris: Julliard, 1964), p. 78.

9. Ibid., p. 77.

10. Ernst Bloch, *Man on His Own* (New York: Herder & Herder, 1970), p. 191.

11. Ibid., p. 192.

12. Ibid., p. 165.

13. Ibid., p. 191.

14. Ibid., p. 156.

15. Ibid., p. 156.

16. Leszek Kolakowski, *Chrétiens san Eglise* (Paris: Gallimard, 1969), p. 379.

17. Ibid., p. 366.

18. Ronald Knox, *Enthusiasm, A Chapter in the History of Religion with special reference to the XVII and XVIII Centuries* (Oxford: Oxford at the Clarendon Press, 1959), p. 3.

The Framework for Absolute Knowledge

19. For these details, see Norman Cohn, *The Pursuit of the Millennium: Revolutionary Millenarians and Mystical Anarchists of the Middle Ages*, rev. ed. (New York: Oxford University Press, Inc., 1970).

20. Frances A. Yates, *Giordano Bruno and the Hermetic Tradition* (New York: Vintage Books, 1969), p. 360.

21. Ibid., p. 369.

22. As usual in utopian literature, the processes of procreation are controlled from above so as to control family life. In *The City of the Sun* one of the Sun Priest's assistants, Love, is in charge. In Cyrano's *Voyages to the Moon and the Sun* (1657 and 1662) the state physician visits all families before they retire for the night and prescribes to them to mate, specifying the number of times, or to abstain.

23. Earlier I mentioned *Allgemeine und General Reformation der gantzen weiten Welt*, published in Cassel in 1614. It was probably also written by Valentin Andreae.

24. For details of life in utopia and for an analysis of the structure of utopian thought, see Thomas Molnar, *Utopia, the Perennial Heresy* (New York: Sheed & Ward, Inc., 1967).

25. This was also Lessing's view, as quoted in "The Philosopher's Magic Quest," Bergson's is not dissimilar, as quoted later in this chapter.

26. Immanuel Kant, *Réponse à la question: Qu'est-ce que "les lumières"?* in Kant, *La Philosophie de l'histoire*, (Paris: Ed. Gonthier by Ed. Montaigne, 1947), p. 55.

27. Ibid., p. 48.

28. Note that for Sartre, too, the socialistic society of the future will be primarily a *public* who read the intellectuals' books.

29. *Kants Opus Postumum*, edited and published by Erich Adickes. Quoted in Theodore M. Greene, *Kant Selections* (New York: Charles Scribner's Sons, 1929), pp. 373 and 374.

30. Quoted in Melvyn J. Lasky, "The Sweet Dream: Kant and the Revolutionary Hope for Utopia," *Encounter* 33 (October, 1969): 4.

31. Immanuel Kant, *Le Conflit des facultés* in Kant, *La Philosophie de l'histoire* (Paris: Ed. Gonthier by Ed. Montaigne, 1947), p. 177. My translation.

32. Ibid., p. 173. My translation.

33. Immanuel Kant, "Idée d'une histoire universelle au point de vue cosmopolitique" in Kant, *La Philosophie de l'histoire* (Paris: Ed. Gonthier by Ed. Montaigne, 1947), p. 40.

34. G. E. Lessing, *The Education of the Human Race* in *Lessing's Theological Writings*, Selected and translated by Henry Chadwick, Stanford University Press, 1967, p. 97.

35. *Lessing's Theological Writings*, Introduction by Henry Chadwick, pp. 12-13.

36. In paraphrasing Jean Wahl's terms, they become "consciences

God and the Knowledge of Reality

heureuses." *Le Malheur de la conscience dans la philosophie de Hegel* (Paris: Presses Universitaires de France, 1951), p. 167.

37. In *The Future of Christianity*, Hegel represented Judaism as the belief in a radical opposition between this-worldly nothingness and the fullness of the beyond; Jesus came to unite the two.

38. The difference is that the apparent end in Hegel's system is the state; in Bloch's, the end is "openness."

39. Karl Barth, *Protestant Thought from Rousseau to Ritschl* (New York: Simon and Schuster, A Clarion Book, 1969), p. 156.

40. The episode of the Tower of Babel is perhaps the most strongly focused antiutopian statement of scripture next to Jesus' words "my kingdom is not of this world."

41. Saint-Simon, *Le Système industriel* (1821).

42. Saint-Simon, *Le Nouveau Christianisme et les écrits sur la religion*, choisis et présentés par Henri Desroche (Paris: Ed. du Seuil, 1969), p. 32. My translation.

43. Auguste Comte, *Catéchisme positiviste* (Paris: Garnier-Flammarion, 1966), p. 299. Literally the statement by Ernst Bloch.

44. It is astounding to what an extent it is possible to reconstruct Marxist thought in referring to Hegel and to Saint-Simon. Hegel's notions of the duel between master and slave, the reflection of their material condition in the mind, the role of work and struggle, the final reconciliation, and other ideas more than prefigure, they literally prescribe, Marxist notions of history, the class struggle, the role of the proletariat, and the classless society. The less systematic Saint-Simon foreshadowed much of Marx's analysis of industrial society, bureaucratic centralization, pattern of leadership, and world unification.

45. Teilhard de Chardin, *The Human Sense*, trans. W. H. Marshner, quoted in Marshner, "The Teilhard Papers," *Triumph* (December 1971): p. 30.

46. F. W. Nietzsche, *Letters*, in *L'Antechrist* (Paris: Union Générale d'Editions, 1967), p. 163.

47. F. W. Nietzsche, *Ecce Homo* in idem, pp. 150–51.

48. F. W. Nietzsche, *Par delà le bien et le mal* (Paris: Union Générale d'Editions, 1965), p. 59, par. 32.

49. Rudolf Bultmann, *History and Eschatology*, forming the Gifford Lectures for 1955 (Edinburgh Univ. Press, 1957), p. 150.

50. Ibid., p. 44.

51. Simone de Beauvoir, *Pour une morale de l'ambiguïté*.

52. Martin Heidegger, "A Call to the Students," *Freiburger Studentenzeitung* (3 November 1933). My translation. "Discours et Proclamations," *Mediations*, Automne 1961, p. 139.

53. Martin Heidegger, "The Self-Affirmation of the German University," idem, pp. 145–48.

The Framework for Absolute Knowledge

54. Elsewhere he wrote: "The noosphere tends to constitute a single closed system in which each element sees, feels, desires and suffers for itself the same things as all the others at the same time. . . . We are faced with a harmonized collectivity of consciousness equivalent to a sort of super-consciousness. The idea is that of the earth not only becoming covered by myriads of grains of thought, but becoming enclosed in a single thinking envelope so as to form, functionally, no more than a single vast grain of thought on the sidereal scale, the plurality of individual reflections grouping themselves together and reinforcing one another in the act of a single unanimous reflection." Teilhard de Chardin, *The Phenomenon of Man* (New York: Harper and Brothers, 1959), p. 251.

55. Teilhard de Chardin, *Sauvons l'humanité*, trans. (1937) W. H. Marshner, quoted in Marshner, "The Teilhard Papers" *Triumph*, November 1971, p. 13.

56. Rudolf Otto, *Mysticism East and West* (New York: Macmillan Co., 1970), p. 59.

Part Four

THE POSSIBILITY
AND LIMITS OF
KNOWLEDGE

AT the end of Part Three I spoke of the modern philosopher's "crisis-approach" to reality—to *being* and to *history*—which, in the framework of his discourse, amounts to a crisis approach to philosophy itself. The intense desire to give a noetic expression to his absolutized self leads the philosopher to the construction of an ideal community in which absolute *noesis* is embodied so that while the community's members, or at least its leaders, are ontologically higher-than-human beings, the structure of the community *is* the true structure of higher-than-human cognition.

We have found this approach in a wide variety of cases: Indian, Neoplatonist, and medieval mystics; adepts of esoteric doctrines from Hermes Trismegistus to Paracelsus; and philosophers from Nicholas of Cusa to Hegel, the existentialists, and the Bergsonians. Can this variety and this wideness of the speculative current be accounted for by the play of influences? Rudolf Otto, studying the similar, at times even identically inspired, mysticisms of Sankara in India and Meister Eckhart in Europe, concluded that across the chasm of distance, time, and milieu an identical problematics explains the close resemblance of the two systems and the similarity of the problems of the soul. In other cases, like that of the alchemists and other semisecret movements like the Free-masons, the more or less tight organizational web and a jealously guarded and transmitted symbolization provide the explanation. Claude Tresmontant, Georg Misch, Eric Voegelin, C. G. Jung, and others speak of the permanence of Neoplatonist, monist, and Gnostic themes in the Western philosophical tradition, which would explain the persistence and at least periodic popularity of the immanentist line of speculation.

A third, very powerful link among thinkers of diverse back-grounds who reach similar conclusions is the common desire *to save Christianity* from the burdens placed upon it by its origin and the orthodox interpretation of its doctrine. It would take us very far to examine the critique of Christianity in all its details, so let me mention only a few of the points raised by thinkers and movements described on these pages in other contexts. The Her-metics and Neoplatonists objected to incarnation and resurrec-tion as contrary to their condemnation of the flesh (*sarx*) and ex-clusive stress on the spirit (*pneuma*). The medieval mystics, such as Eckhart and his followers, found that the God rendered an-thropomorphic by scholastic debates ought to be transcended by the Godhead, at once purer (more spiritual) and more intimately linked to the soul of man. The Joachites regarded the church as excessively earthly and wanted to save the core of Jesus' teach-ing by transferring it to a pure and definitively sacred community where all the faithful are monks. The Renaissance magi thought that, by returning to the primal sources in Egypt, they would purge Christianity of the accumulated inventions of priests; Gior-dano Bruno, according to what was reported of their conversa-tions by the librarian of the Abbey of St. Victor in Paris, "greatly admired Thomas Aquinas but condemned the subtleties of scho-lastics 'about the Sacraments and the Eucharist, saying that St. Peter and St. Paul did not know of these, knowing only that *hoc est corpus meum'* ["This is my body"]. He says that the troubles in religion could be very easily taken away if these questions were taken away, and he says that he hopes that soon there will be an end of them."[1]

Luther himself proposed above all a simplified religion for which the minds had been prepared by an undercurrent of evangelistic preaching with origins in Meister Eckhart. The Reformation was, in general, a hoped-for way of arranging the Christian religion in such a manner as to become acceptable to enlightened minds who meant to do away with its proofs grounded in reason and to anchor it in faith alone. It was a question of reserving reason for the pursuit of other than religious endeavors and rescuing Christianity, whose proofs in reason could no longer, as it was alleged, sustain scrutiny. The second of these objectives constituted the central efforts of several German, Dutch, and Swiss "spirituals" of the sixteenth and seventeenth centuries. These Christians often "without a confession" wanted basically to reduce religion to a purely internal affair because they regarded it as a cause for scandal that mankind, increasingly maturing in Christianity (since Luther's reform, that is, which renewed the direct link with Christ), should still belong to an organized, thus for them pagan, *ecclesia*. As Jung mentioned, the alchemists too intended to hasten the arrival of a true *ecclesia spiritualis*, emerging from the "chemical wedding" of opposites that would constitute a reborn Jesus Christ.

Karl Barth reminds us that German Protestant theology, as it grew in vastness and respectability, also turned to the task of saving the Christian religion from a transcendent and personal God who holds emancipated man in an embarrassing mental bondage. The reduction of the meaning of the encounter with God proceeds in the direction of a "personal experience of the human subject"; the term *anthropology* comes to be used as a substitute for the articulation of "creatureliness"; the power of the human mind slowly prevails over God and his revelation; the heart, that is again subjective experience, becomes the seat of divine wisdom in man. In short, Barth asks the question whether these theological currents did not lead in a direct line to the overt antitheology of Feuerbach, and whether "the theologians themselves [were in the position to protest] that he [Feuerbach] had mistaken their intentions."[2]

It is obvious under these circumstances that, contrary to the widespread impression, the God-problem and with it Christianity as a subject have suffered a serious eclipse in the mind of prominent thinkers. We find that believers and unbelievers alike continued the work of "rescuing Christianity" and the concept of God from earlier and orthodox, but resiliently surviving, interpretations. Examples from Saint-Simon to Teilhard de Chardin have shown it. In our days, more perhaps than at any previous time, philosophers have striven to bring about what earlier thinkers dared only suggest: the transformation of Christianity into an ideal community. The argument runs like this: God has matured in man by the gradual absorption in the soul; the concept of a transcendent God belongs to earlier, less mature, phases; the time is *now* to give full scope to the immanent God who authorizes the setting up of a permanently structureless community, innerly directed by ontologically promoted (human) beings. Men making efforts in this direction have never been lacking, from Joachim de Fiore to Thomas Münzer and to Lessing. Some of these men were aided by historical circumstances to express, indeed *to live*, their aspiration, and their efforts were realized, like Münzer's community, which believed in the elimination of the "old world," and even of God, so that they might build one Christian community. Others who made similar efforts were more circumspect with their proposals; but all regarded the moment ripe to substitute the *community* for *God* as the final accomplishment of a now internalized deity. Ernst Bloch sums up many of these issues when making the reproach to Marx that he ignored the role of theology in bringing about utopia. In Bloch's view, theology, together with its secular version, philosophy, has no other raison d'être but a chiliastic one: in utopia, theology (and philosophy) will vanish—replaced, no doubt, by an anthropology of God.

My conclusion is that while influences certainly played their role in formulating the *corpus* of immanentist speculation, such a *corpus* came into existence in the Western tradition mainly through the philosophical ambition inherent in all the doctrines mentioned to absolutize the *self*. Rudolf Otto goes as far as to write that "mystical conceptions lie behind the higher speculation of more modern times, behind the thought of Descartes, the Occasionalists, Malebranche, Spinoza, Shaftesbury, Leibniz and Kant."[3] As long as the ambition of absolutization remained confined within speculative systems and esoteric movements, its scope was imperfectly evaluated by observers. Indeed, it benefited from the sympathy due to a form of speculation that tries to come to terms with what it perceives as an oppressive situation. The existence of a transcendent God *can be* perceived as such a situation, particularly when the other attribute, personalness, forbids the speculative removal of God into the distant region of the *dei otiosi*. In such a case the tension is felt as unendurable: God appears as a lofty master (Hegel, as we saw, insists on this point) so that he risks becoming a dry abstraction for the intimate recesses of the soul, but at the same time he is also said to be personal, that is, constantly interfering with our freedom. For example, Yahweh for the prophet Isaias is powerful and majestic, frightening yet attractive; before him man experiences reverential fear, dread, awe, and confidence. He is an all-holy God, yet one who acts in history through his chosen people. True, for Otto, this is no obstacle to faith, he even sees in the words "Our Father who are in heaven" a harmonious reconciliation of the tension between the personal and the transcendent element.[4] Yet for many thinkers, when such tensions are allowed to build up inside a religious system, positive religion displaying itself in a systematized faith and in a church comes to be seen as an impediment for all human faculties, particularly the ones having to do with emotions and will. Positive religion becomes the object of contempt for immanentists; these are then the times when variants of existentialism and other systems are proposed that search for the inner God, for the sense of the oneness of the soul with the world spirit, for the leap toward the Godhead. Kierkegaard's example is perhaps the most typical in this respect.

Modern philosophy, on the other hand, is not constrained to confine its ambition to absolutize the self behind the bars of dreams and esoteric language. If it regards a transcendent and personal God as the creator of an oppressive situation, it may say so aloud and with vigor, and it may search publicly for ways of relieving the situation. The logical end to the search is the ideal community, a sign that the philosopher regards as urgent the noetic promotion of human beings. In one sense, he finds in the ideal community the possibility of the kind of immersion in being that archaic man sought in the *past model*. But the archaic method of recuperating the past was made impossible by the Christian concept of a linear history and personal responsibility for acts. The philosopher, unable to revive, and believe in, the concept of cyclical recurrence, has no choice other than *to arrest* history at an arbitrarily chosen point and construct there (from the available conceptual materials) a *utopian model*. In it and through it he does not recuperate the past, but obtains identity with God, nevertheless (*unum esse cum Deo*). As in the case of archaic man, this amounts to "a rejection of the profane world, a lack of interest in human history."[5]

In another sense, the ideal community is a noetic construct, signifying (and not merely symbolizing) the achievement of perfect knowledge through reabsorption in God. This course too amounts to the rejection of the profane world, the profane world not only as history, but also as the milieu of extramental things.

Possibility and Limits of Knowledge

In the ideal community the kind of knowledge is realized that is no longer knowledge—an illusion below the level of real knowing—but a "seeing of all in all," without separation and distinction, without the antitheses of knower, known, and the act of knowing. To express this in Hegelian language, the transcendent universal (God) is replaced by an immanent universal where man is not merely recognized (as a slave is "recognized" by the master), he is actually the only one who is "recognizable"— namely, by other men, now all of them his equals.[6] This situation, Hegel adds, can only come about in the terrestrial kingdom, that is, in the state.

Thus today, more than ever before, we meet the full impact of immanentist speculation, and we meet it mainly in the multiplying constructs proposing an ideal community. As I said in Part Three, such constructs are now daily manufactured, often with hardly any thought given to what they entail in the cognitive order, merely because it has become an intellectual fashion to produce them. Emerson noted that in his youth it seemed that everybody walked around with the blueprint of a perfect society in his pocket; such blueprints are today displayed in all the media of art, literature, politics, and religion as the daily intellectual sustenance of sagging hopes and faded myths. Their increasing coarseness and evident unworkableness are in direct proportion with the presumed urgency of the "crisis approach" to reality; but the breathless feeling of urgency translates well the increasing disarray of the philosophical enterprise that finds itself in a double trap. The first trap is the suggestion that philosophical problems may be made to disappear when the reality that philosophy is supposed to interpret is ontologically transformed so that the problems vanish from the purview of reality, hence from the horizon of philosophy too. Reality, however, refuses to change, and philosophy remains saddled with all its problems. The second trap is that insofar as the philosopher assumes the magician's role and manipulates the constitution of being, he liquidates the phil-

[201]

osophical enterprise, which is then reabsorbed in the *praxis* of the ideal community. Thus we are led to ask a question: if philosophy has become a self-liquidating enterprise, by which we mean that its last distilled answer is that "reality itself must change"—then can the philosophical quest be so redefined as to save philosophy from its own attempt at self-destruction?

Phrased otherwise, what are the conditions of rehabilitating the philosophical discourse that has reached an impasse with the absolutization of knowledge and self and with the consequent absolutization of the community? If Hegel reached the summit of immanentist philosophy with its logical end, the absolute knowledge embodied in the universal and necessary state, can we not, faced with a political impasse behind which we detect the much vaster self-liquidation of philosophy, unravel the thread and decompose the notion of the ideal community so as to find the way back to the philosophical enterprise? To do so, it is not necessary to retrace the course of arguments from the absolutization of the self to that of the community. This has been done in Part Three. It is sufficient to focus once more on cognition and its structure as seen by immanentist speculation—followed by the restorative analysis of knowledge by genuine realism.

This book begins by distinguishing among the three positions we may adopt regarding the God-problem. Let us remember our conclusions. In position *A*, the removal of God from man's scope renders the world fragile, evil, divided, illusory, and ultimately meaningless because unknowable. In position *B*, the immanentization of God in man's soul similarly reduces the extramental world to a state of imperfection, porousness, division, and vanity—facing a self that, as a maturing being on the way to divine status, will carry the world along to an ontologically perfected status. The outcome will be neither the same self nor the same world. What I called position *C* represents the equilibrium. God's tran-

Possibility and Limits of Knowledge

scendence blocks the self's absolutization and compels it to face its inherent limitations, which the constitution of being daily demonstrates as anchored in reality, and God's personalness guarantees the reality of the world and of the self, the knowledge and the meaning.

The ever-renewed popularity, or at least the intriguing character, of positions *A* and *B* is derived from the experience of discursive reason itself. In the course of aligning arguments, discursive reason inevitably finds chasms it cannot bridge by its own powers. It seems then that the flow of rational terms does not always refer to a real substratum, that there is a gap between reality and reason's efforts wholly to espouse and express it. This experience does not justify, however, either a contempt for human cognition or the elevation of the chasms for which reason cannot account to the status of being. Philosophy, writes Etienne Gilson, "is simply not a kind of conceptual poetry called philosophical system."[7] Thus not only is rational discourse dismissed for its limitedness, but another kind of cognition is sought, above the alleged illusoriness of the former kind, a "true" cognition found only in the divinely inhabited soul. The advantage of such a knowledge is that it operates without embarrassment since its materials are what reason produces as a servant of the spirit. Real beings and beings of reason are for such operations equivalent, as one may see in the liberties that immanentist thinkers take with concepts like time, history, the categories of the real, the ontological leap, and the absolutization of the self. It is quite correctly that Eliade finds in the alchemists' ambition to supersede *time* an "anticipation of what is the essence of the ideology of the modern world."[8] This essence Eliade locates in the eschatological enthusiasm of the *homo faber*, who has limitless faith in his technological possibilities. I think one should rather locate this essence further back, in the divinized soul and its claim to a superior knowledge. But one must be careful in describing this superior knowledge. Archaic man distinguished between profane knowledge, which was used in everyday matters, and sacred knowledge, which could refer also to everyday objects and actions but which, as part of the regeneration ceremonies, acquired, for that reason and in the sacred time and place, a higher status. It is in this sense that Eliade speaks of the "religious man who at times becomes the contemporary of the gods."[9] The other kind of superior knowledge, Meister Eckhart's, for example, has its origin in the permanent dissatisfaction with the *status creaturae*, which cannot be temporarily abolished as for the archaic man and which can only be liquidated once and for all by becoming *unum cum Deo*.

Positions *A* and *B* imply this overcoming of human limitations, primarily the noetic limitations. This is understandable. The immanentist thinker could give preference to the breaking down of other limits; but he is an immanentist through his spiritual (*pneumatic*) substance, which is part of the One, waiting to reintegrate the One. The overcoming of other limitations is secondary in the order of his priorities, and indeed they follow from his successful breakthrough to noetic superiority. This is how Rudolf Otto formulates the monistic doctrine that is at the basis of immanentist speculation: "True Being is *Sat* alone [for Sankara], Being itself, the eternal *Brahman*, unchanging and unchanged, undivided, and without parts. . . . This Eternal One is wholly *atman*, pure consciousness, pure knowledge . . . beyond the three antitheses, Knower, Known, and the act of Knowing."[10] Thus the One precedes both God and the soul, and the latter's objective is not actually divinization but merger with what is higher than God, the *One*, or Super-God. The way up to Oneness is a long apprenticeship because the soul is troubled by its own temporarily accepted creatureliness, which imposes upon it the yoke of perceiving other created things, also separated from the One. The One is so precious that, as Otto writes, the full content of the mystical experience is comprehended in its mere beholding and in the "becoming One." The name of God is not more than a convenient, because conventional, reference, an embarrassing one because it evokes personalness when the true objective is to become pure Being. Let us bear in mind that for Eckhart, *Esse* (Being) comes before *Deus*; the second is the predicate of the first.

The question is then legitimate: is the soul's absolutization a higher ambition than its search for divine status? Does the glorified soul need such an appellation as God? The answers, coming from the Gnostics, from India, from medieval Christian mystics of the monist type, are too concordant to tolerate doubt: in its ascent the soul goes beyond God; it aims at the merger with the supradivine, with Being. The Gnostics Valentinus and Basilides describe God in exclusively negative terms; he is neither Yahweh nor Christ, only abyss and silence. The medieval philosophers Denys the Areopagite and John Scotus Erigena purposely refer to God as superessence and supergoodness so as to place the divinity above description. The Hindu mystics speak of the *Brahman* (Being), high above the personal Lord, with which the soul is identical. Eckhart exclaims, "Had I a God whom I could understand, I would no longer hold him for God." Similarly, the nineteenth-century philosopher Friedrich Schleiermacher speaks of a "Godhead" and of the "high spirit of the universe." What Eckhart calls primordial essence and what Nicholas of Cusa calls universal essence have the soul as a receptacle. Through the mystic ascent, Eckhart's "enlightened man" becomes the entity determining good and evil; Nicholas of Cusa no longer feels that he is a thing among things, but a form in which the universal essence has its life; and Eckhart's disciple, Johannes Tauler, transcends God (an idealized human figure) so as to think divinely.

Parts Two and Three showed us that it is justified to quote the monist mystics in describing the philosophers' noetic adventure up to and including our own time. Mystical exaltation that regards the *status creaturae* as illusion and nothingness quite naturally ascends to the next phase where the mystic's experience is mistaken for an ontological fact and all being and all knowledge are attributed to God and to the soul that left behind creatureliness so as to merge in God. We have seen, however, that this absolute desire to reach God is not limited to the mystic. It is also the immanentist thinker's ambition, although he does not ordinarily express it in salvational terms but in terms of heightening man's ontological status.

Yet it is difficult to draw the line that would indicate where mystic endeavors end and philosophical speculation begins. The theistic mystic Ruysbroeck was exempt of Eckhartian aspirations; he recognzed the report of the senses as valid; he admitted the reality of things. Consequently, he recognized also that the world is diverse, so that reality is not the monopoly of a primordial One but is fully bestowed on all creatures. This is, of course, a decisive point since the whole debate turns on whether creatureliness is a fault, an imperfection, a nonbeing, *or* a limited, but in its limitedness a full, essence. Ruysbroeck condemned those mystics for whom all things are emanations of one essence, that is, who took the Plotinian position. In the third place and very importantly, he denied that things can become what they are not through a judgment of the intellect, that is, through what I have called the act of conjuring up "beings of reason" and through the passage of one *genus* to another (*metabasis eis to allo genos*).

Ruysbroeck's thought is a huge step away from the confusion of the soul with God, with the Godhead, with pure Being. This thought represents an important moment not only in the history of mysticism, but also, in view of subsequent developments, in the history of philosophy. In his *Kingdom of the Lovers*, Ruysbroeck used the expression "union without difference" as the culmination of the encounter with God. Later, the theologian Jean Gerson was to make violent accusations against him on this ground, but already in his own days Ruysbroeck was obliged to reply to more friendly but nevertheless puzzled inquiries. Thus the Carthusian Gerard de Herinnes suggested that the expression "without difference" had astonished him and his friends because it seemed to mean "without inequality" between God and man, "without distinction," "without alterity." Ruysbroeck found the issue so important that, although he was very old by then, he visited the Carthusian convent to explain in person that it is not in the divine essence that the difference between God and man disappears, but in the (subjective) joy of beatitude. No absorption of the human into the divine essence takes place, the experience remains purely one of faith and love. Yet, two centuries after Ruysbroeck, a man with a philosophical reputation, Cornelius Agrippa, was still victim of this confusion. In his *De occulta philosophia*, he asks, "Who can give life to inanimate objects?" and answers, "He who has cohabited with the elements, vanquished nature, mounted higher than the heavens . . . to the archetype with whom he then becomes co-operator and can do all things." Is Agrippa the mystic and Ruysbroeck the philosopher? At any rate, Ruysbroeck was not the first to advocate realism in cognition from within the mystic tradition; he apparently recognized that all immanentism—hence the denial of the reality of the extramental world, of creation, and of God himself in favor of a Super-God—originates in this confusion. The same view had been held by the Old Testament writers: God's spirit descends on the prophets and moves them, but they do not become divine. It had also been held by the scholastic philosophers, who could not accept the notion that God entered into them and spoke therefrom. God is in the soul only through his image, but as a reality he is outside man, a fact necessitating a communication, that is, a revelation. Correspondingly, the scholastic position was that knowledge is unable to climb the ontological ladder either as cognition in the ordinary sense or as a *docta ignorantia* into which, according to Nicholas of Cusa, knowing "flows." Where knowledge ends—because end it must—faith takes over, based on a supernatural communication.

This means that knowledge has limits. How does one arrive at

[207]

this conclusion, and what consequences follow from it? The whole issue of valid knowledge turns around the metaphysically prior issue whether there is a guarantee for knowledge when one is in the *status creaturae*. For radical mysticism the creature is what God is not; since God is all that is, full being, the creature has no being, no value, no essence; the creature is unreal, nonbeing. This view is based on the mystic's, of all mystics', desire to go beyond rational knowledge, to deepen to the farthest possible limit the penetration into the being of the Creator; in this sense the aspiration is legitimate. What is not legitimate is when the ascent is not followed by a descent back into creatureliness, and when the mystical experience is taken as a simultaneous ontological transformation of reality outside the mystic. As we saw in the case of Meister Eckhart, *esse* is God, therefore only *non-esse* "remains" for the creature, an unwarranted radical stance based on the self's insatiableness. The second consequence is that knowledge is also denied to creature, as long as he is creature. Only when it is understood that God and creature are not mutually exclusive, although radically distinct, does the need to establish their merger disappear. *Distinct* they remain, but their distinctness and separateness leaves a comfortable room within which, although not beyond it, creaturely *noesis* moves with certitude *closer* to the knowledge of God. We understand now that not only the mystic, but the immanentist thinker also cannot accept what appears to him a compromise, a halfway house, for the soul, hence for the human situation circumscribed by human cognition. Rejecting the possibility of *limits*, he sees man either as deprived of being (position *A*) or as total being (position *B*). Only position *C* offers an ontology and an epistemology harmonizing with our actual experience, namely, that man is a full being within limitations and that he possesses full (reliable, valid) knowledge, also within limitations. In religious discourse this can be understood as meaning that man's being and its modalities, including the cognitive faculty, are given to him by God—*this* is the precise significance

[208]

of creation—but that these gifts do not make him a god. In *Sententiae*, Thomas Aquinas put it into these words: "God is said to be in each and every thing, in as much as he gives to things their own being and nature." Since God does not give them his own being but gives them *their* being, the separation remains intact, as between parent and child.

The status of man is then an in-between-ness: between the human and the divine. The divine part makes him similar to God, but, to put it very plainly, he has so little of it that he cannot aspire to a higher status, nor can he increase his gift by any kind of subtle operation that would put him in the place of the giver. Plato's term for the consciousness of this status is *metaxy*, a concept applicable to *noesis* also. As he suggests in *Euthydemos*, the mind can know things as they are, although it cannot know them exhaustively. But, in order to "complete" the knowledge of things, the mind is in no need of inventing mental constructs ("beings of reason" in my earlier description) and distorting knowledge into something artificial. It may accept with confidence that God meets its noetic desire with his own movement (*kinesis*) toward man. Thus *knowing* implies neither contempt for creaturely reflection while being absorbed in God nor a self-produced reality; it implies a finding or discovery of preexisting things, separately created and distinct from the knower. Thus the intelligibility of things is *in* the things, in the real world. The knower draws it out by a process described in Aristotelian epistemology as abstraction. According to this epistemology, there is in objective reality an indwelling rationality that human intelligence is capable of retrieving.

The question, nevertheless, still remains: Is this *knowledge?*— when what we would like to believe is that knowing is so evident and so absolute both as a process and as its result, that to speak of *limits* of knowledge following from man's limitedness, in-betweenness, makes surely for disappointment, even anguish and misery in the feeling of existence, beyond the imperfection of cognition itself. Hence the temptation, apparently at the other pole from the mystic's own temptation, to make reason the sole instrument of knowledge and to proclaim its sovereignty over all possible knowledge. Whatever cannot be legitimately included within the territory of this sovereignty, is then declared unknowable, and as such nonexistent. This theory is a variety of position A, today, as often in the past, very popular because it excludes, together with the personal God of religion, metaphysics too and because it presents these centuries with a seemingly sober guarantee for scientific investigations. Moreover, this philosophy—in modern times essentially Kant's—also flatters itself with having put an end to the eternal tug-of-war between subject and object, although the price of this peace—better called truce—is the relegation of the object-world into the unknowable *Ding-an-sich*.

As I have said before, this position was prefigured in the posthumously published works of Valentin Weigel, who was deeply influenced by Paracelsus. Let us remember that Paracelsus achieved his greatest fame by the scientific (mostly medical) demonstration of an intimate and all-penetrating correspondence between microcosmic man and macrocosmic universe; epistemologically this meant that we *know* only what we *are*. Thus for Weigel too: knowledge is derived from the knowing subject, not from the object-world, because the object-world, since it is outside the subject, does not exist. The subject learns what it is, learns its own identity, in the cognitive operation itself.

Thus the origin of the Kantian speculation lies in the question "Is philosophy a legitimate enterprise of knowing the world as created, and knowing—within limits—the world's creator?" Kant's answer is to investigate the limits of reason, equate the activity of reason with the totality of the field of knowledge, and to establish the *ideality* (nonreality, inaccessibility) of the extramental world. He perceived well that to posit the reality of objects is to posit God's reality too; hence he excluded both from reason's purview: the object-world is unknowable in itself, and God

Possibility and Limits of Knowledge

is knowable only to practical reason. The subject, with its reasoning processes, remains separated from being, locked up, as Ferdinand Alquié remarks, within the narrow limits of phenomenal cognition.[11] Reality, God, and metaphysics are thus exorcised. All that we legitimately know outside of synthetic a priori judgments, that is, mathematics, are phenomena. The Kantian theory then also posits a limited cognition, but its difference from realistic epistemology is that for Kant there is nothing knowable outside reason's limits, whereas for realistic theory the extramental world is not merely conditionally real, but absolutely so, even if man cannot cognitively exhaust it. The Kantians—and much of modern philosophical speculation down to Wittgenstein—hold that all one can say of the outside world is that it is there (even this is vigorously denied by Fichte, for whom not only the outside world but the Kantian subject too are unreal), but it is there as an amorphous magma. In this way, the subject *is* limited, but only because there is nothing outside it that it could know. It creates its own world—phenomenologically or linguistically circumscribed—so that its, the subject's, temptation becomes overpowering actually to construct its world out of the only available, subjective, materials. Again, as Alquié writes, practical reason "is not directed at a knowable object, but at a task to be fulfilled, a world to build. . . . The aim of the Kantian cogito is to create an opus [*une oeuvre à réaliser*]."[12]

In contemporary speculation, the logical positivists and the linguistic analysts continued the Kantian thesis. This was directly acknowledged by Wittgenstein and such of his commentators as David Pears, but others, like Carnap, Hempel, Stebbing, Philip Franck, Moritz Schlick, Hans Reichenbach, and others also draw their philosophical sustenance from Kant's conclusions. The judgment of the Belgian neoscholastic Maurice De Wulf applies to them very well, although it was made at the beginning of the century, long before Wittgenstein's *Tractatus* and the foundation of the Vienna Circle in 1921–22: "At least three-fourths of con-

God and the Knowledge of Reality

temporary philosophers have felt the influence of Kantian subjectivism in their studies on epistemology."[13] Indeed, the linguistic analysts accept as their starting point the phenomenism of Kant, but they do not stop there: first, they draw a line around the system of factual knowledge so as to exclude any phenomenon not reducible to experimental (or psychological, or linguistic, or physical) verification, after which they have a relatively easy task reducing, at least in theory, the phenomenon so isolated to its components. Thus nothing remains even vaguely reminding us of the old assurance that thought and the extramental reality reliably fit together (*adequatio rei et intellectus*); as Stebbing insists, all we can ask of a system is that its constituent elements should be compatible.[14] A similar opinion is heard from Rudolf Carnap: only experimental verification confers meaning, and the ultimate verification must be of a physical nature.[15] And from Philip Franck, who claims that it is impossible to decide whether the extramental world exists because neither the affirmative position (the realists) nor the negative position (the idealists) is able to conceive the experiment that would arbitrate the question.[16] Moritz Schlick, the founder of the Vienna Circle, held that truth is not in facts but in the concordance of protocol sentences or factual propositions and in the absence of contradiction among hypotheses. Meaning is obtained by, first, reducing all statements of fact to their component data, then performing the operation that verifies these data.[17]

One could go on quoting such identifying statements by the proponents of this Kantism in the fashion of the twentieth century. Their overall ambition is to develop a systematic critique of human thought, but they are unable to dispel the following danger: this critique is inevitably absorbed into the science closest to the linguistic or positivist thinker's heart, a kind of privileged science chosen for nonscientific reasons whether it be biology, physics, geometry, or grammar, as in the Middle Ages it would have been, and indeed was, theology. Then this particular science assumes the function of a metaphysics, and so on indefinitely, because to judge its own assumptions, a third science must be formulated, and so on. Wittgenstein himself was aware of this pitfall, namely, that he might re-create a metaphysics through his theory of language; consequently, he abandoned that particular direction of his research since he did not believe that metaphysical theories may be true at all. If such is the case presented by these late successors of Kant, could a final critique of Kantian (and their own) phenomenism not be the Aristotelian recommendation to "consider Being as such, and the attributes of Being as such"?[18]—in other words, consider that reality does exist. Greenwood expressed the same thought for moderns: behind the signs and symbols there must be a reality, an essence of things that is not grasped by a combination of symbols, only by an analysis of the things themselves.[19]

Kant may not have derived the seeds of his theory of knowledge from Valentin Weigel; both men are in the great current of the Protestant tradition from Luther to Hermann Dooyeweerd, which shies away from a philosophy that includes God in the scope of its investigations. Luther, Calvin, and Barth agree that the knowledge of God via our natural reason is impossible. The only wisdom is what God says, although he may say it through the mouth of his elect, and then the Word is not philosophy; it is closer to revelation. Two Catholic theologians, Louis Bouyer and Etienne Gilson, are of one opinion that Barth is even more categorical than his two great precursors, and Bouyer adds that he is more of a Calvinist than Calvin himself. For Barth, God is totally hidden in nature, and philosophy, a purely human speculative effort, ought to remain in its appropriate "mundane" sphere, renouncing all religious pretensions: "It should confess its profane nature, its being without God."[20] Hermann Dooyeweerd is the latest important thinker in the Calvinist line to formulate this position: "Philosophical thought is bound to the temporal horizon of experience with its modal diversity of aspects. It does not, therefore, include the God-man relationship. Yet, it must deal with the *ego*, the center of all reflection, otherwise it must deny all validity to theoretical thought."[21]

The deficiency of the Kantian approach to the problem of knowledge is as obvious as the deficiency of the mystical approach—and both stumble on their refusal to acknowledge as real the extramental world and God as its creator. If God is conceived as radically different from man but not distant, and as accessible and knowable to him but not identical with him, then creation will be understood as being of a limited nature but in confident contact with the creator who guarantees it and *presents* it when lending it existence. This, in turn, means that animate and inanimate things properly inferior to God in the hierarchy of beings are finite and therefore distinguished from other entities. In spite of their finiteness, each "is marked by an intelligible structure"[22] and, as we shall see further on, the property of intelligence is, precisely, to bring out this intelligibility, which is inherent in finite things and which is not the task of reason to imprint on them.

This way of looking at the process of cognition and its result does not pass by the problems of immanentist thought without turning an understanding eye on them. It must be recognized, for example, that total knowledge is possible only to God. But it does not follow that the soul is capable of so uniting with God as to share in this knowledge. In modern times, with the fading of religious faith, when God remains a mere adjunct of the soul (self), the absurdity of the notion that the soul shares in total knowledge becomes manifest. It is similarly true that the only completely adequate object of knowledge is God as a thing that really and wholly *is*. Yet, why should this fact entail the rejection of the knowledge of other things as illusory and vain, indeed as so base that it borders on sin and evil? The nature of the creature is such that he cannot encompass God entirely, *per essentiam suam*, because "the understanding of a creature is itself created."[23] All finite entities, as Plato said, are limited, but this is not the same thing as evil: evil is the lack of something obtainable, whereas unlimited knowledge cannot be obtained by a limited entity.

Does this view exclude the knowledge of God by the creature? A positive answer to this question would imply a denial of, for example, the mystic's central quest and would frustrate the legitimate, although often miscarried, enterprise to penetrate the essence of being. On the other hand, it would also imply the impossibility of the philosophical quest, which would thus be compelled, as Barth seems to wish, either to turn into a purely theological quest ("religious quest" would be a better expression) or to liquidate itself. Since my arguments on these pages aim *to save philosophy* from both extremes and to demonstrate its legitimacy, they must try to define the legitimate field within which knowledge is validly pursued.

It was said above that the only completely adequate object of knowledge is God. According to Thomas Aquinas—and Meister Eckhart would not disagree—this is granted to the creature only in a state of rapture. The error of Eckhart and of other immanentists is to postulate this state as something regularly and habitually attainable until it becomes man's possession. This is what the Gnostic and Hermetic ascent postulates. This is also what Hegel holds: that truth is only truth if the reality it reveals is complete with all the possibles realized. Since, in Hegel's view, this is not given to man from the historical beginning, the process of completion of history means that man "bites off," so to speak, chunks of Being and that this process permits him to become complete as Being is thus gradually reduced to nothingness. The Platonic tradition and Thomistic thought agree at this point with Hegel and, generally, with immanentism, namely, that man partakes *also* of nonbeing and that this follows from his *status crea-*

turae. The difference is that for Eckhart and Hegel this is a sin, an evil, a void to be frantically filled, and that meanwhile man is defined by the void and by the desire to fill it (*Begierde*). In their respective idioms Eckhart and Hegel insist that man temporarily burdened with the mundane element in his constitution cannot be what he is, fill out his essence, which is, in reality, the same as the divine essence. They regard creatureliness as a wound and the human being as a patient to be restored to a higher ontological status, beyond creatureliness.

In contrast, the void in man that realistic philosophy discovers and formulates is a permanent state and therefore an explanatory principle of the human experience. It was said above that only in God do essence and existence coincide, that only in him is there no void. In man, however, the void is not a lack, unless we measure man against God, an unwarranted operation. It is the negative view of the *status creaturae*, as if the latter were not a God-willed fullness in itself. In spite of what we call man's "limitations," he is capable of knowledge. "The secret paradox of all intellectual substance," Gilson writes, "is that it is a finite power virtually capable of an infinite object."[24] We should add: but not infinitely, because, as Gilson himself states, "God himself has created a paradoxical disproportion between the only object able to appease man's desire, infinite being, and the finite powers of the human understanding."[25] Voegelin describes this "paradox" as an "existential tension" between the humanity of man and the divinity of God that the philosopher's eroticism tries ever to bridge, but in full awareness of its impossibility. Thus the Platonic *eros* is not the same as Hegel's *Begierde*, it describes a state of permanent tension and search, whereas Hegel, as we saw, puts an end to the search and thereby to man's humanity.

As Plato maintains in the *Phaedros* (249 E), the nature of man is such that the soul beholds real being; no physical identification with the object of cognition is implied, but, remarks John Wild, "a noetic identification with the whatness, the *quiddity*, of things."[26] This is the function of intelligence, which, like a Don Quijote, would indeed aimlessly agitate its arms facing nonexisting targets if it did not have before it an intelligible object, a real being, the whatness of which is reliably cognized. Garrigou-Lagrange writes, "Knowledge is the knowledge of something, and must be determined by its object, otherwise it is the knowledge of nothing. . . . After grasping its object, intelligence returns towards itself and grasps itself as a force motivated by being."[27] The first apprehension is *being*, the things that exist outside the self, and only afterward does the self understand its own distinctness from the world it has grasped as nonself. This, writes Garrigou-Lagrange, is the first breakup (*morcelage*) of being into object and subject.

This view must appear as a relativization of knowledge to those who, like Descartes and others, desire subjective evidence and who regard the "intrusion" of the object as debilitating that evidence. Also to those who, like Meister Eckhart and Fichte, fail to deduct the multiplicity of the creature-world from the One Being and therefore, particularly and vigorously Fichte, deny multiplicity. It is precisely the permanent and final breakup of the process of understanding into subject and object that they find intolerable, and for the abolition of which they descend in the philosophical arena. It must appear, on the contrary, as an absolutization of knowledge to those who argue, like the Kantians, the followers of Wittgenstein, the structuralists, and others, that were the intellect differently constituted or the language it chooses differently structured, the evidence of the extramental world would be something else than it is now. Here again, the only counterargument of a realistic philosophy is that what is true for us is true even for God, although he knows *more* and more *deeply* of it than we do. This argument contains the answer to those also who, like some existentialists, contend that the world, unless it is organized and given meaning by us, intellectual beings, does not make sense, that in itself it is absurd.

God and the Knowledge of Reality

"Nothing will make me ever understand," writes Maurice Merleau-Ponty in the *Phenomenology of Perception* (French edition, p. 494.), "what a nebula might be which is not seen by any human being. The nebula of Laplace is not behind us, before the origin of man, but before us, in the world of culture." A storm, wrote Sartre, is not a storm in the primeval forest; it only becomes one when man appears who fears its unleashed forces, looks for shelter, mourns his lightning-struck dead, and tries magically to avert its recurrence. According to this view, man adds gratuitously to the *en-soi*, tries to fill its void through a gratuitously invented meaning and through sets of meaning (structures, linguistic patterns). But why should man and his meanings be considered gratuitous? Can the world not possess intelligibility to be apprehended by intelligent beings who, in turn, try to understand God through the reality of lesser beings?

For an immanentist like Fichte, for example, this question is manifestly absurd. Outside of the Divine Being, he writes in *The Guide to the Blessed Life*, all that appears to us as having existence—things, bodies, souls, we ourselves as single subjects, so far as we ascribe to ourselves an independent and self-sufficient existence—is not truly there; it exists only in the empirical consciousness as something felt and thought. Dialogue here is evidently impossible: intelligibility assumes an underlying being (*ens*), and intelligence, as observed above, is the instrument searching it out, discovering it in the extramental objects. Not only is Fichte thus refuted, but the more moderate Kantian distinction between *Ding-an-sich* and phenomena also disappears, because it is found now that we do have access to the former *without*—let me repeat the point—exhausting it. It is artificial to call what we know merely phenomena, when it is real knowledge as far as it goes—without going all the way.

For the obverse reason, I cannot agree with Husserl for whom the phenomena are all that is, and for whom this *all-that-is* is accessible in the eidetic reduction. There is more than the *all-that-*

is as understood by phenomenology; the transcendental ego will never be able to reach this *plus*, a fact that, however, does not discredit the "psychological ego" whose (limited) grasp of reality is a true grasp of real being. Even though we never catch a straight line or a perfect circle with our senses, we know what a straight line and a perfect circle are. Let me quote again Maritain: "The Idealists . . . are wrong in believing . . . that every interpretation, or more exactly, every judgment of our faculty of knowing is a distortion or a construction. Interpretation and judgment is a more or less perfect and profound way for this faculty to assimilate the object, to conform to what *is*."[28] This is what Marcel De Corte calls "submission to reality," ready to admit, like Maritain, that the line then followed by the intellect does not go far and that the intellect cannot follow it to its end.[29] It must be once again affirmed with Voegelin that "in historical reality a philosopher's truth is the exegesis of his experience: a real man participates in the reality of God and the world, of society and himself, and articulates his experiences by more or less adequate language symbols."[30] Experience is, of course, always finite, and its exegesis, the essence of the search, also only *tends* toward completion.

Does the finiteness of this experience mean that it is imperfect? Without being an "intersubjective" experience, it is a shared one; it is not completed since the sharing of experience does not amount, as the Gnostics believe, to a divine, noetic experience, but it obtains, nevertheless, the reassurance of general participation. The experience of search is ultimately based on the philosopher's wonder faced with the ever-open gap between the "plus of Being" and the "sum of beings" unable to contain it.[31] Confronted with this gap, many thinkers hope to bridge it by reducing philosophy to an anthropology that regards man as an all-embracing reality, not, as Hans Urs von Balthazar notes, "wrapped in Being and not measured by it." But Being is more than man, although man has his own reality and the conmensurate knowledge: not, of course, supraconceptually tailored to the exclusive grasp of Being (like Eckhart's "unknowing knowing" and Fichte's "blessed life" or Hegel's *wirkliches Wissen*), but one that accomodates the multiplicity of being, confident that it is real.

It is the same with the objects, or rather situations, of the *moral world*. They are grasped by our moral intelligence, which decides and acts in a manner similar to the cognitive intelligence although with considerably less certainty. It too rejects two extreme positions.

One position has been intermittently referred to on these pages: the Gnostic position, to be found in the monistic and Indian mystics, and then down to Fichte. Since the world is evil, the so-called ethical commands are issued by the demiurgos or lower, anthropomorphic God; hence, they are not to be followed because they further ensnare man in this world, making of him a cooperator in the prolongation of an evil state of affairs. The elect may then choose asceticism (abstinence from the created material things and situations and from the things of the flesh) or dissoluteness in the name of the indifference of his spirit (*pneuma*) to what happens to his flesh (*sarx*). This view corresponds to what I have described as position *B*.

The other position, corresponding to position *A*, may be identified as moral subjectivism. It is best seen in the Kantian system, and its coarser form is found in today's popular "situational ethics." For Kant, the moral law cannot derive from any external object or source as a law imposed from outside (natural law) because then morality, the moral choice and behavior, becomes a mere means to reach an end. The human being obeys, but not by a motivation welling up inside him; he is not morally free. On the contrary, in Kant's view man ought to give the law to himself so that he may have a subjective (moral) evidence for its validity. We have seen (in Part Three) that this view drove him quite logically to the necessity of placing God inside man and of identifying him with "the human morally self-determining Reason." The situational moralists hold the same view when they argue that the subject is the judge of the situation in which man finds himself.

This position leads to a dismemberment of the moral world; it justifies any and all moral positions provided the agent possesses an inner evidence, indeed a god, dictating him the choice. Kant was aware of this difficulty, and he tried to solve it by seeking an external validation—not in the commands of God as an "external substance" but in the hope that the individual moral choices may ultimately find themselves in accord since each ought to want what all others want also. One surmises that Rousseau's influence and the pietist background account for this trust in intersubjectivity *avant la lettre*. Let me underline that this supposed harmony of moral choices is not a consequence of the recognition by all agents of a moral intelligibility inherent in situations (this, for Kant, would be the essence of an external imposition), but of the supposition that all subjects are made the same way and therefore reach the same (inner) evidence. In other words, it seems that the moral subject possesses a structure the same way as the cognitive subject does; while the latter organizes his world of cognition, the moral subject (or practical reason) constructs his own world of moral acts. Kant further expects a synthesis between the two, the reconciliation of the world of values and of the world of nature. Since man constructs both, in principle there is nothing to oppose it.

Such a reconciliation is, nevertheless, illusory, and Kant derives the idea and the project from the supposed exigency of reason. In other words, he builds on the subject's ability to construct the world. Yet, the subjects vary from one to another: true, as the Catholic tradition indicates, the moral demand is founded on the objective reality discernible in the moral object (not directly on revelation), yet the world is diverse and it is also the scene of good and evil; furthermore, individuals possess intelligence and moral sense to varying degrees, and not all can extract from the surrounding world the same meaning that is objectively *in* the world. Therefore, as Hans Urs von Balthazar writes, "there can be no question of a convergence or harmonizing of the history of the world and the history of the Kingdom";[32] world history is not a gradual Christification of the cosmos, "the theological virtues do not orient mankind's common terrestrial tasks."[33] The gap we understood as irreductible between the knower and the known in the cognitive sphere is present and irreductible also in the moral world: what in the first is error or wrong conclusion derived from an intelligible reality is, in the second, impatience and passion, the will to be transferred swiftly, magically, into another reality. Hence, as von Balthazar notes, the importance of patience in the New Testament, the basic constituent of Christianity, "the power to wait, to persevere, to endure to the end, not to transcend one's own limitations."[34] To accept the moral law grounded on the structure of human nature, but with its source elsewhere.

The gap mentioned before is then the experiential transcription of man's distance from God, mitigated by God's nearness. Von Balthazar speaks of patience; I would add modesty: the awareness that we cannot reach a higher ontological status, a divine *noesis*, or a historical utopia originates from the articulation of the same experience.

Arrived at the term of our inquiry, the question must be asked: Can philosophy be saved? In one sense, the question needs an immediate answer since, according to many students of philosophy, Western universities themselves teach today that there is no validity in the philosophical enterprise, and that philosophy must either resolve itself in revolutionary or other kind of praxis or become an ancilla of positive science, moved, as Berdyaev once said, by a "black envy" of that science. In one way or another, philosophy today is promised to the vilest form of extinction: self-liquidation. This is what I stated earlier in this chapter when I spoke of the "crisis-approach to reality," which demands that since philosophy apparently fails to transform reality, reality ought to change so that philosophy may become unnecessary, the commodious and inconsequential chatter of sophisticated company.

Beyond the immediate need to save philosophy, what is the long-range or rather permanent meaning of this enterprise? I have shown that philosophy in the West is composed of two main themes that have had adepts throughout the whole course of its history, since its so-called dawn in Greece. The two are better described as a double theme because, since each is an extreme position, each calls forth the other's response. Nevertheless, no synthesis arises from this strange duet. The two positions may be identified as rationalism and mysticism, conceptualism and immanentism, the Parmenidean position and the Heraclitean position, or, simply, my own formulation of position *A* and position *B*.

There seem to be two lessons that can be drawn from the antagonisms and forced syntheses of these themes. The first lesson is that philosophy cannot be allowed to continue to ignore discourses not naturally excluded from its purview. The philosophical enterprise has been systematically impoverished since late scholasticism, Descartes, Spinoza, then decisively since Kant, and down to the contemporary variants of positivism and linguistic analysis, and of ideologies. The first evidence is the need to restore not only metaphysics to its prominent place but also religious discourse, with its mystic element, and myth as articulator of experience. Philosophy must draw upon all human experience before it defines its own conceptual categories to which, naturally, it must return as the privileged vehicle of its discourse. It follows from this reenriched view of philosophy that it may

[223]

be allowed, as in Plato's conception, to diagnose society's disease from symptoms of the soul's sickness, and vice versa; hence philosophy's curative function, not of *being*, but of the soul.

The second lesson is that no forced synthesis (no "chemical wedding," to use the alchemistic term) can be usefully effected between the antagonistic positions mentioned above. The character of esoteric speculation is the attempt to confuse the expressions of sentiment, legitimate in themselves, with their unauthorized translation as concepts. The result is, as Rudolf Otto wisely pointed out, the fabrication of a system, a "monstrous science," which is equally misleading whether an Eckhart, a Paracelsus, a Boehme, a Hegel, a Mrs. Besant, or a Bergson formulates it.[35] I have illustrated this kind of system-building in the case of the "Super-God": the exalted soul, contemptuous not only of the world but also of God, who is assumed to be anthropomorphic (multiple and material) since he created it, feels impelled to fabricate a being higher and more spiritual, the only one worthy to ascend to and to merge with. Not only systems known as esoteric are built in such a manner, but, as Otto observes and as I have showed it repeatedly throughout this book, also philosophical systems, or at least substantial parts of them. Such systems automatically engage in what I have called the ontological promotion of man and the noetic promotion of his knowledge.

In consequence, the two antagonistic positions should be understood as not reconcilable in any kind of synthesis; they must yield to a third position if philosophy is to be saved from liquidation. The two positions must be rejected because in the last analysis (see also the conclusion of Part One) both rely unduly on the human being's self-sufficiency and arbitrariness and both deny the extramental world its proper reality and place.[36] From this angle, rationalism appears as a consequence of position *A*: if God is distant, the support is removed from creation, from the extramental world, and the subject persuades itself that it produces the world. Mysticism appears as the consequence of position *B*:

if God is one with the soul, the extramental world becomes illusory, it finally vanishes before the sole Being, the One. The being and cognition of man appear in both cases as carrying a greater burden than what they were made to carry in the *status creaturae.*

Only a philosophically third position corresponds to the *status creaturae.* The term *moderate realism* may be conveniently used to characterize this position. While accepting the testimony of our various cognitive channels, it sets up a control: experience itself, which reports in one continuous process the approximate nature of our judgments. Thus the awareness of limitations keeps all absolutistic claims at a permanent distance. The inflated subject and the compressed object are made equally untenable. The subject, which is not a pure spirit but rather an active intelligence, must conform to what *is* in order to report order, and the object, existing in its own right, must be the orderly substratum about which our intelligence informs us.

Whence the approximate nature of these reports and of our judgments? As soon as the vain concept of individuality disappears, wrote Fichte, the former ego sinks into the divine existence. So long as man desires to be something himself, God does not come to him. But as soon as he destroys his own self wholly and to the root, God alone remains. Now our experience tells us the opposite, namely, that we are intended to be individuals. The self cannot sink for longer than a moment of rapture into the divine existence; he is sustained in his ontological status by the conferral on him of an appropriate nature. The same way, the extramental world does not sink into man's soul; it has its own nature, and its function is to fulfill it as a separate entity. Individuality is thus not an accident; it is the principle by which all beings obtain and express their dignity. To the multiplicity of perceiving selves there corresponds the multiplicity of perceived things, and all these tend to persist in their status without climbing a kind of ladder of perfection. If the soul were *one*, and oneness, in turn, could only be predicated of Being, individualities would indeed collapse in the totality. There would be no error, no approximate judgment—because there would be no knowledge. Knowledge presupposes *degrees* of knowing, hence approximations and errors. Knowledge is predicated on detachment; there can be no knowledge between identical or fused entities. The subject must be able to distinguish itself from the object as different from it and superior to it. Thus even if the soul, as in the mystic's case, is possessed of high noetic ambitions (anyway, a temporary state), the soul *qua* knowing subject is prevented from emulating these ambitions.

A theory of knowledge does not have the task of proving God's existence. It can, however, postulate a situation in which its own assumptions are best served. Such a postulated situation for moderate realism obtains if a God exists who is transcendent and personal. What is the role of such a God in epistemology? I have formulated the epistemological problem as inseparable from the ontological one. To postulate a transcendent and personal God is to prevent man from climbing the ontological ladder and transmuting himself into a higher being with a higher knowledge. Since, in this view, the relationship between him and God remains one of *distance*, and it is, at the same time, *intimate*, it is inconceivable that man's experience of God should contain more than the experience of prophets, mystics, and *spoudaioi* (virtuous men), namely, the divine majesty descending to him and inspiring him through a numinous yet personal presence with confidence and love.[37] Luther gave expression to this double source of our experience with his teaching that the *deus revelatus* (the revealed God) would be an open mouth without the *deus absconditus* (the hidden God), and that without the *tremenda majestas* grace would not be so sweet.

What the religious experience transcribes is true also of the cognitive experience. A transcendent and personal God excludes the possession by man of divine insight into things and excludes also man's absorption in Being. God reminds us that man is not the creator of nature, nor is nature the creator of man; both were created distinct and limited. In multiple ways God thus stands in the way of man's self-identification with God or with the extramental world: God is exclusively the divine being with whom merger is impossible; and he created the extramental world as an entity distinct from the human being. Hence cognition is enclosed within wide but firm limits.

I have no illusion that this manner of *saving philosophy* will satisfy everybody. Holders of positions *A* and *B* have almost always been the majority, for reasons amply explained before. Religious thinkers may also disagree with the proposition that an "anthropomorphic" God is the prerequisite for balanced and moderate thought about being, knowledge, and community. Rationalists may denounce my enterprise for letting "God" unnecessarily intrude in a discussion where other ways of justifying the limits of knowledge have long been found. Mystics might find that my position truncates the soul and thwarts its desire to soar nearer to Being. Finally, partisans of utopia will say that whoever seeks to discredit their ideal, also mutilates the elementary human desire not to set limits to the enthusiastic vision of raising man and his community to not-yet-experienced heights.

One cannot meet all opponents at every turn of their argumentation, but it is sufficient to meet them at the fount of their premises. As for the rest of their arguments, they too must appear then untenable. I began by observing that contrary to the claim that the God-problem is obsolete, the main themes of philosophical speculation return to it regularly in every age, if with no other—but revealing—intention than to liquidate it. I then inquired into the reason of this effort at liquidation and of the resistence offered to it. I found that the effort is ultimately motivated by an extraphilosophical desire: the ontological promotion of man and the concomitant noetic promotion of his knowing. Thereafter the problem was to bring the philosophical enterprise

God and the Knowledge of Reality

back to experience, although keeping well in mind that experience must be recognized as being far wider and deeper than what many thinkers would grant it and still call it reliably informative. If, on the other hand, we open up experience to the ontological quest, to the contribution of myth, to the mystic's vision, and so on, we discover that there is no contradiction between man's limitations and the effort to obtain reliable reports from the surrounding reality. But promotion in being and in knowledge is forever blocked by a God-figure. This may indeed be the last word of moderate realism and the beginning of wisdom.

NOTES

1. Quoted in Frances A. Yates, *Giordano Bruno and the Hermetic Tradition*, (New York: Vintage Books, 1969), p. 230.
2. Karl Barth, *Protestant Thought from Rousseau to Ritschl* (New York: Simon and Schuster, 1969), p. 358.
3. Rudolf Otto, *Mysticism East and West* (New York: Macmillan Co., 1970), p. 253.
4. Rudolf Otto, *Le Sacré* (Paris: Petite Bibliothèque Payot, 1969), pp. 125-26.
5. Mircea Eliade, *Myths, Dreams, and Mysteries: The Encounter between Contemporary Faiths and Archaic Realities* (New York: Harper & Row, 1967), p. 190.
6. Other philosophical systems, for example Husserl's, express this notion of equality less in political terms than in properly epistemological terms: intersubjectivity. Marx too would probably accept this version.
7. Etienne Gilson, *The Spirit of Thomism* (New York: Harper & Row, 1966), p. 87.
8. Mircea Eliade, *The Forge and the Crucible* (New York: Harper & Row, 1971), p. 173.
9. Mircea Eliade, *The Sacred and the Profane: The Nature of Religion*, trans. Willard Trask (New York: Harcourt Brace Jovanovich, Inc., 1968), p. 87.
10. Otto, *Mysticism East and West*, p. 19.
11. Ferdinand Alquié, "Introduction à la lecture de la *Critique de la raison pratique*," in *Critique de la raison pratique* (Paris: Presses Universitaires de France, 1966), p. xi.
12. Ibid., p. x.

Possibility and Limits of Knowledge

13. Maurice De Wulf, *Introduction to Scholastic Philosophy* (New York: Dover Publications, 1956), p. 216.

14. S. Stebbing, *A Modern Introduction to Logic*.

15. Rudolf Carnap, "Les Concepts psychologiques et physiques sont-ils foncièrement différents?"

16. Philip Franck, *La Théorie de la connaissance et la physique moderne*.

17. Moritz Schlick, *Enoncés scientifiques et réalité du monde*.

18. Aristotle *Metaphysics* 3. 1.

19. T. Greenwood, *Foundations of Symbolic Logic*.

20. Quoted in Etienne Gilson, "Calvinisme et philosophie," *Itinéraires* (May 1967): p. 37.

21. Hermann Dooyeweerd, *In the Twilight of Western Thought* (New Jersey: The Craig Press, 1968), p. 31.

22. John Wild, *Plato's Modern Enemies and the Theory of Natural Law* (Chicago: University of Chicago Press, 1953), p. 137.

23. A. E. Taylor, *Platonism and Its Influence* (New York: Cooper Square Publisher, 1962), p. 43.

24. Etienne Gilson, *The Spirit of Thomism* (New York: Harper & Row, 1966), p. 50.

25. Ibid., p. 81.

26. Wild, *Plato's Modern Enemies*, p. 90.

27. Reginald Garrigou-Lagrange, *Le Sens commun: La Philosophie de l'être et les formules dogmatiques* (Paris: Nouvelle Librairie Nationale, 1922), p. 135. My translation.

28. Jacques Maritain, *Les Degrés du savoir* (Paris: Desclée, De Brouwer & Cie, 1939), p. 103. My translation.

29. Marcel De Corte, "La Philosophie et la theologie à l'envers," *Itinéraires* (March 1971), p. 102.

30. Eric Voegelin, "On Hegel: A Study in Sorcery," *Studium Generale* 24 (1971): 344.

31. Hans Urs von Balthasar, *Cordula ou l'épreuve décisive* (Paris: Beauchesne, 1968), p. 53.

32. Hans Urs von Balthasar, *A Theology of History* (New York: Sheed & Ward, 1963), pp. 30-31.

33. Von Balthasar, *Cordula*, p. 41.

34. Von Balthasar, *Theology of History*, pp. 30-31.

35. Otto, *Le Sacré*, p. 155. Otto speaks of Hegel's "animistic logic."

36. We are not surprised to find the immanentist position in its modern forms caught in the same dilemma as was Greek philosophy and its origin, with Parmenides and Heraclitus. Only the One *is*, argued the Eleatic school; all change is illusory; the multiplicity of things is a mere name, agreed upon by mortal men. Heraclitus (and Hegel, Bergson, and others) does not recognize the objectivity of knowledge either, since he denies the principle of noncontradiction. Things "flow into one another"; "God becomes and

[229]

disbecomes"; "knowing is superseded by unknowing." The creature is at once being and nonbeing; he is immersed in the process of change, which alone is real. Parmenides and Heraclitus as well as their followers hardly speak of phenomena.

37. Max Scheler's position is essentially the same: the personal God cannot be known to man through his cognitive acts alone. This knowledge is complemented by God's "sovereign condescension" in revelation. Scheler's position is remarkably similar to Plato's, Maritain's, and Buber's. See Scheler, *The Eternal in Man*, p. 334.

INDEX

Index

Index

[233]

Index

Index

Mysticism, 19, 157–159, 187, 196–197; alchemy and, 82–87; genuine vs false, 38, 64; Knowledge and, 64–67; Muslim, 37–38; Otto on, 195–196, 199; philosophy and, 33, 206–207, 223–225; reality and, 64–67; union with God and, 33–47. *See also* Alchemy; Cabala; Esoterism; Gnosticism; Hermetism; Magic
Myths: cosmogonic, 6–8, 11–12; God and, 54–55

NAPOLEON: Hegel and, ix xii, 133, 149, 151, 187n
Natural religion, 160, 164, 175
Nature, 135; alchemy and, 85–86; Hermetism and, 89–90; Knowledge of, 19–21, 25, 44–45, 76–77; manipulation of, 98
Naudon, Paul, 94n
Nazarenes, 56
Nicholas of Cusa, 14, 18, 20–22, 45, 102, 205; epistemology of, 41–42
Nietzsche, Friedrich, 23, 105, 181–183
Novalis, 50n

OCKHAM, WILLIAM, 19–20, 21–22, 44–45, 156, 157, 162
Oldenburg, Heinrich, 23–24, 25, 45, 68n
Olivi, Peter John, 91, 156
Ontological promotion, xiii
Origen, 28, 37, 58, 102
Ortiz, Francisco, 158
Otto, Rudolf, 7, 33, 36, 39, 42, 187, 224; on immanentist speculation, 204–205; on mysticism, 195–196, 199
Otto, Walter, 7, 54, 55

PAINTING, esoteric symbols in, 84, 89
Pan-en-henic (all-in-one), 5, 33, 95. *See also* Immanent God

Pantheism, 5, 32–49, 59–60
Paracelsus, Philippus, 42, 45, 83, 86, 90, 91, 210
Parmenides, 229n
Paul, Saint, 76, 158, 196
Pears, David, 211
Pera, Fr. Ceslas, 39
Personal God. *See* Anthropomorphic God
Phenomenology, 117–120
Philosophical stone, 85–86, 95n, 100. *See also* Alchemy
Philosophy: alchemy and, 99–102; Being and, 112–113; future of, 222–228; German, 103–105; God's existence and, 48–49, 55, 67; Greek, 126; history and, xii, xiii–xiv, 148–152; impasse of, xiii, 202; Knowledge and, 127–132; maturation and, 131–132; mysticism and, 33, 206–207, 223–225; reality and, 172–173; utopia and, xiii, 171–178. *See also* Existentialism; Gnosticism; Hermetism; Mysticism; Subjectivism; names of specific philosophers
Pico della Mirandola, 78–79, 83, 90, 103
Plato, 12, 53, 63, 74, 78, 150, 216; on Knowledge, 209
Plotinus, 12, 27, 74, 75, 111; mysticism of, 17–18, 64–65
Postel, Guillaume, 91
Proclus, 19, 82
Puech, H. C., 48

QUISPEL, GILLES, 48, 55–56

RAHNER, KARL, 133
Ranters, 158–159
Rational discourse, 202–204
Rationalism, 223–225
Realism, moderate, 225–228
Reality: epistemology and, xv–xvi;

Index

[236]

Index